LIGHTS OF
THE SPIRIT

LIGHTS OF THE SPIRIT

Historical Portraits of
Black Bahá'ís in North America:
1898–2000

edited by
Gwendolyn Etter-Lewis
and
Richard Thomas

Bahá'í
PUBLISHING

WILMETTE, ILLINOIS

Bahá'í Publishing
415 Linden Avenue, Wilmette, Illinois 60091-2844

09 08 07 06   4 3 2 1

Chapter 2 contains "The Pupil of the Eye: African-Americans and the Making of the American Bahá'í Community," to be published in Gayle Tate and Lewis Randolph, *The Black Urban Community: from Dusk Till Dawn* (New York: Palgrave Macmillian, 2006), reproduced with permission of Palgrave Macmillan.

Library of Congress Cataloging-in-Publication Data
Lights of the spirit : historical portraits of Black Bahá'ís in North America, 1898–
    2000 / edited by Gwendolyn Etter-Lewis and Richard Thomas.—New ed.
        p. cm.
    Includes bibliographical references and index.
    ISBN-13: 978-1-931847-26-1 (alk. paper)
    ISBN-10: 1-931847-26-6 (alk. paper)
      1. African American Bahais—History. I. Etter-Lewis, Gwendolyn. II. Thomas,
    Richard Walter, 1939–

BP350.L54 2006
297.9'308996073—dc22
                                                                    2005057117

Cover photo key, clockwise, starting from left: Sadie Oglesby, Alain Locke, Dorothy Champ, Coralie Franklin Cook and George William Cook, Dizzy Gillespie, participants at the second Bahá'í race amity convention in America, December 1921, Elsie Austin, Louis Gregory; *center:* Robert Turner

Cover design by Robert A. Reddy
Book design by Patrick Falso

Bahá'u'lláh once compared
the colored people
to the Black pupil of the eye
surrounded by the white.
In this black pupil
you see the reflection
of that which is before it,
and through it
the light of the spirit shineth forth.

—'ABDU'L-BAHÁ

Contents

Preface

This book grew out of different experiences that ultimately brought the editors to the same conclusion. In 1992 Richard Thomas was invited to a conference convened by the Schomburg Center for Research in the Black Culture entitled, "The Diversity of the African-American Religious Experience: A Continuous Dialogue." He presented a paper on "The Black Experience in the U.S. Bahá'í Community, 1898–1992." For many of those present, it was their first time hearing of the Bahá'í Faith. At approximately the same time, Gwendolyn Etter-Lewis was invited by Louhelen Bahá'í School to give a presentation on notable Black women at one of its first conferences on the equality of women and men. While the majority of the people in the audience were very familiar with the Bahá'í Faith, few of them had heard of the distinguished Black women who were Bahá'ís in the early days of the religion. Professor Etter-Lewis published her presentation entitled, "African-American Women in the Bahá'í Faith, 1898–1919," in the Winter 1993–94 issue of *World Order* magazine and in *Black Women in America: An Historical Encyclopedia* (1993), edited by Darlene Clark Hine. As a result of these seemingly disparate experiences, both Richard and Gwendolyn concluded that the Black Bahá'í story needed to be told.

Both were concerned about the lack of interest in African-American Bahá'ís among scholars of African-American religious history. For example, *Afro-American Religious History: A Documentary Witness* (1985), edited by Milton C. Sernett, which contains documents on Black Judaism in Harlem and African-Americans' involvement in Islam, would have been enriched by inclusion of historical documents on African-American Bahá'ís, particularly in the section of the book entitled "Twentieth Century

Religious Alternatives."[1] Unfortunately, the only mention of African-
American Bahá'ís in this work is from a chapter in E. Franklin Frazier's
book, *The Negro Church in America* (1694), entitled, "The Negro Church
and Assimilation." According to Frazier, "Some middle-class Negroes in
their seeking to find escape from the Negro identification have gone from
the Catholic church to the Christian science church and then to the Bahaist
church."[2]

The late C. Eric Lincoln, one of the premier scholars of the Black
religious experience in the United States, did not mention African-
American Bahá'ís in either edition of his book, *Race, Religion, and the
Continuing American Dilemma* (1984, revised edition 1999). Yet he
discussed African-American Muslims and even referred to African-
Americans in the Mormon Church.[3] Considering the vast differences
between the teachings of the Bahá'í Faith and of the Mormon Church
on race and the role of African-Americans within their respective
communities, Lincoln's neglect of African-Americans in the Bahá'í Faith
is problematic. While the Mormons, until 1978, banned African-
Americans from the priesthood and, as acknowledged by Lincoln,
denigrated Blacks as a race,[4] the Bahá'í teachings elevated Blacks and
referred to them as the "pupil of the eye." Bahá'u'lláh, the prophet-founder
of the Bahá'í Faith, "once compared the colored people to the black pupil
of the eye surrounded by the white. In this black pupil is seen the reflection
of that which is before it, and through it the light of the spirit shineth
forth."[5]

According to Lincoln, "There are three religious communities outside
the Christian mainstream with which Blacks have unusual relationships.
While these relationships may vary in their impact on the black estate,
they all reflect directly or indirectly aspects of the American Dilemma. I
refer to black relations with Mormons, Muslims, and Jews."[6] His rationale
for selecting these religions is understandable, but limited in scope. Had
Lincoln included the Bahá'í Faith, he would have discovered a different
type of "unusual relationship" with Blacks, a relationship not based upon
biased theology, but upon the belief in the oneness of humanity and the
image of Blacks as endowed with tremendous spiritual gifts. Also, most
unusual, he would have discovered that unlike the three religious com-

munities he included, the American Bahá'í community had historically demonstrated its commitment to building unity among all races in the United States.[7]

Anthony B. Pinn's book, *Varieties of African-American Religious Experience* (1998), which by its title should have included African-American Bahá'ís, covers Vodun, Orisha, Islam, and Humanism, yet fails to include the Bahá'í Faith. Most certainly African-American Bahá'ís should be represented in any scholarly work focusing on the "varieties of African-American religious experience."

Unfortunately, the problem has persisted. Albert J. Raboteau's book *Canaan Land: A Religious History of African-Americans* (2001) includes African-American Catholics and Muslims, but nothing on African-American Bahá'ís. This could leave readers with the impression that African-American Bahá'ís have no place in "the religious history of African-Americans."

Lights of the Spirit is designed to fill the gap created by previous studies. This book, the first of its kind, breaks new ground by investigating the roles of Black people in a new religion that originated in the Middle-East in the mid-nineteenth century and, within a few decades, had spread to all parts of the globe. As the essays in this volume demonstrate, African-Americans were not in the background, but rather have been and continue to be key players in the growth and development of the Bahá'í Faith, both domestically and internationally. The editors are both Bahá'ís and scholars in their respective fields and bring to this task a wealth of information never before published in a single volume, much of it never previously published.

The Bahá'í Faith is an independent world religion that originated in Iran in 1844. Its first public mention in North America came at the World's Columbian Exposition in Chicago in 1893, and by 1900 the Faith was established in several localities in the United States and Canada.[8] Robert Turner, a butler, was the first African-American to enroll in the Bahá'í Faith, probably in late 1898.[9] In 1899 Olive Jackson, a dressmaker in Manhattan, became the first African-American woman to convert to the Bahá'í Faith.[10] As coauthors Will C. van den Hoonaard and Lynn Echevarria have pointed out, "the Bahá'í faith took hold among Blacks in North America not only in the United States, but also in Canada."[11]

These early Bahá'ís were the trailblazing members of a community that now numbers more than five million worldwide, has adherents in nearly every country in the world, and includes members of every race and social class.

Black Bahá'ís in Canada and the United States from the early days to the present represent a wide range of humanity. They include the famous as well as the unknown, the wealthy and working class: butler Robert Turner; Broadway actress Dorothy Champ; upper middle class couples George and Rosa Shaw (San Francisco); attorneys Alexander and Mary Martin (Cleveland); Sadie and Mabry Oglesby (Boston); attorney Louis Gregory; poet Robert Hayden; and Canadian singer and electrician Eddie Elliot.

What attracted Blacks in North America to the Bahá'í Faith? Who were they? What roles did they play within the Faith and within their respective African-American communities? This volume provides answers to these questions through historical documents, oral histories and testimonies, and primary documents such as letters, diaries, and journals. It sheds light on a history that deserves recognition and study.

Acknowledgments

We have so many people to thank for helping us bring this book to completion. Obviously, we thank the contributors to the volume, especially those who worked and waited patiently since 1987. Fran Fowler contributed her share in typing, calling, and maintaining connections between Gwen and Richard throughout this long process. We owe Linda Hanson a great debt of gratitude for countless hours typing the final draft to send to the publisher.

Roger Dahl and Robert Stockman were always available for questions concerning research and documents. We thank the Local Spiritual Assemblies of Washington, DC, San Francisco, and New York, the staff at the Moorland-Spingarn Research Center at Howard University, and the editors at the Bahá'í Publishing Trust, particularly Terry Cassiday and most especially Alex McGee for his long hours of faithful and expert editing. We are still in wonder and awe over the beautiful cover design by Bob Reddy. Others to whom we are grateful are Diane Taherzadeh, Lecile Webster, Ouida and Frances Coley, Viola Wood, Adrienne Reeves, and Wilma Ellis.

And finally and most importantly, we are grateful to our families and friends for their unwavering support.

I

The Black Experience in the North American Bahá'í Community

Introduction

Part I begins with a brief introduction to the Bahá'í Faith by Richard Thomas. In chapter 2, "The 'Pupil of the Eye': African-Americans and the Making of the American Bahá'í Community," Thomas discusses the role of African-American Bahá'ís in building a multiracial religious community and how the Bahá'í teachings on the spiritual qualities of Blacks led to the formation of racial identity among African-American Bahá'ís. In chapter 3, "Radiant Lights: African-American Women and the Advancement of the Bahá'í Faith in the U.S.," Gwendolyn Etter-Lewis tells the story of the first African-American women—the "spiritual foremothers"—to become Bahá'ís. Etter-Lewis expands on the theme of African-American Bahá'í women in chapter 4, "Race, Gender and Difference: African-American Women and the Struggle for Equality." This chapter documents the various responses of African-American Bahá'ís to address issues of racial prejudice within the Bahá'í community. In chapter 5, "Spreading the Divine Fragrances: African-American Bahá'ís in the Global Expansion of the Bahá'í Faith, 1937–63," Thomas further examines African-American participation in the global expansion of the Faith. Etter-Lewis, in the next chapter, shows how African-American women enthusiastically left the comforts of their homes in order to teach the Bahá'í Faith in foreign lands. Even though this volume focuses mainly on African-American Bahá'ís, because of the historical interaction of the Bahá'í communities in Canada and the United States—hence the inclusion of "North America" in the title—this final chapter by Canadian scholars completes the circle of part I. "Black Roses in Canada's Mosaic: Four Decades of Black History," by Will C. van den Hoonaard and Lynn Echevarria recounts the exciting stories of the first African-Canadian Bahá'ís.

1

Introduction to the Baháʼí Faith
Richard Thomas

The Baháʼí Faith, the youngest of the world's independent religions, is arguably the most diverse organized body of believers in the world. Worldwide, Baháʼís total more than five million believers, boasting members from greater than two thousand tribes, races, and ethnic groups.[1] "From its obscure beginnings in Iran during the mid-nineteenth century, it has now spread to virtually every part of the world, has established its administrative institutions in well over two hundred independent states and major territories, and has embraced believers from virtually every cultural, racial, social, and religious background."[2]

Basic Teachings of the Baháʼí Faith

The Baháʼí Faith is based on the teachings of Baháʼuʼlláh, whose writings emphasized three basic spiritual principles that are at the core of the Baháʼí doctrine: the oneness of God, the oneness of humankind, and the oneness of all religions. Throughout his writings, Baháʼuʼlláh emphasized that all human beings are the creation of one God and are one people, and that all religions share the same basic spiritual truths.

Other basic teachings of the Faith also reflect the ultimate goal of establishing unity and love among all races, nations, and religions. These include the equality of women and men, the elimination of all prejudices, the elimination of the extremes of wealth and poverty, the independent investigation of truth, universal education, fostering a world commonwealth of nations, and adopting a universal auxiliary language.

Bahá'ís believe that throughout history God has sent a succession of Divine Messengers to educate humanity, a process which Bahá'ís refer to as "progressive revelation." Among these "Manifestations of God" who have brought God's guidance to mankind are Abraham, Krishna, Moses, Zoroaster, Buddha, Jesus, the Báb, Muḥammad, and Bahá'u'lláh.[3]

Another way of understanding the Bahá'í concept of progressive revelation is to compare it with the stages of education in school.

> Just as children start with simple ideas in the primary grades, and are given increasing complex knowledge as they move on through secondary school and college, so humanity has been "educated" by a series of Manifestations. In each age, the teachings of the Messengers of God have conformed not to Their knowledge but to the level of collective maturity.[4]

According to Bahá'í belief, humanity has reached a level of collective development where its future well being is intricately tied to the recognition of its organic unity. Based upon this belief Bahá'ís throughout the world see as their supreme mission the unification of humankind.

Bahá'u'lláh is the latest (though not the last) in the succession of Divine Messengers who are part of the "gradual unfoldment of one Divine Revelation."[5] Shoghi Effendi, Bahá'u'lláh's great-grandson and appointed leader of the Bahá'í Faith from 1921 until his death in 1957, explained Bahá'u'lláh's revelation in relationship to earlier ones:

> [T]he Revelation identified with Bahá'u'lláh abrogates unconditionally all the Dispensations gone before it, upholds uncompromisingly the eternal verities they enshrine, recognizes firmly and absolutely the Divine origin of their Authors, preserves inviolate

the sanctity of their authentic Scriptures, disclaims any intentions of lowering the status of their Founders or of abating the spiritual ideals they inculcate.[6]

In addition, the Bahá'í revelation "clarifies and correlates their [other religious dispensations] functions, reaffirms their common, their unchangeable and fundamental purpose, reconciles their seemingly divergent claims and doctrines, readily and gratefully recognizes their respective contributions to the gradual unfoldment of one Divine Revelation."[7] The Bahá'í Faith "unhesitatingly acknowledges itself to be but one link in the chain of continually progressive Revelation, supplements their teachings with such laws and ordinances as conform to the imperative needs, and are dictated by the growing receptivity, of a fast evolving and constantly changing society."[8] Furthermore, it "proclaims its readiness and ability to fuse and incorporate the contending sects and factions into which they have fallen into a universal Fellowship, functioning within the framework, and in accordance with the precepts, of a divinely conceived, a world-unifying, a world-redeeming Order."[9]

Bahá'í Teachings on the Unity of Mankind

Bahá'u'lláh's writings on the unity of mankind clearly show that not only are all people of the same origin, but that this means that everyone has a responsibility to support unity and brotherhood:

> Ye are the fruits of one tree, and the leaves of one branch. Deal ye one another with the utmost love and harmony, with friendliness and fellowship. . . . So powerful is the light of unity that it can illuminate the whole earth.[10]

A unity that embraces the entire world is at the heart of Bahá'í belief. According to the Bahá'í teachings, "The purpose of religion . . . is to establish unity and concord amongst the peoples of the world; make it not the cause of dissension and strife. The religion of God and his divine law are the most potent instruments and the surest of all means for the dawning of the light of unity among men."[11]

Racial unity continues to be a pressing issue for the North American Bahá'í community. Though the Bahá'í teachings on equality are unequivocal, individuals and communities have struggled to understand how best to put them into practice, particularly in historical contexts where the Bahá'í teachings of equality were the opposite of the practice of general society.

> Know ye not why We created you from the same dust? That no one should exalt himself over the other. Ponder at all times in your hearts how ye were created. Since We have created you all from one same substance it is incumbent on you to be as one soul, to walk with the same feet, eat with the same mouth and dwell in the same land, that from your inmost being, by your deeds and actions, the signs of oneness and the essence of detachment may be made manifest.[12]

Such statements were further elucidated by Bahá'u'lláh's son, 'Abdu'l-Bahá. He explained the importance of unity and its counterpart, diversity:

> Consider the flowers of a garden: though differing in kind, color, form and shape, inasmuch as they are refreshed by the waters of one spring, revived by the breath of one wind, invigorated by the rays of one sun, this diversity increased their charm, and addeth unto their beauty. Thus when that unifying force, the penetrating influence of the Word of God, taketh effect, the differences of customs, manners, habits, ideas, opinions and dispositions embellisheth the world of humanity. This diversity, this difference is like the naturally created dissimilarity and the variety of the limbs and organs of the human body, for each one contributeth to the beauty, efficiency and perfection of the whole. When these difference limbs and organs come under the influence of man's sovereign soul, and the soul's power pervadeth the limbs and members, veins and arteries of the body, then difference reinforceth harmony, diversity

strengtheneth love, and multiplicity is the greatest factor for coordination.[13]

Between 1911 and 1913, 'Abdu'l-Bahá made an extensive tour to visit infant Bahá'í groups in North America and Western Europe. He visited the United States in 1912, a country whose first Bahá'í community had been formed in in 1894. During his time in the United States he devoted several talks on the need to promote unity between Black and White Americans, including a talk given at the fourth annual meeting of the NAACP. After his return to Palestine, he encouraged a White Bahá'í, Agnes Parsons, to establish conferences on racial amity. He took even further steps to promote the practice of racial harmony, such as his endorsement of a marriage between two Bahá'ís, an African-American man and an English woman, to demonstrate the Bahá'í principle of the oneness of the human race.

Studying the history of the Bahá'í community reveals people who are working simultaneously to understand the meaning and the implications of equality, while attempting to make it a reality first in their own communities and gradually in the world around them. The Bahá'í Faith has been established in North America for just over a century and in that time has grown from a handful of individuals of mainly affluent whites to a body that reflects the diversity of American society as a whole. Approximately thirty percent of the American Bahá'í community is non-White, with African-Americans making up an estimated 8–12 percent of the some 150 thousand Bahá'ís in the United States.

History and Development of the Bahá'í Faith

THE BÁBÍ MOVEMENT

During the nineteenth century a wave of messianic expectation swept over the Islamic and Christian worlds. Some Shia Muslims were eagerly awaiting the return of the Imam Mahdi, the appointed successor of Muḥammad,[14] while in Europe and the United States many Christians were expecting the return of Christ. In 1844, a young merchant in Shiraz,

Persia (now Iran), named Siyyid ʿAlí Muḥammad (1819–50), claimed that he was the Twelfth Imam and the promised Qaʾím awaited by Shia Islam. Before long he set up a new system of holy law to replace that of Islam. He took the title "the Báb" (meaning "gate") and inspired a new religion. The Báb "proclaimed that the central purpose of his mission was to prepare for the coming of the universal manifestation of God,"[15] whom he referred to as, "He whom God will make manifest." His followers were called Bábís, and the faith rapidly spread throughout the country, attracting thousands of followers from all ranks of society.[16]

A massive, bloody reaction ensued, as the Persian government and many of the ulama (the Islamic priest class) moved to crush the new religious movement. Leading Bábís were tortured and killed, along with thousands of others who joined the ranks of this young revolutionary religious movement. On July 9, 1850, the Báb himself was publically executed by firing squad.

By this time, the ranks of the leading Bábís had been decimated by violent deaths. In 1852 an unsuccessful attempt by two crazed Bábis to assassinate the Shah led to a murderous general persecution of the Bábis. The only recourse for the survivors was to go underground. However, this brief and bloody history was heroic and far-reaching.[17] This was only the first stage in a marginal religious movement that would evolve into a world religion.

The Baháʾí Faith

The Bábí movement was infused with a new spirit when one of its most prominent members, Mírzá Ḥusayn-ʿAlí Núrí (1817–92), later to become known as Baháʾuʾlláh, (meaning "Glory of God" or "Splendor of God"), became the spiritual leader of the Bábís. He joined the Bábí religion and played a leading role in promulgating the new movement. He was also persecuted during this time and spent four months in the infamous horrible prison, the "Black Pit" in Tehran. After his release, he and his family were forced into exile in Ottoman Iraq, where he spent some time in Baghdad as well as in the mountains of Sulaymaniyyah. Concerned that Baháʾuʾlláh's presence would reignite the Bábí movement, the Iranian authorities asked their Ottoman counterparts to send Baháʾuʾlláh and his followers to Constantinople (now Istanbul, Turkey). Before leaving, Bahá'u'lláh and his followers held a special meeting in a garden situated on the outskirts of Baghdad which they called the Garden of Riḍván (meaning "paradise"). It was during Bahá'u'lláh's twelve days in this garden (April 21–May 2, 1863) that he proclaimed to his companions that he was a prophet of God.[18]

From there, Bahá'u'lláh and his party were further exiled to Constantinople and soon after were exiled again, this time to Adrianople (now Edirne, Turkey). Here Bahá'u'llah made public his claim to be "a divine messenger and the promised one foretold by the Báb." The majority of Bábís accepted Bahá'u'lláh's claims and became Bahá'ís (meaning "followers of Bahá"). It was at this time that the Bahá'í Faith became a religion distinct from the former Bábí faith. Two years later, Bahá'u'llah was once again exiled, this time to the prison-city of Acre in Ottoman Syria (now Israel). According to Bahá'í scholar Peter Smith, "It was during this period of Bahá'u'lláh's exile in Syria (1868–92) that the Bahá'í Faith was consolidated as a religious movement."[19]

This would be the last place of exile for Bahá'u'lláh. After several years of imprisonment, his situation was changed to house arrest. Exiled in one of the most desolate prison-cities in the Middle East, Bahá'u'lláh continued to explain the teachings he had begun during earlier periods of exile. For example, between 1857 and 1858, he had written a book entitled the Hidden Words (Kalimát-i-Maknúnih), in which he "emphasized the practical, moral and spiritual demands of man's relationship with God." In another book, written in 1862, the Book of Certitude (Kitáb-i-Íqán), he "outlined in clear language the Bábí (Bahá'í) doctrine of prophetic succession . . . assured his readers of the continuing bounty and guidance of God, and described the basic requirements for those who wish to become 'true seekers' after God."[20]

While in exile in Adrianople between 1863 and 1868, Bahá'u'lláh focused his writing on several major themes, foremost among them was his claim to be a messenger from God who had brought divine guidance to prepare humanity for the next stage in its collective evolution. He began to "prescribe the pattern of life which his followers should adopt, and prepared the first of a series of proclamatory letters to the rulers of the world in which he announced his mission and admonished them to work for justice and international conciliation. He also forbade religious militancy and instructed his followers to avoid sedition."[21]

Bahá'u'lláh continued these themes during the exile period in Acre. He sent letters proclaiming his mission to the rulers of Britain, Iran, the Ottoman Empire, Russia, and France, and to Pope Pius IX and some major Islamic leaders.[22] In 1873, he completed the Kitáb-i-Aqdas, literally, the "Most Holy Book." William Hatcher and Douglas Martin explain the significance of this historical event in their book *The Bahá'í Faith: The Emerging Global Religion:*

> The ten-year period beginning in 1863, which constituted the formal declaration of Bahá'u'lláh's mission, culminated in the completion of the book that today serves as the core of what Bahá'ís regard as the revelation of Bahá'u'lláh, the Kitáb-i-Aqdas. . . . [which] provides for the establishment and continuation of the authority Bahá'u'lláh called upon humanity to accept.[23]

This book "begins with a reiteration of his claims to be 'the King of Kings,' whose mission is none other than the establishment of the Kingdom of God on earth. Its two major themes are the proclamation of the laws which are to transform individual souls and guide humankind collectively, and the creation of institutions through which the community of those who recognize him is to be governed."[24]

It is important to note, as Hatcher and Martin point out, that "the system of the Aqdas entirely replaced, for Bahá'ís, both those Islamic laws which the Báb had left unabrogated and the strict code which the Báb himself had laid down. . . . The completion of the Kitáb-i-Aqdas opened the final period of Bahá'u'lláh's ministry."[25] Bahá'u'lláh devoted the rest of his life to producing a vast body of writings—encompassing more than a hundred volumes—that explained his vision of the future of humankind. As he entered the last years of his ministry, he devoted time to writing and meeting Bahá'í pilgrims, who traveled great distances to be in his presence. He entrusted to his eldest son, 'Abdu'l-Bahá (1844–1921), the management of the growing Bahá'í community. On May 29, 1892, Bahá'u'lláh died of natural causes.

'ABDU'L-BAHÁ: THE CENTER OF THE COVENANT

After the passing of Bahá'u'lláh, the Bahá'í Faith entered a new stage of its development. This stage was facilitated by way of a "covenant" previously authored by Bahá'u'lláh that appointed his son, 'Abdu'l-Bahá, as his successor and the authorized interpreter of his teachings. Bahá'í scholars and commentators have argued that it is this covenant, which has no parallel in religious history, that has protected the Bahá'í Faith from separating into sects and divisions:

> Bahá'u'lláh had raised His peerless Son to be the Centre of His Covenant. In a document which He designated *Kitáb-i-'Ahdi—the Book of My Covenant*—a document the like of which cannot be found in the whole range of the Scriptures of humankind, he made His purpose indubitably clear that 'Abdu'l-Bahá was to be the head of His Faith, the Expounder of His Word, the Unerring Balance by Whom falsehood was distinguished and separated from truth.[26]

This direct line of authority was essential in protecting the unity and growth of the faith. "This was Bahá'u'lláh's explicit conveyance of authority for the establishment of an institutional system designed to guide, protect, and enlarge the emerging Bahá'í community."[27]

Notwithstanding the direct guidance by Bahá'u'lláh appointing 'Abdu'l-Bahá as his successor, opposition arose from among some members of his family and their supporters. However, the Bahá'í Faith continued its growth and development under the leadership of 'Abdu'l-Bahá, who began the process of building an international religious community based on the teachings of Bahá'u'lláh.[28] A key component of this process involved nurturing Bahá'í administrative institutions. As called upon under the terms of Bahá'u'lláh's covenant, "'Abdu'l-Bahá encouraged the establishment of what he called 'spiritual assemblies' in both North America and Persia."[29] This stage of Bahá'í institutional development was crucial for the future growth and consolidation of the Faith. These spiritual assemblies constituted "elected bodies . . . authorized to supervise activities such as publishing literature, teaching programs, and devotional services at both the local and national levels. They were to serve as forerunners of what Bahá'u'lláh had termed 'Houses of Justice.'"[30]

In describing the historical significance of 'Abdu'l-Bahá's visits to Europe and North America, Shoghi Effendi wrote: "'Abdu'l-Bahá's historic journeys to the West, and in particular His eight-month tour of the United States of America, may be said to have marked the culmination of His ministry, a ministry whose untold blessing and stupendous achievement only future generations can adequately estimate."[31] The greatest achievement of 'Abdu'l-Bahá's ministry was the establishment of the Bahá'í Faith in the Western Hemisphere. As Shoghi Effendi wrote in his history of the Bahá'í Faith in 1944:

> The establishment of the Faith of Bahá'u'lláh in the Western Hemisphere—the most outstanding achievement that will forever be associated with 'Abdu'l-Bahá's ministry . . . set in motion such tremendous forces, and been productive of such far-reaching results, as to warrant the active and personal participation of the Center of the Covenant Himself in those epoch-making activities which His Western disciples had, through the propelling power of that Covenant, boldly initiated and were vigorously prosecuting.[32]

During World War I 'Abdu'l-Bahá addressed a series of letters to the Bahá'ís of Canada and the United States called the "Tablets of the Divine Plan."[33] 'Abdu'l-Bahá addressed these "Tablets" to North American Bahá'ís for "the worldwide proclamation of Bahá'u'lláh's message to humankind."[34] In them, the Bahá'ís of Canada and the United States "were called upon to take the lead in establishing the faith in every part of the globe."[35] These letters provided the foundation for the international teaching plans by which the Bahá'í community has grown and the teachings of Bahá'u'lláh have been promulgated throughout the world.[36]

SHOGHI EFFENDI: GUARDIAN OF THE BAHÁ'Í FAITH

On November 28, 1921, 'Abdu'l-Bahá died in Haifa, Palestine. He appointed Shoghi Effendi (1897–1957), his eldest grandson, to succeed him as the "Guardian of the Cause Of God." Members of the community designated as "Hands of the Cause" would provide assistance and support for the Guardian.

The Guardianship conferred the sole authority for the interpretation of Bahá'í teachings on 'Abdu'l-Bahá's eldest grandson, Shoghi Effendi Rabbani. As was the case with the appointment of 'Abdu'l-Bahá in Bahá'u'lláh's Covenant as the Center and designated interpreter, the Guardian was designated the one to whom all the believers were to submit questions on any matter of Bahá'í belief.[37]

Shoghi Effendi was the spiritual head of the Bahá'í Faith from 1921 until his death in 1957. As Guardian of the Bahá'í Faith, he had two major functions: to interpret the Bahá'í teachings and guide the Bahá'í community. "From the beginning of his Guardianship," Hatcher and Martin explain,

Shoghi Effendi made it clear that not only had the Bahá'í Faith entered a new stage in its growth, but that the authority conveyed by ['Abdu'l-Bahá's Will and Testament] involved a function quite different from the charismatic leadership of the community characterized by 'Adbu'l-Bahá. What he called the "apostolic era" had passed, and the "formative age" had begun.[38]

Shoghi Effendi described the formative age or period thus:

The Formative Period, the Iron Age, of that Dispensation was now beginning, the Age in which the institutions, local, national and international of the Faith of Bahá'u'lláh were to take shape, develop and become fully consolidated, in anticipation of the third, the last, the Golden Age destined to witness the emergence of a world-embracing Order enshrining the ultimate fruit of God's latest Revelation to mankind, a fruit whose maturity must signalize the establishment of a world civilization and the formal inauguration of the Kingdom of the Father upon earth as promised by Jesus Christ Himself.[39]

It was during the period of Shoghi Effendi's leadership that the worldwide Bahá'í administrative structure was developed. Soon after he assumed the leadership of the Bahá'í community, Shoghi Effendi, drawing on the writings of Bahá'u'lláh and 'Abdu'l-Bahá, instructed the Bahá'ís to establish Local Spiritual Assemblies in all areas in which nine or more adult Bahá'ís resided. All Bahá'í activities were to be under the auspices of Local and National Spiritual Assemblies. Through countless letters, He carefully and lovingly guided these fledgling assemblies as they struggled to become functioning Bahá'í institutions.[40]

Shoghi Effendi invested an enormous amount of time and energy into developing the administrative institutions of the Bahá'í Faith. The reason for this careful development of local and national institutions during the early stages of his ministry was because the

> administrative institutions of the faith provided the necessary instruments for the implementation of 'Abdu'l-Bahá's "Divine Plan" to spread the Bahá'í message around the world. Before the widely scattered community could undertake so great a task, it was essential that adequate time be allowed for these institutions to learn the rudiments of Bahá'í administration and consultation.[41]

By 1937, Bahá'í administrative institutions were now ready to become vehicles for the implementation of 'Abdu'l-Bahá's "Divine Plan." Systematic plans were now the order of the day; detailed and targeted goals were developed for the expansion and consolidation of the Bahá'í community as part of a strategy of worldwide expansion. At first, only the North American Bahá'í community was assigned plans. As other Bahá'í national communities developed and became better organized, they were given their own plans and goals. In the first American Seven Year Plan (1937–44), "[T]he Bahá'ís were called to establish permanent residence in all of the states and provinces of North America and in each of the Latin American republics." After this period, the Bahá'ís were given a two year period to consolidate their gains. They were then given a second Seven Year Plan (1946–53). The goals for this plan included further expansion in the Americas and the widening of the social base of the community, the creation of new National Spiritual Assemblies in Canada and in Central and South America, and the beginning of a systematic teaching campaign in post-war Europe.[42]

Between 1951 and 1957, Shoghi Effendi appointed a number of Bahá'ís of outstanding character and dedication as "Hands of the Cause of God." They were responsible for both teaching the Faith and protecting the institutions. They were also charged with assisting selected National Spiritual Assemblies in achieving the goals of the later Ten Year Crusade.[43]

No sooner had the second Seven Year Plan been completed than Shoghi Effendi launched another plan, the most ambitious one in the history of the Bahá'í Faith. He called this global teaching plan, a "Ten Year World Crusade." It would end in 1963, marking the centenary of the Declaration of Bahá'u'lláh in the Garden of Riḍván. By the end of this plan, the Bahá'í Faith had spread to 132 new countries and territories; established communities in 120 countries and territories; National Spiritual Assemblies had been established in the majority of the countries in Latin America and Europe; and there was a great increase in the numbers of new Bahá'ís, assemblies and property endowments. Among the many impressive accomplishments of the Ten Year Plan was the dramatic increase of languages into which the Bahá'í literature had been translated and printed. The number had more than doubled. Most of this increase had occurred in the Asiatic and African Continents, adding to the racial and cultural diversity of the Bahá'í world community.[44] This was, indeed, a great accomplishment for the Bahá'í Faith.

Unfortunately, Shoghi Effendi did not live to see the fruits of his most ambitious Global Crusade. He died unexpectedly in November 1957. His death stunned the Bahá'í community; but under the leadership of the Hands of the Cause collaborating with National Spiritual Assemblies, both acting on the guidance that they had already received from the Guardian, the Ten Year Plan was completed and the Universal House of Justice was elected in 1963.[45]

THE UNIVERSAL HOUSE OF JUSTICE

The Universal House of Justice is "designated to be the primary legislative and administrative authority of the Bahá'í community."[46] As the supreme administrative body of the community, its elected members would be chosen from among the adult Bahá'ís—those of age twenty-one and older—of the world at an international congress of all the national spiritual assemblies. The first election of the Universal House of Justice on April 21, 1963, on the hundredth anniversary of the declaration of Bahá'u'lláh's mission, was a great moment in Bahá'í history. This young religion, based upon the principle of the oneness of all races, religions, and nations, had survived a century of struggle, persecution and internal conflicts, and succeeded in proclaiming its message of love and unity around the world. It had now, in 1963, elected through a democratic process involving fifty-one National and Regional Spiritual Assemblies, the supreme administrative body of the Bahá'í World Faith. Shoghi Effendi claimed the Universal House of Justice "is to be the exponent and guardian of that Divine Justice which can alone insure the security of, and establish the reign of law and order in, a strangely disordered world."[47] From 1963 to the present, the Universal House of Justice, based in Haifa, Israel, has provided spiritual guidance for the Bahá'í Faith as it has continued to grow and develop throughout the world.

2

The "Pupil of the Eye": African-Americans and the Making of the American Bahá'í Community

Richard Thomas

The Black "Pupil of the Eye": The Foundational Bahá'í Teaching of the Spiritual Qualities of Blacks

When Bahá'u'lláh proclaimed his prophethood and declared his mission in Baghdad during the spring of 1863, President Lincoln had already set free over three-fourths of the slaves in the United States.[1] Before Bahá'u'lláh's death in 1892, however, these newly freed slaves were well on their way to losing much of their freedom due to what historians John Hope Franklin and Alfred A. Moss, Jr., call "the Triumph of White Supremacy" in the South.[2] The partitioning of Africa among the European powers during the Berlin Conference of 1884–5 contributed to the further globalization of White supremacy over Africans and people of African descent.[3]

Notwithstanding the growing influence of the ideology of White supremacy in the United States, Europe, and colonial Africa, with its emphasis upon the inferiority of Blacks,[4] the prophet founder of the Bahá'í Faith "compared the colored people to the black pupil of the eye surrounded by the White. In this black pupil, he declared, is seen the reflection of that which is before it, and through it the light of the spirit shineth forth."[5] This spiritual description of "colored people," later to be applied mainly to people of African descent, soon became the cornerstone of Bahá'í teachings on the spiritual qualities of Black people and their historical role in the growth and expansion of the Bahá'í Faith.

The association of people of African descent with the "pupil of the eye" has had far-reaching positive implications for Black Bahá'ís throughout the diaspora. Along with other Bahá'í teachings, this image of them as the pupil of the eye greatly enhanced their sense of racial pride and connection to a worldwide religious movement dedicated to the unification of all races, nations, and religions. It also challenged racist images and stereotypes of Black people and encouraged a radical reevaluation and transformation of traditional White racial thinking within the Bahá'í community. For example, in the second edition of her book, *The Pupil of the Eye: African Americans in the World Order of Bahá'u'lláh*, Bonnie J. Taylor, a White Bahá'í, thanked Drs. May Khadem Czerniejewski and Rick Czerniejewski, Persian-American and Polish-American Bahá'ís, respectively, "who lovingly prepared the beautiful description of the pupil of the eye that is included in this book." The following description is a testimony to the influence that this specific teaching has had on the "racial" thinking of non-Black Bahá'ís.

The pupil of the eye is a portal which admits and regulates the flow of light to the retina. Without this passage, no images are perceived. At the retina, our consciousness is intimately in contact with physical reality, for the brain's cells themselves flow out to the retina to receive information through the illumination modulated by the pupil.

The pupil has the dual function of light gathering and modulation. Light, which unites all colors and is composed of all colors, illumines physical reality, but at the same time its intensity can destroy the delicate structures of the eye. When light levels are high, it constricts to protect the retina from intense and even damaging exposure. Since sight is often described as our most precious sensory ability, we can say that the pupil helps to protect this most precious gift. On the other hand, when there is very little light the pupil admits more light through dilating, thus permitting sight even in very dark places.

The black appearance of the pupil is deceptive. The pupil appears black only until the inside of the eye is illumined. Than it becomes radiant, filled with a warm, reddish-orange glow. With this reflection from the inside of the eye, the pupil itself become a source of illumination.

The most remarkable quality of the pupil is that despite its vital service, it is the embodiment of "the hollow reed from which the pith of self hath been blown," for it is the absence of physical structure that permits it to facilitate the harmonious functioning of all the other components of the eye that make sight possible.[6]

This description of "the pupil of the eye" by two non-Black Bahá'ís, one an opthalmologist, is their way of exploring the physical or material meaning of the term, and in so doing, enhancing its spiritual significance. By exploring the physical characteristics of the eye, they opened up new ways of seeing and appreciating "blackness" in a society where it has always had a negative connotation.

The spiritual leaders of the Bahá'í Faith often referred to the "pupil of the eye" when discussing or addressing Blacks. For example, 'Abdu'l-Bahá, Bahá'u'lláh's son and leader of the Bahá'í community from 1892 until

1921, wrote in a letter to the prominent African-American Bahá'í Louis G. Gregory: "O thou who hast an illuminated heart! Thou art even as the pupil of the eye, the very wellspring of the light, for God's love hath cast its rays upon thine innermost being and thou hast turned thy face toward the Kingdom of the Lord."[7]

After receiving a photograph of Robert Turner, the first African-American Bahá'í, 'Abdu'l-Bahá responded with loving praise for both his racial traits and spiritual qualities.

> O thou who are pure in heart, sanctified in spirit, peerless in character, beauteous in face! Thy photograph hath been received revealing thy physical frame in the utmost grace and best appearance. Thou are dark in countenance and bright in character. Thou are like unto the pupil of the eye which is dark in color, yet it is the fount of light and the revealer of the contingent world.[8]

Imagine, if you will, being an African-American during the first decade of the twentieth century, when White supremacist ideas and White images of Black inferiority permeated American culture, and receiving such praise for your race and your character from the spiritual leader of your religion. "I have not forgotten nor will I forget thee," 'Abdul-Bahá wrote to Gregory, "I beseech God that He may graciously make thee the sign of His bounty amidst mankind, illumine thy face with the light of such blessings as are vouchsafed by the merciful Lord, single thee out for His love in this age which is distinguished among all the past ages and centuries."[9]

Rúhíyyih Khánum, the widow of the Guardian of the Bahá'í Faith, Shoghi Effendi, wrote in 1961:

> When Bahá'u'lláh likens the Negro race to the faculty of sight in the human body—the act of perception with all it implies—it is a pretty terrific statement. He never said this of anyone else. . . .
>
> I thought the American Negro's humility, his kindness, friendliness, courtesy and hospitableness were something to do with his oppression and the background of slavery. But after spending weeks,

day after day in the villages of Africa, seeing literally thousands of Bahá'ís and non-Bahá'ís, I have wakened up to the fact that the American Negro has these beautiful qualities not because he was enslaved but because he has the characteristics of his race.[10]

Rúḥíyyih Khánum explained how other Bahá'í teachings on spiritual qualities helped her to understand why "the Guardian so constantly spoke of the 'pure-hearted' African." She pointed out how "the emphasis on the heart in our Bahá'í Faith is overwhelming, 'My first counsel is this; possess a pure, kindly and radiant heart.' 'Thy heart is my habitation'— 'All in heaven and on earth have I ordained for thee except the human heart which I have made the habitation of my Beauty and Glory.'"[11]

As applied to Blacks, she concludes, "It is this spiritual quality defined as 'heart' in our teachings which I think is one of the priceless gifts the Negro race is going to share with others in the [Bahá'í] community."[12]

The First Generation of African-American Bahá'ís

Bahá'u'lláh's teachings emphasizing the oneness of the human family have always had a special appeal to African-Americans. He proclaimed that all people were "created from the same dust . . . [t]hat no one should himself over the other."[13] Due to the long experience with White racial discrimination at the hands of State and Church, many African-Americans were attracted by the spirit of universality reflected in the words of Bahá'u'lláh from their first exposure.

During the 1890s, when the Bahá'í Faith was first introduced to a small group of White Americans, a much smaller group of African-Americans were also being swept up in this new universal faith that promised to unite the world peoples into one family. Several decades later, the Bahá'í Faith in the United States would capture the hearts and minds of a range of African-Americans. The first African-American Bahá'í was Robert Turner, the Black butler of Phoebe Hearst, who was one of the early American Bahá'ís and the mother of the famous publisher William Randolph Hearst. Turner's first exposure to the Bahá'í Faith occurred as he listened to an early American Bahá'í, Lua M. Getsinger, teach the Bahá'í Faith to his employer. Turner was so affected by these teachings that he pursued opportunities to hear more. He learned more about the Bahá'í Faith and eventually became a firm believer sometime around late 1898.[14]

Turner's exposure to the Bahá'í Faith and its teachings deepened when he accompanied Mrs. Hearst on her journey to Palestine (in what is now northern Israel) to visit 'Abdu'l-Bahá, the son of Bahá'u'lláh, who became the head of the Bahá'í Faith after his father's death. When Mrs. Hearst and her party arrived in the Holy Land, several of them noticed 'Abdu'l-Bahá's great affection for Turner, which transcended the normal social etiquette of race relations in Western societies. Obviously embarrassed by all the attention 'Adbu'l-Bahá was bestowing upon him, Turner felt that he was unworthy to be present, no doubt because he was not only Black, but also a butler. However, 'Abdu'l-Bahá embraced Turner and then gave a talk that included an obvious reference to the Black butler: "We can all serve in the Cause of God no matter what our occupation is. No occupation can prevent the soul coming to God. Peter was a fisherman, yet he accomplished most wonderful things; but the heart must be turned always toward God, no matter what the work is: this is the important thing; and then the power of God will work in us."[15]

'Abdu'l-Bahá's demonstration of love and affection for Turner was a lesson in the Bahá'í approach to racial and social equality for all the White members of the party. Here was a pure demonstration of how a true Bahá'í should act towards all members of the human race. Yet there was much more to 'Abdu'l-Bahá's demonstration of love for the Black butler. 'Abdu'l-Bahá saw Robert Turner playing a vital role in the history of the spiritual development of Black people. According to one source, he assured Turner that "if he remained firm and steadfast until the end, he would be the door through which a whole race would enter the Kingdom."[16]

Mrs. Hearst was so influenced by 'Abdu'l-Bahá's affection for her butler that soon after she returned home, she invited a group of prominent Black educators to meet with her. They were lavishly entertained and served great food while she told them about the Bahá'í Faith.[17] Robert Turner remained a Bahá'í to the end of his life[18] and thus became the "door," as 'Abdu'l-Bahá had told him, through which thousands of African-Americans entered the American Bahá'í community.

For several decades, a small but steady stream of African-Americans passed through that door opened by Robert Turner into the Bahá'í Faith, particularly African-American women. It was only a year after Robert Turner became a Bahá'í that Olive Jackson of New York City joined the Bahá'í Faith, becoming the first Black woman in the United States to join the faith. In 1911, Susie C. Stewart of Richmond, Virginia, became a Bahá'í, followed by Leila Y. Pane in 1912, who had heard 'Abdu'l-Bahá speak at the Metropolitan AME Church in Washington, DC, during his tour of North America. Ms. Stewart was also notable as she was one of the first African-American Bahá'ís involved in raising funds for the building of the Bahá'í House of Worship in Wilmette, Illinois. Another African-American woman, Harriet Gibbs-Marshall of Atlantic City, New Jersey, also became a Bahá'í in 1912. She was one of the most impressive women, Black or White, to join the early American Bahá'í community. Not only was she very well educated for both her race and her sex for the time in which she lived, but she was also musically talented, and established a conservatory for African-American students in Washington.[19]

The Martin family of Cleveland was one of the first Black families in the United States to embrace the Bahá'í Faith. After hearing a talk by Louis Gregory, the most prominent African-American Bahá'í during these early years, Mary Martin, a school teacher, and her husband, Alexander, a lawyer, studied the faith for a year before joining the Bahá'í community. Alexander Martin completed law school at Western Reserve in 1898 "and was one of the first Black Americans elected to Phi Beta Kappa in the nineteenth century."[20]

One of the most impressive examples of an African-American's attraction and devotion to the Bahá'í Faith was seen in Dorothy Champ. She was a designer, singer, model, and a dancer in the popular Hall Johnson play Green Pastures. She also performed in one of Earl Carroll's shows. Champ was so inspired by the Bahá'í teachings that she gave up her career to devote her life to teaching the Bahá'í Faith after joining the Bahá'í community in 1919. Later she became the first Black to be elected to New York City's Local Spiritual Assembly, the governing body of the

Bahá'í community in that city. From that moment on, Champ devoted herself to lecturing on the Bahá'í Faith throughout the country. When she died in 1979, she had established herself as one of the greatest teachers of the Bahá'í Faith in the United States.[21] A report on Dorothy Champ, written in 1950, commented that in the year 2050, "Somebody will read of Dorothy Champ and her service to the Bahá'í Faith, in the *Syracuse Daily Orange*, the daily newspaper of the University of Syracuse, in which the analysis of [her] talk was carried, was buried in a time capsule beneath the bank in Syracuse, alone with other important examples of Syracuse University in the year 1950, to be unearthed in 2050."[22]

Louis Gregory and the Racial Challenges in a New Religion

It was a lawyer named Louis Gregory who had the most exemplary role among African-Americans in the making of the early American Bahá'í community. As pointed out by Gayle Morrison in her excellent biography:

At the heart of the most challenging issue for the American Bahá'í community—the problem of obliterating racial prejudice—stands Louis George Gregory. A highly regarded teacher, writer, and lecturer throughout the first half of the century, and the first Black to serve on the national administrative body of the Bahá'ís of the United States and Canada, Louis Gregory is a major historical figure. Few Blacks of his era were ever elected or appointed repeatedly to positions of national leadership in organizations with a White majority. None worked more tirelessly for the removal of racial prejudice.[23]

He first heard about the Bahá'í Faith from a Southern White man; he was taught the Bahá'í Faith by Joseph and Pauline Hannen, two White Bahá'ís. He was also the second African-American to meet 'Abdu'l-Bahá in the Holy Land, though 'Abdu'l-Bahá, the spiritual head of the Bahá'í Faith, had known of the young Black spiritual seeker two years earlier. The Hannens mentioned him to 'Abdu'l-Bahá during their trip to the

Holy Land in 1909. 'Abdu'l-Bahá told them to continue teaching Gregory and that he would soon become a Bahá'í. They followed 'Abdu'l Bahá's instructions and Louis Gregory joined the Bahá'í Faith in April that year.[24]

Gregory wrote to 'Abdu'l-Bahá soon after he became a Bahá'í and received a reply in November of that year. 'Abdu'l-Bahá's reply included one of the greatest challenges given to anyone in the Bahá'í community in the United States with regard to racial harmony: "I hope that thou mayest become . . . the means whereby the whites and colored people shall close their eyes to racial differences and behold the reality of humanity, and that is the universal unity which is the oneness of the kingdom of the human race, the basic harmony of the world and the appearance of the bounty of the almighty."[25]

Realizing the tremendous burden he was placing upon this new African-American Bahá'í, who was at the time experiencing racism not only from the larger White society, but also from some White Bahá'ís, 'Abdu'l-Bahá encouraged Gregory not to "look upon . . . thy limited capacity; look thou upon the Bounties and Providence of the Lord of the Kingdom, for His Confirmation is great, and His Power unparalleled and incomparable."[26] In loving language, 'Abdu'l-Bahá, who had himself endured a lifetime of oppression and hardship, encouraged Gregory to "rely as much as thou canst upon the True One [God], and be thou resigned to the Will of God, so that like unto a candle, thou mayest be enkindled in the world of humanity and like unto a star, thou mayest shine and gleam from the Horizon of Reality and become the cause of the guidance of both races."[27]

Louis Gregory accepted this challenge and, as a result, greatly influenced both the interracial history of the Bahá'í community and the larger society. Accepting such a challenge, however, meant a great deal of sacrifice, as his biographer explains:

> In 1909, at the age of thirty-five, he turned his back on a secure economic position as a lawyer within the small elite of Black professionals, directing increasing degrees of attention to a new unpaid calling. For the rest of his long life, he put his Bahá'í activities foremost, finally abandoning his profession altogether to become a

"racial amity worker," as he often referred to himself, surviving on
a bare subsistence, devoting himself to the self-imposed demands
of his work: constant travel, writing, and lecturing in the cause of
racial unity.[28]

Born in Charleston, South Carolina, on June 6, 1874, during the era
of Reconstruction and growing into adulthood amid the emergence of
the era of Jim Crow segregation,[29] Gregory accepted the responsibility of
building bridges between Black and White Americans in a predominantly
White religious community still resistant to the radical social implications
of the Bahá'í teachings on the oneness of the human race. The biggest
spiritual and racial challenge for Gregory which began before he was
encouraged by 'Abdu'l-Bahá, was what Morrison describes as "the partially
segregated Bahá'í community of Washington, DC."[30] Such racial practices
within the Bahá'í community did not help Gregory's credibility among
his African-American friends. "As soon as I became a believer and began
to teach [others about the Bahá'í Faith] . . . my colored friends got on my
back and began to press me with troublous questions. If this were a New
Religion which stood for unity, why were its devotees divided? Why did
they not meet together in one place? Were the Bahá'ís not full of prejudice
like other people?"[31]

As concerned as he was about the obvious shortcomings of some of
the White Bahá'ís in the area, Gregory did not allow them to dampen his
spirit. The White couple that had taught him about the Bahá'í Faith
always welcomed him and his African-American friends to their home,
and this no doubt encouraged Gregory to continue as a Bahá'í, and it
sustained him until he received 'Abdu'l Bahá's encouragement and spiritual
challenge.

Louis Gregory not only received much encouragement in letters from
'Abdu'l-Bahá, but in 1911 met with him in the Holy Land. Whatever
concerns Gregory might have had about the race issue within the
Washington, DC, Bahá'í community were addressed by 'Abdu'l-Bahá
during their first meeting, when 'Abdu'l-Bahá himself raised the issue.
On one occasion, 'Abdu'l-Bahá asked Gregory about conflict between
the Black and White races. 'Abdu'l Bahá's question made Gregory smile,

and he later wrote, "I at once felt that my enquirer, although he had never in person visited America, yet knew more of conditions than I could ever know."[32] Gregory told ʻAbduʾl-Bahá that much friction existed between Blacks and Whites and that "those who accepted the Baháʾí teachings had hopes of an amicable settlement of racial differences while others were despondent. Among the friends were earnest souls who wished for a closer unity of races and hoped that He might point out the way to them."[33] ʻAbduʾl-Bahá inquired further, "Does this refer to the removal of hatreds and antagonisms on the part of one race, or of both races?" "Both races," Gregory answered. ʻAbduʾl-Bahá replied that it would be done.[34]

Gregory's answer seems to have been calculated to protect the feelings of White American Baháʾís. He was not one to speak ill of others even if they were violating Baháʾí teachings on the oneness of the human race. He had been concerned about the racial segregation in some of the Baháʾí meetings in Washington, DC, yet Gregory chose not to place the total burden of racial antagonism on Whites, thought he knew they were the main perpetrators of racial antagonism in the United States. No doubt, ʻAbduʾl-Bahá understood Gregory's reluctance to place most of the blame on Whites. This humble and forgiving characteristic of Gregory's endeared him to ʻAbduʾl-Bahá, who must have sensed the anguish of this Black spiritual pioneer reluctant to burden his spiritual leader with the racial problems of the United States.

During this discussion, someone in the party mentioned that a suggestion had been made that the "central meeting"—a public meeting—in Washington, DC, should be open to all races, but that group meetings—those for Baháʾís only—should be set up along racial lines, meaning racially segregated. ʻAbduʾl-Bahá replied, "There must be no distinction in Baháʾí meetings. All are equal."[35] ʻAbduʾl-Bahá then expressed his approval of the working committee, an administrative body of the Washington, DC, Baháʾís, for providing representation to African-American Baháʾís and said that he would pray for them. In response to the question: "What should the colored race do to improve its material and spiritual condition?" ʻAbduʾl-Bahá's response was: "[T]he best thing for it is to accept these teachings. In this way they will gain the confidence of the Whites and differences will fade. The Bahá'í teachings reveal the means of both material and spiritual progress."[36]

'Abdu'l-Bahá had already demonstrated his keen interest in the racial problems in the United States. Gregory had not come to 'Abdu'l-Bahá complaining about racial discrimination in the American Bahá'í community. Instead, 'Abdu'l-Bahá had asked Gregory about the situation, and both Gregory and his White fellow Bahá'ís must have been a bit surprised when they discovered the full social implications of some of the Bahá'í teachings on race, since those teachings extended far beyond the imagination of the majority of White and Black Bahá'ís. For example, during this period in American history, racially integrated meetings constituted a giant step forward in social relations between the races. Furthermore, many White Bahá'ís could not bring themselves to accept interracial marriage, which was taboo in American and was even legally banned in twenty five states.[37] Yet 'Abdu'l-Bahá's position on interracial marriage was clear. As he told Louis Gregory and the other pilgrims: "If you have any influence to get the races to intermarry, it will be very valuable. Such unions will beget very strong and beautiful children. If you wish, I will reveal a Tablet in regard to the wiping out of racial difference."[38]

Gregory's pilgrimage to the Holy Land and his discussions with 'Abdu'l-Bahá would prepare him for a life of teaching the Bahá'í principles in the United States.

During 'Abdu'l-Bahá's tour of the United States in 1912, he never missed an opportunity to proclaim the Bahá'í teachings on the oneness of humanity as it related to unity among racial groups, particularly Blacks and Whites, such as this excerpt from a public meeting in New York:

God maketh no distinction between the white and the black. If the hearts are pure both are acceptable unto Him. God is no respecter of persons on account of either color or race. All colors are acceptable to Him, be they white, black, or yellow. Inasmuch as all were created in the image of God, we must bring ourselves to realize that all embody divine possibilities. If you go into a garden and find all the flowers alike in form, species and color, the effect is wearisome to the eye. The garden is more beautiful when the flowers are many-colored and different; the variety lends charm and adornment. In a flock of doves some are white, some black, red, blue; yet they make no distinction among themselves. All are doves no matter what the color.[39]

In order to impress upon the Bahá'í community in the United States the importance of interracial marriage as a reflection of the Bahá'í belief in the oneness of the human race, 'Abdu'l-Bahá encouraged Louis Gregory to marry Louisa Mathew, a White Bahá'í from England. Their union was the first interracial marriage among the Bahá'ís in the United States[40] and served as a living example of the Bahá'í belief in racial unity. Notwithstanding 'Abdu'l-Bahá's explicit teachings on the benefits of interracial marriage, most Black and White Bahá'ís in the Washington, DC, area, in which the Gregorys lived for a while, found "it difficult to accept the marriage or to imagine its survival in a segregated society."[41]

By 1912, Gregory was rapidly emerging as the foremost African-American teacher of the Bahá'í Faith in the country. He would remain so for many decades, just as he would spend his life working for racial unity between Blacks and Whites.

Though the institution of Hands of the Cause did not function formally during Gregory's lifetime, he was posthumously named a Hand of the Cause by Shoghi Effendi. He was one of nine others who had rendered exemplary service to the Faith during 'Abdu'l-Bahá's ministry and were given the title to recognize their position in Bahá'í history.

Bahá'í Teachings on the
Oneness of Humanity and Racial Unity

Given the long history of racism which C. Eric Lincoln called "the racial factor in the shaping of religion in America,"[42] it is only natural that the Bahá'í teachings on the oneness of humanity and interracial unity have been the major attraction for African-Americans who became Bahá'ís, from Dorothy Champ to Dizzy Gillespie, from college professors to sharecroppers. The power of those teachings can be seen in that even

African-Americans who did not become Bahá'ís have been impressed by
the Bahá'í teachings and have participated in Bahá'í activities on the
oneness of humanity and racial amity and unity.

The great African-American teacher and scientist Dr. George Washington Carver expressed great admiration for the Bahá'í Faith in a letter
to Roy C. Wilhelm, a White Bahá'í in New York who had discussed the
Bahá'í teachings with several African-American intellectuals. Carver wrote,
"I am so happy to know that the Christ-like gospel of good will is growing
throughout the world. You hold in your organization the key that will
settle all our difficulties, real and imaginary."[43]

Dr. Carver was only one of many non-Bahá'í African-Americans who
found much to respect in the Bahá'í teachings and activities centering
around the basic principles of the oneness of humanity and interracial
unity. Other African-Americans were exposed to Bahá'í teachings through
a series of talks on Bahá'í topics organized by Louis Gregory in his capacity
as president of the Bethel Literary and Historical Society, the oldest
African-American organization in Washington, DC. One such talk, given
in 1910 by two Bahá'ís, a White American and a Middle-Easterner, focused
on "The Race Question from the Standpoint of the Bahá'í Revelation."
It was the fourth talk by Bahá'ís presented at this center of African-
American intellectuals. According to Gregory's biographer, this was
Gregory's way of challenging segregation within some Bahá'í circles by
increasing the "number of Bahá'ís or serious students of the faith from
the gifted and influential circle of blacks in which . . . [he] moved."[44]
'Abdu'l-Bahá also spoke to this "gifted and influential circle of African-
Americans at the Bethel Literary and Historical Society" during his visit
to the United States in the early twentieth century.[45]

'Abdu'l-Bahá's uncompromising position on racial equality and unity
within the American Bahá'í community, his great demonstration of love
and respect for African-Americans, and his frank and honest lectures
and talks on the racial problems in the United States, warmed the hearts
of African-Americans. At every opportunity, he encouraged Black and
White Americans to solve the racial problems before it was too late.
Wherever he spoke, if there were Blacks and Whites in the audience, he
praised them. When he spoke at Howard University in April 1912, one

of his companions reported: "[H]ere, as elsewhere, when both white and colored people were present, 'Abdu'l-Bahá seemed happiest."[46] As he looked over the racially mixed audience at Howard, 'Abdu'l-Bahá remarked: "Today I am most happy, for I see here a gathering of the servants of God. I see white and black sitting together."[47]

'Abdu'l-Bahá spoke in White and Black homes and at the fourth annual meeting of the NAACP in Chicago.[48] When 'Abdu'l-Bahá returned to the Holy Land, he had left a legacy of goodwill within the African-American community. But his next move would be even more historically significant for African-American Bahá'í's and non-Bahá'ís.

Once back in Palestine, 'Abdu'l-Bahá arranged to set in motion one of the most far-reaching campaigns for the proclamation of the oneness of humanity and the promotion of racial amity in the history of race relations in the United States, which consisted of a "series of large, well-publicized interracial meetings, conducted not to promote a specific grievance or to seek improvement of the lot of American Blacks in some particular way, but to proclaim the oneness of mankind and to promote 'racial amity' between Black and White Americans."[49] He gave the responsibility for arranging this first race amity conference to Agnes Parsons, a wealthy White Bahá'í in Washington, DC. This conference was held in 1921 and included such impressive African-Americans as Joseph Douglass, the grandson of Frederick Douglass, and Dr. Alain Locke, along with many prominent Whites. 'Abdu'l-Bahá sent a special message to those gathered at the event: "Say to this convention that never since the beginning of time has one more important been held. This convention stands for the oneness of humanity; it will become the cause of enlightenment of America. It will, if wisely managed and continued, check the deadly struggle between these races that otherwise will inevitably break out."[50]

The first race amity conference attracted many African-American organizations, leaders, and scholars. It provided African-American Bahá'ís with a forum from which they could not only teach the basic principles of the Bahá'í Faith to their fellow African-Americans, but could also provide support for such groups as the NAACP and Urban League. John Weldon Johnson attended a Bahá'í race amity meeting held in New York City in March 1924. The NAACP and the National Urban League were among the major organizations at the conference. A succession of "similar conferences, interracial dinners, and fellowship meetings through the years" attracted other prominent African-Americans who were interested in the race amity work of the Bahá'ís, such as W. E. B. Du Bois, A. Philip Randolph, Samuel Allen, and James H. Hubert.[51]

For decades, other race amity and race unity conferences followed with a few short interruptions. These Bahá'í race amity conferences brought together African-Americans both within and outside the Bahá'í community, along with Whites, to share mutual concerns for the oneness of the human race and interracial unity. They also provided African-American scholars opportunities to expose large racially mixed gatherings to the fields of African and African-American history. In August 1931, Professor William Leo Hansberry of the History Department at Howard University presented his research on the "Negro Civilizations in Ancient Africa," at the Bahá'í-run Green Acre School, in Eliot, Maine. In December 1932 in New York, Arthur A. Schomberg, director of the Schomberg Collection, along with other African-Americans, such as Dr. Ira DeA. Reid, director of the research department of the National Urban League, and Dr. Alain Locke, took part in a race amity conference jointly sponsored by the National Bahá'í Committee for Racial Amity and the Urban League of New York.[52]

Bahá'í race amity (later called "race unity") conferences and activities created and maintained strong bonds between the American Bahá'í community and African-American leaders, organizations, and institutions. These conferences and activities also helped African-American Bahá'ís maintain social links with the broader African-American community. Without these linkages provided by such events, many African-American Bahá'ís might not have been able to overcome some of the racial barriers that yet remained in the Bahá'í community life.

The Role of African-American Bahá'ís in Building a Multiracial Religious Community

The development of the Bahá'í community in the United States from a predominantly White, upper class, partially segregated religious community, to one of the most racially diverse religious communities in the United States, depended in large part on the role of key African-American Bahá'ís. They persisted in focusing upon the teachings of Bahá'u'lláh and ignoring the periodic expressions of racism on the part of many White Bahá'ís. Unlike the White couple that taught Louis G. Gregory the Bahá'í Faith and hosted racially integrated meetings in their home, some White Bahá'ís did not understand or were unwilling to accept the basic Bahá'í principle of the oneness of the human race as meaning racial equality. Although 'Abdu'l-Bahá had instructed the Bahá'ís in Washington, DC, to hold racially integrated meetings "both in public places and in private homes," some White Bahá'ís would not "either because racial mixing was uncustomary or because it was distasteful to them personally." These White Bahá'ís had been attracted to the Bahá'í Faith "by one principle or another, or by the Person of 'Abdu'l-Bahá [and] would have been horror-struck to discover that to be a Bahá'í meant to be a proponent of racial equality."53

In the Washington, DC, Bahá'í community, Louis Gregory proved to be an agent of change by working to increase the number of Bahá'ís from "the gifted and influential circle of Blacks in which [he] moved."54 Had he decided to leave the Bahá'í community after experiencing racial segregation, some White Bahá'ís no doubt would have been quite content to have the American Bahá'í community remain lily-white. The present Bahá'í community would have looked no different than the vast majority of all-White and predominantly White churches. For three decades Gregory worked tirelessly teaching the Bahá'í Faith to all people, but particularly devoting much time and energy traveling throughout the South where the majority of African-Americans still lived, telling them about the Bahá'í Faith.

Beginning in 1910, Gregory took many trips to the South where he taught the Bahá'í Faith to thousands of Blacks. These included students and faculty at major African-American colleges. On one of these trips he had the chance to discuss the Bahá'í Faith with Booker T. Washington and students at Tuskegee Institute. Along with other African-American teachers of the Bahá'í Faith, such as Elsie Austin, Matthew W. Bullock, and Ellsworth Blackwell, who were elected at various times between 1922

and 1961 to serve on the National Spiritual Assembly of the Bahá'ís of
the United States, Gregory played a key role in laying the foundation for
the development of a multi-racial religious community.[55]

Many African-American Bahá'ís—as well as many White Bahá'ís—
made great sacrifices to overcome blatant racism, in order to build a
multiracial religious community based upon the principle of the oneness
of the human race. Notwithstanding the great work both Black and White
Bahá'ís were doing in the area of race amity conferences and activities,
some African-American Bahá'ís believed the Bahá'í community was losing
ground among interested African-Americans. Sadie Oglesby, an African-
American Bahá'í from Boston, remarked at the 1927 Bahá'í National
Convention that Bahá'ís were no longer attracting new African-American
believers and were losing those African-Americans who had once been
interested in the Bahá'í Faith.[56]

The major reason for this decline of interest in the Bahá'í Faith among
African-Americans, and probably the decline in Black membership as
well, could be attributed to a brief "abandonment of [race] amity work
in 1925 and 1926" and an emphasis on "world unity" work. While both
Black and White Bahá'ís appreciated the importance of world unity,
"inevitably, the world unity conferences, however well intentioned and
important in themselves, diverted attention from racial amity work to a
concern both less specific and less controversial." According to Morrison,
these "[w]orld unity conferences thus offered any individual or Bahá'í
community not fully committed to racial amity, yet another opportunity
to turn aside from the hard realities of racial adjustment."[57]

Fortunately for the American Bahá'í community, African-American
Bahá'ís continued to press the community to live up to the principles of
Bahá'u'lláh and the challenges given to them by 'Abdu'l-Bahá to address
the racial problems in the United States. When White Bahá'ís failed to
live up to the Bahá'í principle of racial unity, African-American Bahá'ís
felt betrayed. For example, in 1937, Ellsworth Blackwell, one of the most
prominent African-American Bahá'ís in Chicago, was not allowed to serve
as a guide at the Bahá'í Temple in Wilmette because of his race. In a
letter to the then head of the Bahá'í Faith, Shoghi Effendi, Ellsworth
Blackwell said in part:

From my knowledge of the [Bahá'í] teachings, it appears to me that the Principles of Bahá'u'lláh are being violated within His Temple by the Believers. The only apparent excuse for their policy is that the presence of Colored guides would offend people of the White Race. As you no doubt realize, the aforementioned large touring groups are composed of all nationalities and races. Are we supposed to alter the Principles to accommodate the prejudices of the people outside the Cause, particularly within our own institutions? And, may I ask, when are we to begin to live the Teachings of Bahá'u'lláh?[58]

Fortunately for all concerned, the appropriate Bahá'í local and national institutions responded very well to what had been "a misapprehension and error" on the part of one member of the National Temple Program Committee, who was of the opinion "that it was the policy of the Temple Program Committee not to use colored friends as guides." A careful search of the past minutes of the committee, however, failed to find such a policy. Blackwell consulted with the committee and was impressed by the fact that not only was there no such policy, and but that the discriminatory action was taken "on the part of one Committee member." This obviously satisfied Blackwell, in addition to being informed that several weeks earlier the Committee had asked an African-American Bahá'í to guide at the Temple.[59]

Shoghi Effendi, who was responsible for stewardship, encouragement, and development of Bahá'í communities around the world, recognized the humiliation, pain, and anguish African-American Bahá'ís were experiencing as the results of certain White Bahá'ís' racial attitudes. In a February 1942 letter sent on his behalf to Sadie Oglesby, the first African-American woman to make a pilgrimage to the Bahá'í holy shrines in Palestine, he said that he was "well aware that the conditions within the ranks of the believers in respect to race prejudice is [sic] far from being as it should be. However, he feels very strongly that it presents a challenge to both white and colored believers."

Shoghi Effendi then gave the following advice to his fellow Black Bahá'ís: "[I]t is incumbent upon the Negro believers to rise above this great test which the attitude of some of their White brethren may present. They must prove their innate equality not by words but by deeds." They must, Shoghi Effendi stressed, "accept the Cause of Bahá'u'lláh for the sake of the Cause, love it, and cling to it, teach it, and fight for it as their own Cause, forgetful of the shortcomings of others. Any other attitude is unworthy of their faith." He then reminded the Black Bahá'ís how Bahá'u'lláh had praised Blacks: "Proud and happy in the praises which even Bahá'u'lláh Himself had bestowed upon them, they must feel that He revealed Himself for them and every other downtrodden race, loves them, and will help them to attain their destiny." Pointing to the fact that "the whole race question in America is a national one and of great importance," Shoghi Effendi expressed the concern that "the Negro friends must not waste their precious opportunity to serve the Faith, in these momentous days, by dwelling on the admitted shortcomings of the white friends. They must arise and serve and teach, confident of the future in which we know these barriers will have once and for all been overcome."[60]

Shoghi Effendi's letter to African-American Bahá'ís emphasized the role they had to play in the spiritual unification of the United States. As he explained to another African-American believer: "The more Negroes who become Bahá'ís, the greater the leaven will be within their own race, working for harmony and friendship between these two bodies of American citizens: the white and the colored."[61]

'Abdu'l-Bahá's similar advice to Louis Gregory more than three decades previous had inspired him to transcend the shortcomings of the society around him and demonstrated to younger African-American Bahá'ís how to overcome racial barriers within the Bahá'í community with dignity and grace, and in the process contribute to the development of the Bahá'í community.

Following in his footsteps, a small group of younger African-American Bahá'ís were already playing a major role in the growth and development of the Bahá'í Faith, both on the national and international levels. For example, Elsie Austin, the first African-American woman graduate of the University of Cincinnati College of Law, joined the Bahá'í Faith in 1934. In 1937, she became the first African-American woman to be appointed assistant attorney-general of Ohio. Wilberforce University gave her the honorary degree of doctor of law for "outstanding service as the first colored woman to hold this post." Ms. Austin was a representative of the International Council of Women set up by the United Nations. She lived variously in the Bahámas, Tangier, Nigeria, and Kenya to spread the Bahá'í teachings, and was chairperson of the Bahá'í delegation to the 1975 International Women's Conference in Mexico City, Mexico. In addition to serving as a member of the National Spiritual Assembly of the Bahá'ís of the United States, she wrote brilliant and insightful commentaries of the applications of Bahá'í teachings to the problems of the world.[62]

Dr. Sarah Pereira and Amoz Gibson were two other African-American Bahá'ís who dedicated much of their lives to the spiritual and social development of the Bahá'í community in the United States. They were children of the first generation of African-American Bahá'ís. Even though Gibson did not formally join the Bahá'í Faith until 1944, his father, who had studied for the ministry at Howard University, embraced the Bahá'í Faith in 1912, and his mother joined as well. Pereira was four years old when her parents joined the Bahá'í Faith, in 1913. Both Pereira and Gibson were elected in 1961 to serve on the National Spiritual Assembly of the Bahá'ís of the United States. They were both also elected and appointed as members of international Bahá'í administrative bodies.[63]

In 1963, Amoz Gibson was one of nine Bahá'ís elected by Bahá'í delegates from around the world to serve as a member of the first Universal House of Justice, the supreme ruling body of the worldwide Bahá'í community. In 1973, Dr. Sarah Pereira was appointed by this body to serve on the Bahá'í Continental Board of Counselors. In this capacity she served and represented Bahá'í communities in North and South America between 1973 and 1985.[64] Dr. Wilma Ellis was appointed chief administrative officer of the Bahá'í International Community Offices in New York; Geneva, Switzerland; and Suva, Fiji. Dr. Ellis was also a member of the Continental Board of Counselors, a body responsible for assisting in the development of Bahá'í communities whose members are appointed by the Universal House of Justice.[65]

To the American Bahá'í community's great credit, and owing to its dedication to the Bahá'í teachings on interracial unity, this predominantly

White national community has continuously elected African-Americans to the National Spiritual Assembly of the United States, the governing body of the American Bahá'í community. Louis G. Gregory was elected during the years 1922–4, 1927–32, and 1939–46, at the end of which, he retired. Others who were elected and served included Elsie Austin, 1946–53; Ellsworth Blackwell, 1954–6 and 1958–61; Amoz Gibson, 1960–3; Sarah Pereira, 1961–74; Glenford Mitchell, 1968–81; Magdelene Carney, 1970–92; William Maxwell, 1974–7 and 1984–88; Wilma Ellis, 1981–6; Robert Henderson, 1982–2005; Alberta Deas, 1982–1992; Tod Ewing, 1991–92; William Roberts, 2000–5. Two of the present nine members of the National Spiritual Assembly of the Bahá'ís of the United States are African-Americans, and one, Dr. Robert Henderson, serves as the body's secretary-general.[66]

The elections and appointments of African-American Bahá'ís to decision-making positions on Bahá'í national and international administrative bodies provided clear evidence of the Bahá'ís' longtime commitment to building a multiracial religious community. African-American Bahá'ís in these positions provided invaluable role models not only for African-American Bahá'í children and youth, but also for Bahá'ís' from all racial, ethnic, and cultural backgrounds.

The Spiritual Qualities of Blacks and Their Contributions to the Expansion of the Bahá'í Faith

As the Bahá'í Faith began to expand throughout the world under the ministry of Shoghi Effendi, who lead the Faith from 1921 to 1957, and later under the direction of the Universal House of Justice, which was first elected in 1963 and currently serves as the supreme administrative body of the Bahá'í community, the spiritual qualities attributed to Black people were seen as vital to its global expansion. Such emphasis upon the spiritual qualities of Blacks was in sharp contrast to contemporary White racial views of Blacks in the United States. At a time when the highest court in the land, government agencies, the armed forces, and major-league baseball, sanctioned racial segregation, and most White neighborhoods barred Blacks,[67] Shoghi Effendi was encouraging Black Bahá'ís to contribute their rich spiritual gifts to the Bahá'í Faith.

He also was educating the predominantly White Bahá'í community in the United States to recognize and appreciate these spiritual qualities of Black people mentioned in the Bahá'í writings. In a letter to a Bahá'í written on his behalf in the fall of 1941, Shoghi Effendi explained: "The qualities of heart so richly possessed by the Negro are much needed in the world today—their great capacity for faith, their loyalty, and devotion to their religion when once they believe, their purity of heart, God has richly endowed them, and their contribution to the Cause is much needed."[68]

This letter, among others, written during the first of several expansion plans that took place in 1937–44, enabled Bahá'ís to better appreciate the unique cultural and spiritual contributions Black Bahá'ís were making and would make in the future to the growth and expansion of the Bahá'í Faith. Black Bahá'ís also needed to be reminded that the Bahá'í community needed their "gifts." Writing to two Bahá'ís in December 1942, Shoghi Effendi addressed this issue: "The Negroes, though they themselves may not realize it, have a contribution to make to the World Order of Bahá'u'lláh. His Teachings and the Society He has come to establish are for every race and every nation, and each one of them has his own part to play and the gift of his own qualities and talents to give to the whole world."[69]

A year later, in a letter to individual Bahá'ís written on his behalf, Shoghi Effendi again mentioned the spiritual qualities of African-Americans and expressed delight in their increasing participation in the American Bahá'í community. "The Negro Bahá'ís have much to contribute to the Cause. They are a deeply spiritual people with a great capacity for faith, and possess both patience and loyalty. He is happy to see the way they are increasingly assuming their share of Bahá'í responsibility, and arising to dedicate themselves to the Cause of God in this day."[70]

This steady flow of inspiration and encouragement from the spiritual leaders of the Bahá'í Faith, with its emphasis upon how much the Bahá'í community and the world need the spiritual qualities, the "gifts" possessed by African-Americans, contributed to the formation of a unique racial identity.

Spiritual Qualities of Black People and the Formation of Racial Identity Among African-American Bahá'ís

There is a direct historical and social connection between the Bahá'í teachings on the spiritual qualities of Black people and the cultivation of African-American Bahá'ís' racial identity.[71] Many African-American Bahá'ís of the present generation have internalized the imagery of the "pupil of the eye, through which the light of the spirit shineth forth." as a fundamental component of their racial identity within the larger Bahá'í community. It is not uncommon, therefore, to hear African-American Bahá'ís referring to themselves as "the pupil of the eye."

Nowhere has this been more evident than in Bahá'í conferences focusing on the African-American issues and African-American Bahá'í gatherings. For example, over the last decade or so there has been an increased need among African-American Bahá'ís to explore the spiritual and historical significance of being a Bahá'í of African descent. In November 1994, a Bahá'í conference was held in Chicago called the Vanguard of the Dawning Conference, described by one observer as the "first national Bahá'í conference ever to focus solely on the African-American community."[72]

On the first day of this historic conference, a husband and wife musical duo from Bermuda "opened the session with 'Pupil of the Eye,' an uplifting song proudly telling African-Americans of their destiny. Aided by two artists from the Chicago Bahá'í Youth Workshop, they announced that the time had come! Black girl, Black boy arise . . . you're the pupil of the eye . . . the spiritual light of the world."[73]

In a 1995 publication, *The Black Men's Gatherings: A Spiritual Transformation,* two African-American Bahá'í writers, James A. Williams and Ted Jefferson, referred to Bahá'u'lláh's often quoted statement of Blacks as the "pupil of the eye" in their discussion of Black men's "need for esteem."[74] "These words, spoken by the Blessed Beauty [Bahá'u'lláh] quoted by the Master ['Abdu'l-Bahá] and written by the beloved Guardian [Shoghi Effendi], clearly define our position within the human body of races and ordain that through us the 'light of the spirit' will shine."[75] According to these writers, "God Himself has recognized us and given our existence purpose and meaning. We can truly say that if there is any singular role the Black Men's Gatherings plays, it must be to provide the means for opening 'the pupil of the eye.' . . . In one sense, we are destined to serve a singular purpose as 'the pupil of the eye.'"[76]

Men of African-descent from throughout the diaspora have attended these gatherings held for ten years in rural South Carolina and now in Eliot, Maine, since 1988. It was an African-American Bahá'í, William Roberts, who first saw the need for such a gathering. As explained by one participant:

> For years he had wondered why Black men had not made more significant contributions to the Faith as envisioned by 'Abdu'l-Bahá. He questioned why there were so few older Bahá'í men. He also noticed in Bahá'í meetings something that puzzled and saddened him: Black men appeared to avoid each other deliberately in order to seek the community of White Bahá'ís. . . . Black men were trying very hard to become invisible to each other, especially if non-Black Bahá'ís were around. Dr. Roberts used this telling behavior as sufficient reason for convening the first Black Men's Gathering.[77]

At first glance, an observer might ask: "How could the Bahá'í Faith, a universal religion that promotes 'the oneness of mankind,' sanction what can be viewed only as a 'segregated' gathering?"[78] One has only to witness the support and encouragement from the gatherings from non-Black and women Bahá'ís—as well as the Universal House of Justice—to realize that its purpose is not to segregate, but to heal the spirits of Black Bahá'í men and to better enable them to serve their Faith. Two participants in the gathering explained this need:

> Black men have lived in a state of emotional neglect due to the conditions of this society. Even the Bahá'í community, due to its infancy, cannot adequately compensate us. Some of us were even suspicious of the warmth and affection White Bahá'ís gave in spite of their uncertainty over how to give it. Their uncertainty and our suspicions became allies and blocked effective communication

between us. Because we had not learned to love ourselves, we tended to distrust anyone who showed us love.[79]

The gathering gets to the heart of this dilemma:

At the Gathering, we study our sacred Writings and the timely, awe-inspiring, and loving messages of the Universal House of Justice. Without interference from the outside world, we are able to apply them to ourselves. "Noble have I created thee, yet thou hast abased thyself." Within the prayerful, healing, and cleansing environment of the Gathering, each man is offered the opportunity to claim his own spiritual reality and a previously unknown emotion—love— begins to fill his soul. . . . We can truly say that if there is any singular role the Black Men's Gathering plays, it must be to provide the means for opening "the pupil of the eye."[80]

As Black Bahá'í men at the gathering go through this process of healing, they reenter the larger Bahá'í community with a renewed faith in their unique identity and their special contribution to the whole.

We, the Black men who attend these Gatherings, are like wayfarers who see the new ocean for the very first time. . . . We can reveal the content of our hearts now. . . . With honor and nobility, we can stand before our sons and daughters and teach them the Ways and the Will of God. . . . This Cause is Ours! Not only does it reflect our beauty, it embraces it, it magnifies it, it takes our small but growing light and adds to the multi-colored reflection of the ever-brightening Dawn.[81]

Bonnie Fitzpatrick-Moore, an African-American Bahá'í who moved to South Africa in order to teach the Bahá'í Faith and has lived there for a quarter century, referred to the pupil of the eye several times in her book, *My African Heart*. After a gratifying visit by a group of African-American Bahá'í women arranged by her in June 1994, Fitzpatrick-Moore poured out her feelings on the historical and spiritual meaning of the visit in relationship to the pupil of the eye.

> As I watched them packing and eventually depart, my heart, though broken, swelled with gratitude that I had been chosen to witness the new beginning of our shared history and I had seen what incredible results can be achieved when the pupil of the eye, that part that reflects perfectly what is before it, is looking directly and continually at the Light! Praise be to God, the Lord of all the worlds![82]

Four years later, an African Bahá'í woman writing from Jwaneng, Botswana, sent an open letter to African-American Bahá'ís: "An open letter to all Black Americans from Mrs. L. Warren, Member of the Continental Board of Counsellors of the Bahá'í Faith in Africa."[83] In this letter Warren mentioned the historical significance of the 1994 visit of African-American Bahá'í women and the role that Africans and African-American Bahá'ís must play as the pupil of the eye in spreading the Bahá'í message to Black people.

> In 1994 when the sister's group came to southern African, the general receptivity of the African people to the Faith was good, but now it has gotten even better. This is a critical time in the lives of humanity and souls have been so ready for the Message of Bahá'u'lláh. The century is fast approaching its end and none of us knows what the next century will bring. . . . What better way to bring it to a close than for those who have been affectionately referred to as "the black pupil of the eye" through whom "the light of the spirit shineth forth" to go forth among their brethen, thus proving to all and sundry that Africa is far from being the Dark Continent it was said to be.[84]

As this letter demonstrated, the Bahá'í teachings on the spiritual qualities of Black people and their role in the growth and expansion of the Bahá'í Faith contributed to the formation of a new racial identity among Black Bahá'ís throughout the Bahá'í world. The "pupil of the eye" became the spiritual image which not only united Blacks in their service to their Faith, but also provided Bahá'ís of other racial and cultural backgrounds with a new way of looking at their Black coreligionists. Freed from the traditional anti-Black racist stereotypes, Bahá'ís could move forward in building a truly united multiracial religious community.

African-American Artists and Intellectuals in the Bahá'í Faith

From its early history in the United States, the Bahá'í Faith has held a special appeal for those African-American artists, intellectuals, and musicians seeking a religion that taught and struggled to practice the principle of unity and love among all people. As already mentioned, Dorothy Champ was so attracted to the Bahá'í teachings that she gave up her Broadway career to promote the teachings of her adopted faith. This was not a requirement of the Bahá'í Faith, however. One of her contemporaries, Alain Locke, the first person of African descent to become a Rhodes Scholar and the "father" of the Harlem Renaissance, was "a well-known and respected figure among Bahá'í intellectuals." According to Christopher Buck, the foremost scholar on Alain Locke's life as a Bahá'í, Locke converted to the Bahá'í Faith in 1918. He also helped organize the first Bahá'í conferences for race unity in Washington, DC, New York, and other cities, and wrote several articles published in the biennial record of the international Bahá'í community, *The Bahá'í World*.[85]

There were also two well-known Bahá'í African-American poets: Margaret Danner and Robert Hayden. Danner, a close friend of Hayden and Langston Hughes, became a Bahá'í in 1962 and included the Bahá'í House of Worship in some of her poems. Hayden became a Bahá'í in 1943. "When giving readings of his works, he would preface poems inspired by or referring to the Faith with explanatory information about the Cause." From 1968 until his death in 1980, Hayden was associate editor of the Bahá'í magazine *World Order*.[86]

John Birks "Dizzy" Gillespie, world-renowned jazz musician, joined the Bahá'í Faith in Los Angeles in 1968. In his autobiography, *To Be or*

Not To Bop: Memoirs of Dizzy Gillespie, he discussed the spiritual journey that led to his becoming a Bahá'í and what it meant to him as a person and a musician:

> Becoming a Bahá'í changed my life in every way and gave me a new concept of the relationship between God and man—between his fellow man—man and his family. I became more spiritually aware, and when you're spiritually aware, that will be reflected in what you do. They teach you in the Bahá'í Faith, without the idea of stopping you from doing things, to fill your life with doing something that's for real, and those other things you do, that are not for real, will fall off by themselves . . . the [Bahá'í] writings gave me new insights on what the plan is—God's plan—for this time, the truth of the oneness of God, the truth of the oneness of the prophets, the truth of the oneness of mankind. . . .
>
> There is a parallel with jazz and religion. In jazz, a messenger comes to the music and spreads his influence to a certain point, and then another comes and takes you further. In religion—in the spiritual sense—God picks certain individuals from the world to lead mankind up to a certain point of spiritual development. Other leaders come and they have the same Holy Spirit in their hands, so they are really one and the same. This means that Judaism, Christianity, Islam, Buddhism, and all the major religions are one and the same. . . .
>
> When I encountered the Bahá'í Faith, it all went along with what I had always believed. I believed in the oneness of mankind. I believed we all come from the same source, that no race of people is inherently superior to any other. And they teach unity, I latched on to that.[87]

Champ, Locke, Danner, Hayden, and "Dizzy," are just a few of the well-known African-American intellectuals and artists who were attracted to and inspired by the Bahá'í teachings. Other known and lesser known African-American intellectuals and artists have also found their way into the Bahá'í community, attracted by the teachings of the oneness of all people, races, and religions.

3

Radiant Lights: African-American Women and the Advancement of the Bahá'í Faith in the U.S.

Gwendolyn Etter-Lewis

Social conditions in the U.S. during the 1890s contrasted sharply with the Bahá'í Faith's emphasis on unity.[1] Unchecked practices of blatant discrimination effectively marginalized women and people of color, and targeted them for maltreatment. While most African-American women turned to the church for solace, some, like Olive Jackson, pursued other avenues of religious engagement. Olive became a Bahá'í in or around 1899, the first African-American woman to become a Bahá'í. This is not insignificant, since Black churches offered "a theology of liberation, self-determination, and black autonomy."[2] Ms. Jackson's enrollment marked the beginning of the first generation of African-American women Bahá'ís. In pursuit of sanctuary from a hostile social climate as well as equal participation in religious worship, African-American women began to enter the ranks of the Bahá'í community.

Spiritual Foremothers

Not much is known about the very first African-American women to become Bahá'ís, as historical records are sketchy at best. There are likely more than are mentioned here, but the paper trail thus far has led to only a few. In instances where there are no available written records, data from oral histories are used as an alternative means of documenting women's lives. This sparse group of Black Bahá'í women compensated for its small number through extraordinary deeds that directly influenced the direction and growth of the Faith.

Bahá'ís' adherence to a principle of unity in a world characterized by disunity and their following Bahá'u'lláh's call to heal social ills[3] created a social context wherein many Black women Bahá'ís found themselves at the very center of change. While several women were already active in the Black community and / or various civil rights and women's rights groups prior to their enrollment, becoming members of the Bahá'í Faith merely fueled the intensity of their efforts.

During the early days of the Bahá'í Faith in the U.S., African-Americans learned about the new religion from a variety of sources. Some had direct contact with Bahá'ís while others heard about it from newspapers or through the community grapevine. Though many Bahá'ís were actively involved in promoting the teachings of their religion, it should be noted that Bahá'ís are forbidden to proselytize or to coerce others into joining the religion,[4] so methods of disseminating the teachings of Bahá'u'lláh were often subtle and without pressure. Barred from using aggressive tactics for recruitment, Bahá'ís found that their numbers increased slowly but steadily over time.

As previously indicated, Olive Jackson is believed to be the first African-American woman to become a Bahá'í. The exact date of her enrollment has not been established, but she is listed on the 1899 New York City Bahá'í membership roster.[5] According to the 1900 U.S. census of New York County, Ms. Jackson was a dressmaker.[6] It's not known how she first learned of the Faith, but she may have been introduced to the Bahá'í Faith by one of her clients.

Records at the National Bahá'í Archives suggest that it was not until the early 1900s that a wave of African-American enrollment occurred, in part as a result of the visit of 'Abdu'l-Bahá to the U.S. in 1912–13. Bahá'ís across the country used 'Abdu'l-Bahá's visit as a means of attracting other people to the Bahá'í Faith. Newspaper accounts indicate that members of the press were intrigued by this exotic "holy man." The result was an increase in the number and racial diversity of Bahá'ís.

Among those who became Bahá'ís at this time was Pittsburgh, Pennsylvania, resident Leila Y. Pane, who enrolled in April 1912. Born in South Carolina in 1884, she was married and had one son, Henry P. Pane, Jr.[7] Mrs. Pane briefly described in writing her introduction to the Bahá'í Faith:

> Attended my first Bahá'í meeting in 1912. Metropolitan AME Church, Washington, DC. Accompanied by Dr. and Mrs. James R. Wilder. Here in this assembly 'Abdu'l-Bahá gave one of his soul stirring messages of Bahá'u'lláh through an interpreter.[8]

Leila's brief description was one of many preserved by the Bahá'í census that began in 1935. The data indicated that African-American women became Bahá'ís at a rate almost double that of African-American men.[9]

Some Black women who enrolled during this same time period studied the Bahá'í Faith along with their husbands, and in some cases the couples became Bahá'ís together. Such couples included the parents of Dr. Sarah Martin Pereira (1909–95),[10] a well-known second-generation Bahá'í. In an oral history interview, Dr. Pereira vividly recalls the story of her parents' 1913 enrollment:

> I'm very grateful to my natural parents, who are also my spiritual parents. . . . . ['Abdu'l-Bahá] came to Cleveland, Ohio, where my parents were living. . . . Mr. Louis Gregory, the famous Hand of the Cause, was a young Black lawyer in those days . . . and my father was a young Black lawyer as well as a neighbor, Mr. Fleming. He and his wife were already Bahá'ís. . . . My parents were members of the Congregational Church. And the Flemings had what we now call a fireside[11] evening to introduce Mr. Louis Gregory who had come to town to visit them and to do Bahá'í work. So these three

young lawyers talked about many things among which was the Bahá'í Faith. And after my parents had heard and met Mr. Gregory, they studied the Faith for perhaps a year. . . . We all became Bahá'ís.[12]

Individual communities that 'Abdu'l-Bahá visited, such as Cleveland, made special efforts to take advantage of the interest created by this event and invited notable speakers like Hand of the Cause Louis Gregory for follow-up meetings. The Martin family was particularly active and their efforts to spread the Bahá'í teachings brought in a number of African-American believers.

Zylpha O. Gray Mapp (1890–1970) embraced the Bahá'í Faith in 1916.[13] In 1908 she had become the first African-American woman to graduate from Plymouth High School, following the example of her father, William Johnson, who was the first African-American ever to graduate from the school, in the mid-1880s. While waiting to enter nursing school Zylpha met Alexander M. Mapp, an architect, contractor, and builder from Barbados, West Indies, and the couple married on June 15, 1910.[14]

Mrs. Mapp was elected to the Spiritual Assembly[15] of the Bahá'ís of Boston in 1929 and served on that body until 1934, holding the office of secretary from 1930 to 1934. She wrote about her role as secretary:

I . . . live on a farm seventeen miles from Boston but somehow the Master ['Abdu'l-Bahá] makes it possible for me to travel back and forth to the meetings, and through His will I am to be secretary. I know since He has raised me to that station He will help me carry on. We must not shrink, but always show our willingness to work.[16]

Her daughter, Dr. Zylpha Mapp Robinson (1914–2001),[17] who became a Bahá'í when she was a teenager, remembered her mother's account of a search for spiritual fulfillment. She felt that it was more than a whim—that her mother was destined to find the Bahá'í Faith:

I think that my mother definitely was born to be a Bahá'í. . . . [She went to different Sunday schools] and she would hear from the Catholic and the Baptist or the Episcopalian or whatever church she went to, that [it] was the only way to God. And it began to bother her at the age of six or seven as to why God would leave out so many people in the world who probably had never even heard of Jesus. And so one day she asked her father. . . . He told her not to ask such questions, that that's sacrilegious. . . . So from that tender age she became aware that there was something missing in her life as far as religion was concerned.[18]

As the story continued, it was clear that Zylpha never forgot the feeling that something had been omitted from traditional explanations of Christianity. Even in adulthood the questions that began in childhood still lingered:

And of course it wasn't until after [my mother] had become married, and she must have been in her early twenties [when she heard about the Bahá'í Faith]. She went to a dentist for dental treatment . . . and apparently in all those various visits she had begun to talk to this gentleman about her views on religion. . . . It was in Cambridge, Massachusetts, about 1916. He said, "Madame, I think you're ready to hear a message. Would you like to come . . . and talk to some of our friends?" And she said she was interested, but she would go home and speak to my father. . . . The long and short of it is that evening they went to a fireside. . . . And when she heard the message that evening about Bahá'u'lláh, she immediately accepted the Faith.[19]

Later generations of African-American Bahá'í women found less direct paths to the Bahá'í Faith. Vivian Dunlap Wesson (1895–1994), who later moved to West Africa in order to teach the Faith and lived there for over twenty years, was attracted by the Bahá'í House of Worship in Wilmette, Illinois:

I became a Bahá'í because I lived in Chicago and Bahá'ís were building a temple. I read about it in the papers and I wanted to know what it was all about. . . . I read that this was a worldwide religion and had so many attractions that ordinary religions didn't

have. And I had been restless about religion for a long time. My
father was a minister, his three brothers were ministers; they were
all Baptists. . . . I belonged to a church in Chicago which was the
largest Black congregation in the United States at that time.[20]

Mrs. Wesson's strong background in the Baptist Church for several
generations reflected the deep roots of Christianity in the African-
American community. Thus, it was natural that she began her spiritual
search within the church:

I left the church. . . . I went to many churches after that, but I
didn't become a member. . . . I went to all kinds of churches and
religions that I had never entered into before and looked at them
and decided none of them suited me. And I said, "I'm gonna try
this Bahá'í [Faith] to see what these Bahá'ís teach. A friend of mine
was already a member. She was a White woman married to a Black
man. [She] invited me to come to some of their meetings. I went.
. . . I became a Bahá'í after about three months of study. . . . I
couldn't help it. It was something that took me over. . . . I signed
[my declaration card] when I was twenty-six years old.[21]

The Bahá'í House of Worship in Wilmette was actually under construction when Mrs. Wesson first discovered it.[22] However, enough of
the temple had been erected to give her some idea about the finished
product, and more importantly, she was curious about its builders.
    Erma Hayden (1911–97) found information about the Bahá'í Faith in
a library book by accident:

I first heard about the Bahá'í Faith when I was either seventeen or
nineteen. . . . I had a lot of friends from other denominations, and
I was Episcopalian. And I wondered why there were such differences
in beliefs. . . . So I went to the library to find out why. And it was in
the library that I found it—found the Bahá'í Faith in a book. And
since that answered my question I felt satisfied. I didn't know the
significance of what I'd found. Ten years later after my husband

and I came to live in Ann Arbor I got to know a Bahá'í. . . . One day Chad's wife said, "I've a friend who wants to meet you and wonders if you would come to dinner on Wednesday. . . . I agreed and we went. We had a wonderful time and then all of a sudden she turned to me and no one else and said, "Erma have you ever heard of the Bahá'í Faith?" Now this was ten years later. I remembered nothing about what I had read, but I said yes . . . . And it was from reading *Gleanings [from the Writings of Bahá'u'lláh]*, going to firesides, and coming to know the Bahá'ís that I came to say, "Yes, I'd like to be a Bahá'í."[23]

Even though Erma had discovered the Bahá'í Faith earlier, it was not until she had actual contact with a Bahá'í that it registered in her consciousness. Her husband, award winning poet Robert Hayden, became a Bahá'í one year after Erma, in 1943.

In addition to these women, there were a few early Bahá'ís who believe that they were led to the Bahá'í Faith through dreams and visions. Eulalia Bobo Taylor (1912–95) was one such person. She had always relied on this unconventional source of spiritual guidance, and here she describes one of the visions that initiated her quest for knowledge beyond her previous religious experiences:

I had a vision. . . . I had taught Sunday school and I knew the Bible. . . . So finally I asked the question to myself, why should I worship Jesus? What has he done for my people? Because I was always concerned with the whole race because I knew that if I wasn't able to find something to help the whole race, helping myself wouldn't do any good, because my brother was Heavyweight Champion of the World [Joe Louis] and he couldn't help the race. . . . On the twenty-sixth of May, around three o'clock in the afternoon, I heard a voice say, "Eulalia, you can come out of confusion and come over here with these people and be happy." . . . And when that voice spoke to me I began to see clearly . . . I went to the Bible to find out it actually was Jesus . . . so I began to look for these people of all colors, who had nobody between them and Christ. . . . But I went to other churches because I had been raised a Baptist. . . . So I had to go around to different churches to see if I could find them [the group of people in my vision]. . . . I was walking down the street one day and met a man. He was a mortician and I had known him since I was a kid. . . . When I got to him he said, "Eulalia I'd like you to meet some people." . . . We went to [a woman's home] that night; she had a fireside. . . . They gave me the Hidden Words [of Bahá'u'lláh] and I started reading it. Well, I knew this was the word of God. I [knew I] was a Bahá'í that night. . . . That was in 1954.[24]

Mrs. Taylor considered her strong Christian background an asset to her membership in a new religion and she used her extensive knowledge of the Bible as a means of teaching others about the Bahá'í Faith.

This sampling of early African-American women Bahá'ís indicates that they were unique in their openness to the Bahá'í Faith and corresponding willingness to "go against the grain" by accepting its tenets. Their circumstances as members of two historically disenfranchised groups, African-Americans and women, were not easy, and being affiliated with a non-Christian, relatively unknown religion added yet another layer of possible oppression. However, not being strangers to difficulties, these women were determined to fully participate in the Bahá'í Faith.

Religion, Culture, and Creative Expression

Drawing on the richness of their heritage, many of the early African-American Bahá'í women expressed their spiritual perspectives through art: poetry, song, drama, and personal narratives. The Bahá'í Faith purposefully minimizes religious ritual[25] and thereby provided an excellent outlet for such creative endeavors. It was not uncommon, for example, that Bahá'í gatherings would include dramatic presentations or readings.

Susie C. Stewart from Richmond, Virginia, wrote a letter from her hospital bed to a Bahá'í friend dated May 4, 1911, the same year she enrolled in the Faith.[26] She described her poor health saying, "[I]f I am unable to resume my duties I shall be just as happy, knowing that my physical weakness may lead me to greater spiritual health."[27] In this same letter Stewart explained the process of writing a poem she had been inspired to commit to paper entitled "Perfect Union":

> I am not a poetess, never wrote a poem before; but one night, while I lay awake praying for perfect union among the believers the words appeared to me as if in letters of light. The next morning they continued to ring within my soul until I had to write them, so I sat down amid the whir of the sewing machine and wrote them off without any trouble as to rhyming. I knew God meant that I should write them for some good purpose, so I obeyed.[28]

The poem itself was written in beautiful, flowing handwriting. It focused on creating unity among Bahá'ís and ended with a reference to the much anticipated visit of 'Abdu'l-Bahá to the U.S.:

> In love, and prayer, and service may we all united be,
> That the Coming of our Beloved to these shores we soon may see;
> To prove our perfect union, raise the Temple[29] while we may.
> 'Abdu'l-Bahá calls to union; let us hasten to obey![30]

Mrs. Stewart felt that her success in writing a poem was proof that the Bahá'í Faith was the source of many miracles. In spite of her positive outlook, Susie's health continued to decline and she died the summer of 1911. Susie Stewart was remembered for her efforts to teach others about the Bahá'í Faith as well as for "sowing much seed in Richmond."[31]

The work of Harriet Gibbs-Marshall, who became a Bahá'í in 1912, embodied creative expression. She had held informal discussions on the Bahá'í Faith in her home as early as 1910 and continued these information meetings for several years after she enrolled in the Faith.[32] Mrs. Marshall, born in 1870 on Vancouver Island, British Columbia, was descended from a distinguished family background. She was one of five children of Judge Mifflin Winstar Gibbs (1823–1915) and Marie Alexander (d. 1904). The other children were Horace, Donald, and Ida Alexander Gibbs Hunt (1862–1957), a teacher and civil rights activist (a fifth child died before adolescence[33]). Harriet later married Capt.

Napoleon B. Marshall, an 1897 Harvard graduate who practiced law after serving in the military.[34]

The talented and well-educated Harriet Gibbs-Marshall became, in 1899, the first African-American woman to graduate from the Oberlin Conservatory of Music. She majored in piano, harmony, voice, and pipe organ. Her love of music eventually took her to Paris, where she studied piano with noted pianist and composer Moritz Moszkowski. In 1902 Mrs. Marshall was appointed Director of Music for the Public Schools of Washington, DC.[35]

Harriet realized a lifelong dream when she established the Washington Conservatory of Music in 1903. It was a private institution operated exclusively by African-American musicians and dedicated to providing African-American students with the opportunity to study music through a conservatory approach. When the conservatory expanded in 1906 to include drama and speech, it was renamed the Washington Conservatory of Music and School Expression. Under Harriet's leadership as president of the conservatory, another expansion took place in 1937 when she created the National Negro Music Center as a resource designed to "develop a library of Negro music, present concerts and to prepare books for use in public schools on Black music."[36] The conservatory continued to exist until 1960 when school officials concluded that other institutions were meeting the needs of African-American students.[37]

During the period of its operation, the conservatory was not only an educational institution, but, through Mrs. Marshall's influence, it was used for Bahá'í meetings at a time when few other facilities would permit integrated gatherings.[38] In addition to providing the Bahá'í community with a place to meet, Harriet Gibbs-Marshall also was active in spreading the Bahá'í Faith to other countries. In a letter dated 29 January 1937, Mr. Louis Gregory wrote to Harriet from Haiti: "You are very much loved among them [Haitians] for the constructive services you have rendered them. 'Welcome to Haiti,' said one of the officials upon knowing that I had a letter of introduction from you. The Bahá'í seed sown by you is also having effect."[39]

In later years she suffered from crippling arthritis, but was never known to complain. She was praised for her "loyalty and devotion" and for her sacrificial contributions to the Bahá'í Fund: "The element of sacrifice was indeed in all her acts and work."[40] Harriett died on February 21, 1941 having been preceded in death in 1933 by her husband who was not a Bahá'í.[41]

In the Boston area, Zylpha O. Gray Mapp (discussed above) was another woman who used her many talents to further the advancement of the Bahá'í Faith and to foster her own intellectual and social interests. She appeared to be a Renaissance Woman in every sense of the word. Like many African-American Bahá'í women before her, she believed in giving something back to the community. On her own property and with the cosponsorship of the Boston Urban League, she established a camp for underprivileged children named Camp Azjaowé. The building was constructed by her husband, and each member of the family was involved in running the camp, which became a unifying force for the Mapps. Mrs. Mapp structured the camp program so that each session began and ended with prayers.[42]

While her own children were still in school, Zylpha enrolled in the Portia Law School in pursuit of her dream of becoming a practicing attorney. She completed two and a half years before she had to drop out due to the illness and subsequent death of her father, as well as the economic difficulties created by the Great Depression.[43]

Undaunted by personal difficulties, Zylpha continued a vigorous pace of activities well into her later years. She assumed an active role in the Springfield, Massachusetts Federation of Women's Clubs and in 1960 became its first African-American president, a post she held for four consecutive years. During this time she turned her sewing hobby into a service for one of the club's development projects located at the White Earth Mission in the western U.S. She designed, cut-out and sewed fifty to sixty dresses a year for four years and sent them to Indian children on the reservation at the White Earth Mission.[44]

In addition to all of these activities, she took the time to express herself through poetry. She composed poems about famous people such as Eleanor Roosevelt,[45] historical events, and family. She wrote this poem for her young son in 1941:

To Baby Alexander
A tiny bundle of golden brown, wrapped in a blanket of blue
Black eyes and tresses as soft as down, a bit of loveliness, you.
What can you tell us of the great beyond, and did the Master[46]
    call you here?
Or did curiosity bring you to the War torn sphere?
Whatever your mission, you are heaven sent
And may your life here be well spent.[47]

Much later Zylpha focused on current events of the time. The Civil Rights March on Washington, DC, caught her attention, as noted in this 1963 poem:

Peaceful Revolution
All roads lead to Washington
By plane, by bus, by car
They've come, tens of thousands
From near and far
They join their hands in brotherhood
And singing—march along
At the feet of the Emancipator[48]
They lay their burdens down
Americans of every race, every color, every creed
Are united in this effort
Which is our country's greatest need
The cry for freedom fills the air
And with God's help—they say
We shall overcome—Yes, Now
For this is a New Day.

Embedded in most of her poetry were subtle references to the Bahá'í Faith. "New day" is a concept found in the Bahá'í writings that refers to the unity of mankind and thus a new state of harmony never before witnessed by the world. This is a central teaching of the Bahá'í Faith as well as a prophecy by Bahá'u'lláh: "This is the Day in which God's most excellent favors have been poured out upon men, the Day in which His most mighty grace hath been infused into all created things. It is incumbent upon all the peoples of the world to reconcile their differences, and, with perfect unity and peace abide beneath the Tree of His care and loving-kindness."[49]

Mrs. Mapp's poetry afforded her with a means of expressing her creative disposition, while letter writing provided her with an opportunity to express her wisdom and appreciation of other Bahá'ís. She corresponded regularly with several other Bahá'ís, including Shoghi Effendi, head of the Bahá'í Faith from 1921 until 1957, and Hand of the Cause of God Louis Gregory. In 1968, at the age of seventy-seven, Zylpha went on a trip to Barbados, West Indies, with the intention of teaching people there about the Bahá'í Faith.[50] Her record of enthusiastic, tireless participation in the Bahá'í community is a noteworthy tribute to the first generation of African-American Bahá'ís.

Finally, it is not possible to talk about artistic expression without including Dorothy Champ, a Broadway dancer and actress who gave up her career when she became a Bahá'í in 1919. In that same year, she became the first African-American elected to the Spiritual Assembly of the Bahá'ís of New York City.[51] She was a member of Actors' Equity Association, and appeared in the Broadway productions of *Green Pastures* and *Love in a Cottage*.[52] In spite of her professional success, she found greater fulfillment in the Bahá'í Faith and decided to commit herself full time to Bahá'í activities. She was described in a 1942 newspaper article as "extremely modest" and her devotion to the Bahá'í Faith was illustrated by her own words quoted in that same article: "All my life, I sought a religion which could answer the questions and problems of day to day living and it was not until I found the Bahá'í Faith that I found an answer."[53]

Dorothy was born in Loudoun County, Virginia, on 23 February 1893. In addition to being an actress and dancer, she was a dressmaker who started her own business and designed fashions for her clients in Providence, Rhode Island, and New York until her retirement.[54] In 1942 Champ continued her lifetime of service to the Bahá'í Faith by moving to communities where there were few or no Bahá'ís, in order to help meet the goals of the country's Seven Year Plan.[55] She lived in Wilmington, Delaware; Elizabeth, New Jersey; and East Providence, Rhode Island. In addition to moving to these cities, Dorothy made it a practice to visit various communities throughout the east coast giving lectures on the Bahá'í Faith. Her speaking style was evidence of her theater experience and she had a unique ability to command the undivided attention of diverse audiences. She spoke convincingly about her heartfelt reverence for the Faith: "Her love for God and His Cause was so strong that the fire would flash from her blazing eyes, galvanizing those who heard her speak."[56]

From time to time Ms. Champ would also write poetry and prose about events of the time. She greatly admired Dr. Martin Luther King, Jr., and had this to say about his death:

A plea for justice and freedom was the hope of Dr. King. The night of his last speech he was aglow with a light such as I had never seen before. The sorrows that had weighed so heavily upon him had left his face and vanished, the words he spoke made me think of the words of Emerson, "Goodbye proud world, I am going home." He [Dr. King] was a leaf in the breeze of the Will of God.[57]

Shortly before her own death, Dorothy received a letter from a friend saying, "I remember when we were in the kitchen, how you told us we must be willing to die for the Faith, what I remember is how you said it."[58] Ms. Champ died in East Providence, Rhode Island, on November 28, 1979. She had no survivors. Her husband had passed in 1933 and there were no children. In a eulogy written by Katherine McLaughlin, Dorothy Champ was remembered as "the fire of the love of God."[59]

The Question of Gender

Mary Brown Martin (1877–1939), who became a Bahá'í in 1913, was known in the Cleveland, Ohio, area for her outspoken commitment to securing women's right to vote.[60] For many Black women like Mary B. Martin, the sexism reflected in women's lack of voting privileges was intricately connected to the racism that denied equal rights to African-Americans. These two issues sometimes combined in a way that produced additional dimensions of conflict between groups of women fighting for the same cause. Historian Paula Giddings noted that, "When a group of Black women asked her [Susan B. Anthony] to help in organizing a branch of NAWSA [National American Women's Suffrage Association], she refused—on the grounds, she said, that it would be inexpedient."[61] Anthony's decision to maintain segregation within the suffragist movement alienated many Black women who had considered themselves allies. Coralie Franklin Cook, a Bahá'í professor at Howard University and friend of Susan B. Anthony, described her reaction to being excluded: "I have never been able to join the National Women's Party . . . the old Nat'l WSA of which I was once an ardent supporter and member, turned its back on the woman of color . . . so I have not been 'active' although I was born a suffragist."[62] Coralie and Mary found other ways of advocating for women's rights.

Prior to her involvement in the women's voting rights movement, Mrs. Martin assumed the duties of traditional homemaker and stayed at home with her children until they were old enough to attend school. She then ventured into public life where she played an active role in local efforts to win women's right to vote. During her time at home, Mary used the evenings to tutor young immigrants who needed help learning English. Later she and her husband, Alexander, pursued their interest in languages by joining French and German foreign language clubs. In turn, she taught her children these languages. The oldest daughter, Sarah, eventually became a professor of romance languages, a career which she attributed to her mother's *in vitro* influence.[63]

Mary's family history contained many stories of how she was predisposed to being an independent thinker, a woman outside of the "box" of stereotypes. As a child she was known for her buoyant spirit and love of education. The daughter of Jane and Winfield Scott Brown, she was the only girl in a family of six boys. According to family history: "As soon as she could acquire some bit of new knowledge at school, she would hasten home and try to teach it to her younger brothers."[64] Her love of teaching and learning never subsided. After completing two years of college at Flora Stone Mather College of Western Reserve University and the old Normal School, Mary accepted a teaching appointment at a Black school in Cotton Plant, Arkansas. From that point on teaching became her life's work.

She later returned to Cleveland, Ohio, and on September 27, 1905, married Alexander Hamilton Martin. The couple had four children: Lydia Jane, Sarah Elizabeth, Alexander Jr., and Stuart. Both Lydia and Sarah became Bahá'ís. Mr. Martin completed law school at Western Reserve University (now Case Western Reserve University) in 1898 and was one of the first African-Americans to become a member of the Phi Beta Kappa honorary society.

A consummate educator and community activist, in 1929 Mary Martin was elected to the Cleveland Board of Education. She was the first African-American and only the second woman to serve on the board. She was elected again in 1933 and in 1939 by nonpartisan ballot. Two weeks after the 1939 election Mary died as the result of illness. She was not forgotten. In a 1965 public ceremony the Cleveland Board of Education named a new elementary school the Mary B. Martin Elementary School.[65] Even as her name was immortalized, Mary's daughters, Lydia and Sarah, exemplified her spirit by being active Bahá'ís in their own right.

Language was a special interest of Rosa Shaw (d. 1953) who lived in San Francisco. Rosa became a Bahá'í in 1915 and her husband, John, enrolled in 1919. Both were naturalized citizens originally from the British West Indies. They married on May 9, 1921, and lived with John's mother in San Francisco.[66] Rosa and John Shaw were staunch believers in the Bahá'í Faith and they demonstrated that a couple working together can achieve goals otherwise impossible to reach solely by individual effort.

Rosa was an active member of a local Esperanto Club,[67] a lifelong interest that she maintained by attending study classes held in the Bay area. Like many other Bahá'ís, Rosa's pursuit of Esperanto probably was ignited by the fact that the Bahá'í teachings point to the adoption of a universal auxiliary language as a prerequisite for world peace.[68]

In addition to her work with the Esperanto Club, Rosa and John were active members of the San Francisco Bahá'í community. Individually they served on several Bahá'í committees and sometimes found themselves on the same committee. John was elected to San Francisco's Spiritual Assembly in 1927, 1931, and 1934. Rosa was a member of the Hospitality Committee, the Teaching Committee, and the Housing Committee.[69]

However, the Shaws did not confine themselves to local matters. In 1939, pursuing the goals of the first Seven Year Plan, they moved to Haiti in order to teach the Bahá'í Faith there. They returned to San Francisco a few years later, and in 1943 and 1944 Mrs. Shaw traveled to Halifax, Nova Scotia, where she visited different communities and gave presentations about the Bahá'í Faith. While she was away Mr. Shaw also gave talks and one lecture in particular was entitled, "The Negro as a World Citizen" and published in a local paper, *The People's Advocate*, on January 5, 1944.[70]

Other Black Bahá'í women activists and educators during this early time period included Hallie Elvera Queen, an educator who became a Bahá'í in 1912 or 1913.[71] Ms. Queen earned a bachelor's degree from Cornell in 1908 and a master's degree from Stanford University in 1923. Another lover of language like her cohorts Mary Martin and Rosa Shaw, she taught German, French, and Spanish at Howard University in Washington, DC, from 1915 through 1917.[72]

Prior to her arrival at Howard University, Ms. Queen taught English in Aguadilla, Puerto Rico, from 1909 to 1913. In a letter from another Bahá'í addressed to 'Abdu'l-Bahá in 1913,[73] part of a letter from Hallie was included. In the excerpt she outlined some of her efforts as well as difficulties related to telling others about the Bahá'í Faith:

> During the year 1912–13 I have endeavoured to add an humble mite toward spreading the Bahá'í Principle in Aguadilla, Puerto Rico, where I was stationed. I had three serious handicaps: 1st: Puerto Rico is intensely a Catholic country. . . . 2nd: The language is Spanish. . . . 3rd: I am myself a beginner, striving to work out my own personal problem of salvation, and scarcely fit to take up God's work. . . . I made small mention of the Cause *as a Cause*, but strove to instill its *teachings*. What little I have been able to do, I lay at the Master's Feet ['Abdu'l-Bahá]. . . . I instilled into the minds of my boys that the girls were their equals. . . . I am just beginning; I have

done but little, and if, in this, there be any good, I offer it as a sacrifice at the Throne of my Savior.[74]

Hallie Queen's single-spaced letter was filled with moving descriptions
of her experiences as a teacher in a foreign land. She designed her courses
so that students would be involved the community and have some basic
knowledge of Bahá'í principles:

> I formed a welfare society in my class. At Christmastime we found
> the names of all the needy and deserving women of our city, and
> took them baskets of fruit and clothing. . . . At the time of the
> recent flood in Ohio, we collected forty-two dollars, which we sent
> to the sufferers and for which we were personally thanked by the
> Acting Governor of Puerto Rico, Mr. M. Drew Carrell. . . . We
> held weekly discussions on the Beauty of Universal Peace and the
> horrors of war. . . . An essay on the Life of Qurratu'l-'Ayn[75] was sent
> by one of my pupils to the Insular Fair, and received a first prize.
> . . . I sent out Bahá'í literature to American friends. . . . I myself
> learned how not to be afraid of life.[76]

Hallie's return to the U.S. did not change her energetic approach to
daily living. She was mentioned in the October 1914 issue of the NAACP's
journal, *The Crisis,* as a person frequently requested by the "Latin-
American Legations for translations and interpretations of consular and
diplomatic intercourse."[77] At least one of her essays was published by *The
Crisis.* In 1917 she organized the first chapter of the American Red Cross
at Howard University, and the eighty African-American women who
joined formed the "largest single sewing unit in the organization."[78] Hallie
Queen was elected chair and under her leadership the group volunteered
to make one thousand garments for underprivileged children. Sixty-four
of these garments were completed during the first regular meeting. The
university newspaper reported that this campus chapter of the Red Cross
"promises to be one of the most enthusiastic movements ever made among
women of Howard University."[79]

Mary B. Martin, Rosa Shaw, and Hallie Queen illustrated the capacity of women to initiate change. At a time when few women ventured beyond the boundaries of their homes or communities, each one of the preceding women in her own way stepped outside of traditional women's roles in order to further a larger cause, that of the unity of humanity, through the teachings of the Bahá'í Faith.

4

Race, Gender, and Difference:
African-American Women
and the Struggle for Equality
Gwendolyn Etter-Lewis

Reconstructing the history of African-American women who became
Bahá'ís prior to 1950 is not simply a matter of adding information to a
steadily growing corpus of data previously overlooked and unanalyzed. It
is in fact a means of broadening our understanding of the diversity of
Black life and culture at a time period when it was extremely difficult to
step outside of the prescribed roles for women and African-Americans.
As Darlene Clark Hine says of Black women's history, "We cannot
accurately comprehend either our hidden potential or the full range of
problems that besiege us until we know about the successful struggles
that generations of foremothers waged against virtually insurmountable
obstacles."[1] The obstacles of race and gender present in Bahá'í communities were given fierce attention by Black women who believed in
Bahá'u'lláh's vision of unity. Having experienced the repercussions of
being in a position of double jeopardy, both Black *and* female, African-
American women actively resisted attempts, both active and passive, by
fellow Bahá'ís to make the principle of the oneness of mankind a slogan

rather than a way of life. Thus, their struggles to implement the Bahá'í principles of race and gender equality not only highlight a resistance to maintenance of the status quo, but also reveal the power of an individual, or of a single act, to create positive change.

Even though Bahá'u'lláh's teachings clearly and unequivocally placed unity of the races and elimination of prejudice at the core of its doctrine, Bahá'ís struggled with putting these principles into practice. African-American women who enrolled in the Bahá'í Faith prior to the 1950s found themselves in the midst of this struggle. As a result, many African-American women became discouraged and left the Faith. Others endured quietly, while some accepted the challenge with outspoken determination. Their response took shape in two major forms of action: 1) activities that focused exclusively on uniting Black and White Americans within and outside of the Faith, and 2) socioeconomic projects involving racial uplift that naturally would lead African-Americans to equal status with their White peers.

The Most Vital and Challenging Issue

"As to racial prejudice, the corrosion of which, for well-nigh a century, has bitten into the fiber, and attacked the whole social structure of American society, it should be regarded as constituting the most vital and challenging issue confronting the Bahá'í community at the present stage of its evolution."[2]

Historical accounts of early African-American Bahá'í women's activism is sketchy not because of their lack of interest, but because record-keeping in the Faith was not yet systematic and tended to minimize issues of race. On the other hand, when and where such data exists, it is not easily accessible. Historian Gerda Lerner points out that Black women's history has been neglected and that "Their records lie buried, seldom read, rarely interpreted."[3] The result, she said, is "general invisibility."[4] In spite of this bleak situation, there is a solution—primary sources. Oral histories, diaries, journals, and letters have preserved Black Bahá'í women's words and deeds.

Living Life Where Placed

Howard University professor Coralie Franklin Cook (d. 1942) used principles of the Bahá'í Faith as a means of cultivating more open attitudes toward race on an historically Black college campus. The traditional success of the university in producing highly educated and accomplished Black professionals made the concept of racial integration less critical to students and faculty alike. However, Professor Cook's activism as a Bahá'í had a significant impact on conservative campus viewpoints.

She was born in Lexington, Virginia and was educated at Storer College in Harper's Ferry, West Virginia, Emerson College in Boston, Martha's Vineyard Summer Institute, and the Shoemaker School of Oratory.[5] Her husband, George Cook, was born into slavery on January 7, 1855, in Winchester, Virginia. He escaped from slavery, attended school and graduated from Howard University with a BA in 1886 and a law degree in 1898.[6] George and Coralie married on August 31, 1898, and were the parents of one son, George Will Cook, Jr.[7] Both of the Cooks were faculty members at Howard; Coralie was Chair of Oratory and George held the positions of Professor of Commercial and International Law and Dean of the School of Commerce and Finance, respectively.[8] Coralie and her husband George became Bahá'ís in 1913.[9]

Prior to serving on the faculty at Howard University, Mrs. Cook taught at Storer College from 1882 to 1893 and was superintendent of the Washington Home for Destitute Colored Women and Children from 1893 to 1898. She was an honorary member of Delta Sigma Theta Sorority, a member of the Red Cross, the NAACP, the Book Lover's Club, and the Juvenile Protective Society.[10] In 1914 the Judges of the Supreme Court of the District of Columbia appointed Coralie to the Board of Education, a position she retained until 1926, the longest term held by any board member. Both she and George were known for their social welfare activities in the Black community and won awards and commendations for that work. They brought that same kind of zeal to their Bahá'í activities.

The Cooks heard about the Bahá'í Faith as early as 1910 through Joseph and Pauline Hannen, two very active white Bahá'ís who lived in the

Washington, DC, area. In a letter written to Mr. Hannen, dated March 18, 1910, Coralie described her attraction to the Bahá'í Faith:

> You may be sure that the little booklet from Mr. Wilhelm was received with grateful pleasure. I could not put it down until I had read it thru. The cover design is unique and the entire contents wonderfully appealing. If you can find speakers so impressive as those we listened to Sunday night it will be a *Joy* to me to gather a company to listen to you. My friends were very generally impressed not only with the wisdom of your teaching but with the earnestness and *sincerity* of the teachers.[11]

She was convinced that this new religion would bring many positive changes to the African-American community. She wrote to Mrs. Hannen,

> Mr. Cook tells me that you and Mr. H. heard Mr. Madden last Sunday. Is he not a man of splendid courage and a true servant of the Blessed Perfection [Bahá'u'lláh]? I wish many more could have seen that audience and witnessed the promise in our girls for the future womanhood of the race. It was altogether fitting that a group of *young* women should conceive and carry out the idea of bringing him before a group of those he had recently so defended and protected.[12]

Coralie recognized the importance of exposing young Black women to people who could appreciate their potential and simultaneously provide them with a positive outlook on life. The well-being of Howard's female students was her foremost concern. She regularly organized Bahá'í meetings on campus mainly for the benefit of students.

In addition to her many campus and community responsibilities, she also cared for her elderly mother. The stress associated with such intensive caretaking sometimes created complications in her personal life. Her November 29, 1913, letter to Mrs. Hannen described some of the challenges she had to confront:

Your many kind words and *deeds* have been a great spiritual help to me. If at any time I seem not to appreciate them it is only that it seems [so] I am just beginning faintly to grasp the fact that I need the Bahá'í Faith far more for my daily tasks among unbelievers than I do when sitting at a board meeting. My mother's illness has exhausted my strength. She is now about as well as usual, but *so* subject to cold and relapse. I will talk with you sometime in regard to the writing to 'Abdu'l-Bahá. Dear sister, you see I must live my life where I am placed. . . . I am praying for patience and wisdom to live my life so that I may not bring discredit upon the Teachings that have brought such joy to my weary heart.[13]

The weariness eventually gave way to a more invigorated Coralie Cook. The following year she recovered much of her strength and resumed Bahá'í activities. The "writing to 'Abdu'l-Bahá" she refers to in the preceding letter turned out to be an assessment of race relations in the U.S. The five-page, single-spaced letter written to 'Abdu'l-Bahá and dated March 2, 1914,[14] is a rhetorical masterpiece filled with historical references and numerous examples of the negative consequences of racial prejudice. In the beginning of her letter Coralie states her position without apology:

Perhaps the subject I shall try to write upon is one of such import as to invoke your Presence. However that may be, you will know that I shall write no thoughtless word and shall try to be just and honest in every statement.

We do not make the mistake of supposing that 'Abdu'l-Bahá does not understand far more about this matter than any believer can possibly show him, but we do feel it fitting to put on record and into your hands certain facts as expressing the attitude of the colored people themselves concerning race prejudice. Since we are the ones whose progress it impedes and whose footsteps it hounds surely we must be better prepared to speak than those who view the situation ON THE OUTSIDE.

Race relationship, in the Southern States especially, but more or less thru out the country is in a deplorable condition.

She goes on to explain in great detail racial attitudes and incidents of discrimination across the country. Coralie is unflinching in her assessment of current events and negative attitudes fueled by underlying prejudice. She struck at the heart of the matter with history as her most potent weapon:

No phase of the color question excites so much rancor and misrepresentation as the one of mixed marriage. It is constantly made use of by all classes of whites from the statesman to the boot-black and now includes some so-called Bahá'ís to arouse passion and strife and to flatter Saxon vanity. If the whole truth were told, it must be said that many colored people are as strongly opposed to inter-racial marriage as the whites. . . . This mixing of the two races we are told is biologically unfit. . . . But even from such unholy alliance came the great Frederick Douglass and our gifted DuBois is plainly of mixed blood, the same admixture gave to France her Dumas, to Russia her Pushkin, while some go so far as to claim the African strain courses through the blood of the great Robert Browning and the early American patriot Alexander Hamilton. Surely such examples in no wise incite the alarming theory of race deterioration.

Although Coralie did not mention 'Abdu'l-Bahá's exhortation that Black and White people should marry one another because intermarriage would "abolish differences and disputes between black and white,"[15] her point about the myths of race mixing was well made.

Some Bahá'ís may have been shocked to read the letter's contents, but Coralie spared no one in her assessment. In the conclusion of the 1914 letter, she took the Bahá'ís to task for their slow response to racial ills of that time:

To any one of the Bahá'í Faith to whom the tempter says "temporize" or let the matter work itself out I say beware! When was ever a mighty Principle championed by temporizing or delay. I know some must suffer both white and black, but who better able to wear the mantle of suffering than the real Bahá'í?[16]

Coralie raised the question "why wait?" as many had advised. She exhorted Bahá'ís to take immediate action and become involved because they had the answer to the problem—Bahá'u'lláh's teachings on the oneness of humanity. Years after Coralie's letter to 'Abdu'l-Bahá, Sadie and Bertha Oglesby became the first Black Bahá'í women to make pilgrimage to the Bahá'í shrines in Haifa and Acre. They found that the head of the Faith, Shoghi Effendi, relentlessly focused on issues of race within and outside of the Bahá'í community. Race relations, as Coralie had observed, were far from being resolved.

Essay writing was only one of Mrs. Cook's means of offering input. She also was an eloquent orator who never failed to pay tribute to Black culture. It was her hope that educating the white Bahá'í community in this manner would bring them closer to their Black Bahá'í brothers and sisters:

Coralie Franklin Cook, a Bahá'í and member of the Washington Board of Education, made a fine address on "Negro Poets." She made a sympathetic presentation of the works of Phyllis Wheatley, the slave girl of the eighteenth century who wrote many poems, Paul Lawrence Dunbar, William Stanley Braithwaite, Jessie Faucet and others, showing praiseworthy results of their attraction to the Muse. Greatly to the delight of the audience she read several poems, one of them humorous.[17]

Coralie's flair for public presentations also proved to be an asset to the Bahá'í community in terms of leadership and organization. A report about one such event credited Coralie with its success:

Mrs. Coralie Franklin Cook, that queenly sister of ours, never manifested her ability more gloriously. She was the unique figure, who, with her few master strokes, brought about much of the success of the Convention, and without whose assistance we would have fallen short of accomplishment along many lines.[18]

Many Bahá'í activities in the Washington, DC, area were guided or inspired by Coralie Cook. She opened the doors of Howard University to the Bahá'í Faith and was responsible for attracting many young African-Americans to this new religion. Her work on race unity and racial uplift activities made valuable inroads in the Black community.

To Be a Pilgrim

Mrs. Sadie and Mr. Mabry Oglesby, wife and husband, confronted issues of race in their community from a variety of perspectives. At first unconvinced that they could make a difference, they were completely transformed by the mother and daughter's pilgrimage to Bahá'í holy places in what is now northern Israel. Sadie in particular grew into a skilled public speaker and, as instructed by Shoghi Effendi, made race relations her priority.

Sadie and Mabry Oglesby joined the Bahá'í Faith in 1914.[19] Mabry owned his own real estate company, and Sadie was a homemaker.[20] Both served on the Local Spiritual Assembly of Boston and raised their daughter, Bertha Parvine, in the Bahá'í Faith.[21]

The Oglesbys' concern about issues of race was expressed in frequent letters to other Bahá'ís regarding particular acts of discrimination, especially if violence was involved. After the 1919 riots in Washington, DC, and Chicago,[22] Sadie and Mabry jointly voiced their alarm in a letter to fellow Bahá'í Harlan Ober dated September 1, 1919:

> These hate campaigns are on in every group being fanned into flames so rapidly by the ignorant that it does not require one to be a prophet to see that society is sleeping on an active volcano which shows every sign of eruption at any moment. . . . We believe that the Bahá'ís have a great opportunity as well as a great responsibility to bring this great life-giving information to the world. . . . To this end we suggest the following for your consideration: 1st. United prayers over a continued period. . . . 2nd. Conference initiated by Bahá'ís calling together leaders of races, churches, groups. . . . We believe that the general unrest at this time properly handled can be used to stimulate great Bahá'í activities everywhere and will be the

means of opening many doors for spreading the Cause never before opened. "To sit, to talk, to listen—there is no virtue in that. To rise, to act, to help—that is a Bahá'í life. Deeds are the standard."[23]

Sadie and Mabry indicated that they were not willing to accept talking and listening as a solution to so critical a problem. Instead they referred to the Bahá'í emphasis on deeds and not words as the most effective course of action. They were not alone in their concern. Morrison noted that racial incidents during the "Red Summer" of 1919 "awakened in the American Bahá'ís a heightened sense of responsibility."[24] Between 1921 and 1936 the Bahá'ís embarked on a "Program for Racial Amity" and hosted many activities including race amity conventions in major cities.

Sadie and daughter Bertha made history by being the first African-American women to go on pilgrimage, in 1927, and visit the Bahá'í Holy places in Haifa and Acre. According to Sadie, a few hours after arriving in Haifa on March 11, she and the other pilgrims were greeted by Shoghi Effendi, Guardian of the Bahá'í Faith. He immediately asked her how many African-American Bahá'ís there were in the U.S. When she told him there were only a few, Shoghi Effendi replied, "The Cause needs the colored people and cannot be established without them. . . . The friends should practice all the teachings and not only a part and this will draw the colored people to the Cause." [25]

This initial exchange became an ongoing dialogue throughout her pilgrimage. At a later time in the pilgrimage, Shoghi Effendi asked Sadie if she had been forceful in helping Bahá'ís understand the importance of the oneness of humankind. When she replied that she had not, Shoghi Effendi urged her to take a more aggressive approach:

He said I should be insistent and urgent upon this matter. That I should be persistent and not quiet so that the believers may learn of this great need. He told me I had been negligent, indifferent and had not done my duty upon this subject.[26]

Shoghi Effendi tried to impress upon Mrs. Oglesby of the importance of speaking out about racism, an issue he referred to as "the most vital and challenging issue" facing American Bahá'ís in a letter to the American

Bahá'í community in 1938.[27] He urged her to make that her goal when she returned to the U.S. At first Sadie resisted: "I expressed my great sorrow to him and told him I was quite unprepared, unqualified for the work he wished me to do. I said to him, 'I have no strength or importance in America. I am so sorry.'" Shoghi Effendi persisted, "When you return to America do as I have told you. Be fearless and know that the invisible concourse will assist you and I will supplicate at the Holy Shrine on your behalf."[28]

Sadie's initial discomfort with such a specific discussion about race appeared to be felt by the other pilgrims as well. Although Shoghi Effendi repeatedly stressed the importance of racial unity, some of the pilgrims seemed not to understand:

One day at dinner with the pilgrims, both Eastern [from Persia] and Western [from Europe and North America], Shoghi Effendi, as he discoursed upon the matter of unity between the white and colored people, was interrupted several times and to each of those who sought information upon other matters he said, "That is not important," but urged the need of a center in America composed of the two races. . . . "America's problem is the establishment of unity and harmony between the white and colored people." He said, "Racial prejudice and differences on the part of non-believers is a problem but there should be no racial problem on the part of the believers."[29]

Shoghi Effendi's insistence on discussing race unity was a way of stressing the importance of such a critical issue. He knew that the Bahá'í Faith's unique stance on race unity was a challenge for many Americans who were still recovering from the deep-seated prejudices provoked by the not so distant events of slavery and the Civil War. Nevertheless, he made it clear that race unity was a pivotal principle of the Bahá'í Faith.

The question of how to heal the long-standing wounds inflicted by racism was no easy matter, especially in the context of the explosive racial climate in the U.S. Sadie knew from experience that matters of race were difficult to resolve even within the Bahá'í community where the believers had been given specific instructions in the Bahá'í writings on how to cope with the "most vital and challenging issue."[30] Her concern was not unfounded.

Shoghi Effendi linked race unity to the growth of the Faith and maintained that Sadie must play an important role in the process. According to Sadie's journal, on March 27 he said to her, "My charge to you is that when you go back to America, tell the friends to look within themselves and find there the reason of so few colored people being in the Cause. Until this is removed, the Cause cannot grow. . . . This is vital."[31]

Furthermore, he advised Sadie to take trips to promote the Bahá'í teachings in the South when she felt that she had done all she could to promote race amity in the Northeast. Even though the task was overwhelming, Sadie finally consented to carry out Shoghi Effendi's instructions.

After twenty days on pilgrimage and several private audiences with Shoghi Effendi, Sadie Oglesby left Haifa with a new purpose. In a letter to Mabry Oglesby dated May 23, 1927, Shoghi Effendi remembered Sadie fondly: "My dear co-worker: Just a word that I wish to add in person in order to express my pleasure and delight at having met our dear and devoted Bahá'í sister Mrs. Oglesby, whose pure faith, tender devotion and ardent zeal I shall ever remember."[32]

Subsequent letters exchanged between Shoghi Effendi and Sadie Oglesby demonstrated her commitment to the task of establishing race amity. Upon her return to the U.S., Sadie immediately took action by assuming an energetic role in the 1927 National Bahá'í Convention, an annual meeting held to elect members of the National Spiritual Assembly. During the convention Sadie spoke at length about the theme of her pilgrimage, racial unity. She also revealed the impact of Shoghi Effendi's words on her life, "We are not the same people we were before we went away. . . . So I know what my work is now, as I never knew it before."[33]

Throughout the next ten years Mrs. Oglesby tirelessly devoted her energies to promoting unity between the races. She wrote Shoghi Effendi regularly and told him of her activities. As promised, he answered her letters, supported her and prayed for her success. Although Sadie was not

always certain of the impact of her work, the following account by a
Bahá'í youth is evidence that her efforts were not in vain:

> Sixteen-year-old Mary Maxwell,[34] a beautiful and most refreshing
> girl to know, was Chairman of the Youth Movement in Montreal,
> and she told me how after the Convention with its inspiration
> through Mrs. Oglesby, she had persuaded two other girls and three
> youths to accompany her to a dance given by the Colored People
> for raising money to build a Settlement House. They danced with
> the Colored Young People rather than each other, stayed until the
> lights went out, and felt that their spirit to promote good will
> between the races had been accepted in good faith, for all, both
> white and colored, seemed to have a splendid time.[35]

Testimonies from many Bahá'ís, especially youth, indicated that they
listened to Sadie and put her suggestions into practice. Pilgrimage altered
Sadie's life forever, and she in turn changed others.

The Kings of the Earth

African-American Bahá'í women's reactions to the issue of race were as
varied as their personalities. Most were steeped in the traditions of the
Black church and thus brought to the Bahá'í community much needed
leadership skills. Naomi Oden (1921–88) was one individual whose
grassroots organizing brought many African-Americans to the Bahá'í Faith
in the Detroit area. She sought to address race unity by first preparing
individuals, especially Black males, for the challenges of being productive
members of the community inside and outside of the Faith. In her
obituary, friends and family recalled that "she saw Black men as crucial
to the survival of the race."[36]

Naomi became a Bahá'í in 1949, after close friends introduced her to
the Faith. In an interview she remarked that she thought her friends had
become Communists when they abandoned their regular bridge card party
for Bahá'í firesides: "So I'd go back on Friday . . . a good time to go play

Bridge with them, but they didn't have time for Bridge, they only had time for the Bahá'í Faith."[37]

Naomi continued to question her friends about the Bahá'í Faith until they agreed to take her to a fireside—a meeting to introduce new people to the teachings of the Bahá'í Faith. After over six months of meetings at the home of another prominent African-American Bahá'í, Joy Earl, Naomi enrolled.

Naomi had made a commitment to assist Black males before she became a Bahá'í and carried on that work as part of her Bahá'í activities. Earlier in her life she decided that she would do all she could to elevate her Black brothers. She was even willing to give up her job so that an African-American male could have a managerial position:

> This was in Harlem. . . .The two Black fellas that were in the organization [were] the only two salesmen we had. They were the interracial part of it. They [the corporation] needed a new sales manager . . . and so anyhow I told them [the Black salesmen] . . . "Every evening I'll teach you what a sales manager does." That's what I was doing, sitting up nights teaching them . . . and the corporate members were overhearing this . . . The president of the corporation called me up . . . and she says, "I want you to take over the sales managership of the Newark office. . . ." I said, not me, I can't. Mr. Brown is the one to do it.[38]

Eventually the corporation forced Oden to take the position. She had to accept the promotion or be fired. However, she was successful in getting the corporation to agree to promote one of the Black salesman when the next vacancy occurred.

At another time Oden worked as a secretary for the Health Department of a large city. This time, when she was promoted there was resentment on the part of her Black male colleagues. She recalled that she had envisioned herself as a supporter rather than a leader:

> I never wanted to be [promoted] . . . cause I thought that it was the time of the Black man. I wanted really to support the Black

man, help give him status and be in the background and then I felt that we had a fighting chance as Black people if . . . the Black man who was head, who did things, who's capable of doing things. And if we helped him to become more capable then we as Black women would have someone to lean on rather than somebody leaning on us.[39]

Naomi did not let others' negative opinions distract her. She valued her male colleagues' viewpoint, but also recognized the limitations of administrators in comprehending the wisdom of promoting a Black man instead of a Black woman.

Naomi's commitment to advancing Black males was not unusual, and according to others like author Paula Giddings, it was a necessary step. Giddings notes that Black women historically have believed that racism was the source of problems for African-Americans and that, "As in the past, the thinking was that before they could gain rights as Black women, the rights of Black men had to be assured."[40] Oden's personal philosophy about supporting Black men influenced her Bahá'í work. When she opened her home for public Bahá'í meetings, she targeted young Black males, including gang members. It was in the early sixties that she met members of the the notorious Shaker gang:

I said [to my step son] I want to know your friends. . . . He said they smoke pot and all that kinda stuff. . . . Well, I acted like it was nothing. . . . I said if they are your friends, and you think enough of them to call them your friends, then I want to know who they are. . . . He brought the whole Shaker gang there. They were all older than he was. . . . They were notorious for breaking into people's houses and all that. . . . And so when I got in I expected to see little [boys]. Their leader was nineteen and I expected to see kids fifteen and fourteen and I got there and these grown men sit up. . . . But I walked in that place . . . seems like all my tiredness just left me . . . and I said you are my sons. . . . [I]t looked like energy just flowed in my body. . . . They were wearing their hair Marcel . . . and they had scars on their faces like they were mad . . . and pretty soon their faces melted when I told them I loved them and I said, you know what happens to you happens to me.[41]

This was just the beginning of some popular firesides that at times lasted all night. Even years afterward, Detroit-area Bahá'ís vividly recalled the meetings in Naomi's home, which she had made a point of opening to everyone. As she recalled:

> I lived next door to a couple of doctors. They'd see these old cars drive up and these people were just packed [in]. People were just coming from far and wide. I had [Bahá'] Sunday school on Sunday morning. Children would come and their parents would come and there were these fellows . . . who had been in prison were coming. I'd met them and I didn't see them as prisoners you know. . . . They were welcome at my home. I told them about the Faith. They'd come down and I'd say to some of the people there, you are going to meet the kings of the earth coming here. But you know nothing was ever taken from my house. And many times I would even go out. . . . I'd say I'm going and when you go out all you have to do is pull the door closed. . . . What I'd learned then, the harvest is great but the workers are few.[42]

The unorthodox methods Naomi used to tell others about the Bahá'í Faith resulted in a large number of new believers throughout the 1960s and 1970s in and around Detroit. Many went on to serve the Faith in various administrative capacities. Her daughter, Ernestine Tedla, also became a Bahá'í and eventually moved to Ethiopia in order to teach the Bahá'í Faith there.

Naomi Oden was a unique individual who understood the importance of grassroots organizing. With the elevation of Black men at the core of her activities, she was able to advance the Bahá'í Faith in areas previously untouched. Constantly searching for a way to help Black men, in 1974 she helped establish the Elmhurst Home Inc., a rehabilitation center for substance abusers. In 1986 and 1987 she won awards for her work with youth and substance abuse treatment.[43] Naomi's special connection to the Detroit-area Black community was a lifeline to the positive future that she asked Black men to help create.

A Gathering Silence

Another Detroit Bahá'í, Erma Hayden (1911–97), carried out her ideological goals quite differently. A pianist by training, Erma became a Bahá'í in 1942. Her husband, poet Robert Hayden, became a Bahá'í in 1943. Their daughter, Maya, joined the Faith in 1965 and pioneered in Ethiopia with Ernestine Tedla. In the 1960s Erma volunteered to travel through the Southern states to teach the Bahá'í Faith. Hayden recalled in a 1988 interview the problems she encountered traveling through the Deep South by bus.

> I was on my way to Mississippi again and I had to change buses. I never liked Alabama and I had to change buses in Alabama. And it meant I had to wait about an hour. And so at that time they had said that if people were traveling interstate they could sit anywhere. And whenever there was a law even though I was scared to death, I believed that if the law is here and we must begin to use it or it will fade into oblivion.[44]

By law Erma had the right to be in the White waiting room. African-Americans were permitted to sit in White waiting rooms if they were traveling between states, but the mandate was relatively new and had not been tested. Paula Giddings observes that it was not uncommon for Black women to take on civil rights issues in spite of possible danger: "The courage of these modern-day Sojourner Truths was deeply embedded in a philosophy of life where fear played a secondary role."[45] Erma's narration indicates that this experience was etched deeply in her memory. She not only described the incident itself, but her feelings at significant points.

> So when I got off the bus [in Alabama] . . . I went in [the white waiting room] and somehow I didn't feel altogether certain about this so I sat in the last row. That was the easiest one to get out of [to

the door] if I needed to get out. And I had a book with me and of course I read the same page over and over again. And while I was looking at this book . . . the driver came and said to me I think you have the wrong waiting room. I said, "I'm an interstate passenger," as though I didn't know from anything. And he said let me see your ticket. And so I did. And he said OK you're all right. So I thought I'll sit here comfortably, but I still didn't feel right about it.[46]

She resolved to obey the law in spite of her apprehension. She could not predict what would happen, only what she would do in order to make something positive happen. True to the tradition of Black women activists, she got involved.

Here comes this redneck who's pretending to be drunk. He said, "We made this waiting room over there [the colored waiting room] for you." And I said, "I'm an interstate passenger," but he was too ignorant to understand any of that. . . . And so he stood around trying to talk to me and I was trying to talk to him in some intelligent way . . . [but] was getting nowhere fast so I just stopped it.[47]

Her strategy was to use logic in order to convince the men of her right to sit in the white waiting room. The result was frustration, but she stood her ground on principle:

So he eventually went over further into the waiting room and got a real redneck. . . . He came over with this man and he said, "Alright come on we don't want you in here." I said, "But I'm an interstate passenger," knowing full well he wasn't listening. And he said, "We don't care what you are, we don't want you in here." And he started to pick up my things. And at that point I got mad. I said, "Don't you touch my things." . . . But I was only angry, it wasn't because I was brave. And so I said, "I'm leaving here because I don't want to cause trouble for the rest of these people [the Black porters]." And so I did just that . . . and the redneck and his friend followed me to the door then they pitched me out the door, yes they did. . . . And

of course you're so embarrassed . . . I got my stuff together and I
first went into the Black waiting room. And you know there's a
silence that gathers, that let's you know in the split second of time
that things have been happening that everybody in there knows
what has been happening. . . . Now I know that it was not wise for
me to be traveling around at midnight down in the south alone.
. . . Had I not been going on a mission for the Faith, I wouldn't
have done it.[48]

Hayden's attempt to integrate the white waiting room was motivated
by her desire to implement Bahá'í principles as reflected in the desegre-
gation laws. Without fanfare or publicity Erma Hayden made a bold step
toward change. African-American women were not dispassionate
bystanders, but active participants in issues of racial equality within and
outside of the Bahá'í Faith. Their individual acts of courage inspired
others to take a stand. Through African-American women's leadership,
Bahá'ís were able to set into motion practices of equality that would
forever shape the inner workings of the Faith.

The Question of Gender Equality

Since women were represented at all levels of Bahá'í administration issues
of gender were not as explicitly articulated as issues of race. Dorothy
Champ, for example, was the first African-American elected to the
Spiritual Assembly of the Bahá'ís of New York city in 1919.[49] On a national
level, in 1946 Elsie Austin was the first African-American woman to be
elected to the National Spiritual Assembly of the Bahá'ís of the United
States. She later also served on the National Spiritual Assembly of North
and West Africa from 1955 to 1958.[50] Her contemporary Dr. Sarah Pereira
also served on Local Spiritual Assemblies and was the first African-
American to be appointed to the Auxiliary Board, from 1954 through
1964. She was elected to the U.S. National Spiritual Assembly in 1961
and served until 1973 when she was appointed by the Universal House
of Justice to the Continental Board of Counselors for North America,[51]
again the first African-American woman to hold such a post. Women

serving on these institutions had direct input in the administration of Bahá'í affairs. Both Dr. Austin and Dr. Pereira attained national prominence and were well respected by fellow Bahá'ís. These early gains in administrative positions by African-American women were an indication of progress, but the long path to full equality had just begun.

African-American Bahá'í women were involved in the fight for women's rights because of their sense of justice and knowledge of women's achievements. However, their participation must be understood within the context of their daily lives as well as within the framework of the national climate. Some were outspoken advocates while others led quietly by example. Paula Giddings notes that "Throughout their history, Black women also understood the relationship between the progress of the race and their own feminism. Women's rights were an empty promise if Afro-Americans were crushed under the heel of a racist power structure."[52]

In Giddings' view, Black women did not see themselves in an adversarial position with Black men, but rather claimed their rights as women believing that their advancement meant progress for the entire race. Black women within the Bahá'í community worked tirelessly for the equality of mankind, but they also engaged in the struggle for the equality of women, a major principle of their Faith. Many had already been to the front lines of the so-called "battle of the sexes" before they became Bahá'ís, but learning of Bahá'u'lláh's emphasis on the equality of women intensified their efforts. "In this Day the Hand of divine grace hath removed all distinction. The servants of God and His handmaidens are regarded on the same plane."[53]

Another important aspect to the promotion of women's rights was suffrage. Both Mary Brown Martin and Coralie Franklin Cook, were active in the suffragist movement. Documentation about their specific activities is sketchy but data from diaries, letters and family histories indicate that they took prominent roles in the campaign to secure women's right to vote.

According to a family history written by her daughter Lydia, Mary became active in the suffragist movement at the end of World War I. Equal rights for women was not an unusual concept for Mary because she descended from a long line of independent women who told their heroic stories to their children, so the Bahá'í principle of the equality of women confirmed Mary's personal beliefs and thereby provided a spiritual context in which a social condition could be successfully realized.

Coralie Franklin Cook's involvement with women's equal rights grew out of her natural inclination for activism. She was a member of the Colored Women's League founded in 1892 and a close friend of Susan B. Anthony.[54] However, Coralie was disheartened by white women's reluctance to work with Black women even within the Suffragist Movement. By 1921 she refused to continue the frustrating task of trying to participate in white dominated suffragist activities:

> I have never been able to join the National Women's Party. [I am] heartily in sympathy with its object, [but] I do not subscribe to its methods. I regret also to have to say that I am not an "active" suffragist. The old Nat'l WSA of which I was once an ardent supporter and member, turned its back on the woman of color . . . so I have not been "active" although I was born a suffragist.[55]

She did not give up, but simply changed tactics. She focused her efforts on writing and participating in Bahá'í activities. She was a regular contributor to the NAACP journal *The Crisis* and to Bahá'í publications such as *Star of the West*.[56] In addition, Mrs. Cook held Bahá'í meetings on the campus of Howard University and helped organize race unity gatherings.

On the whole, African-American Bahá'í women tended to live their lives as if the equality of women was a reality. They responded to gender bias with a toughness only prior experience can mold. Early African-American women in the Bahá'í Faith, by definition, became agents of change.

Mothers as Role Models: Vignettes of Exemplary Women

African-American Bahá'í women did not arrive at the principle of the equality of women from utter nothingness. Neither was their activism sudden and unaccountable. They were not "blank slates" ready to be written upon by higher authorities. Rather they were shaped in the image of their foremothers who demonstrated with their own lives, the reality of the equality of women. The following vignettes highlight women who made a difference in some way, however small. These brief sketches by no means do justice to the memory of these extraordinary women, but rather create a bridge for understanding African-American Bahá'í women's commitment to gender equality.

Earlita Fleming (b. 1922) became a Bahá'í in 1944 and in 1953 moved to Morocco in order to teach the Bahá'í Faith.[57] Fleming grew up with a mother who did not conform to the "rules." As a young woman, her mother, Olivia, learned to take the initiative in order to fulfill her own goals regardless of whether or not other women did the same thing.

> She became interested in, and went to work for McMartin and Chamberlain, which was a mortuary. She became the first Black woman to be an embalmer. And she loved [the] work! She really loved it. She never got her license because she could never get the money together to go to Seattle to take her exam. But she did the work.[58]

Olivia was not stymied by the lack of a license. She worked as an embalmer in Walla Walla, Washington, for as long as she could. She married and moved to San Francisco, but never gave up her independent ways.

Zylpha Mapp was another woman whose vision was larger than the immediate present. She was constantly seeking ways to be involved with the world outside of her home. Her daughter recalled that her mother made their home an international center.

> She made her home available to the students at the university. . . . She would open her door and people would come from different parts of the world. . . . Sometimes she would have them sharing their particular cultural dishes. And she would be making dishes from Africa, from India, from South America.[59]

After her four children were in school, Mapp decided that she wanted to continue her education so she enrolled in law school in order to have a career that would put her in a position to help others. As her daughter remembers,

> Well, she was an achiever. Because not only was she concerned about the achievement of her family, but even for herself. After she got us well on the road she went back to school herself and studied law at Portia Law School.[60]

As previously mentioned, Zylpha did not finish law school, but she continued to approach life with others in mind. She went on to the next project, always with service to others in mind. Ultimately she became the president of the Springfield, Mass., Federation of Women's Clubs and held the post for four years.[61]

Dr. Elsie Austin recalled that her mother, Mary, was an outspoken person who was one of the few African-Americans privileged with a college education. Mary believed in hard work and tried to be self-sufficient at a young age:

> [My mother] was the youngest of 13 children. Her mother sent her to Tuskegee. . . . And she was fiercely independent. She did not want her mother, who was in her late years in life, to put her through Tuskegee. So she marched into Booker T. Washington's office and asked if she could have a job. And he gave her a job at the school. And she worked her way through.[62]

From that point on, both Booker T. Washington and his wife took a special interest in the bold young lady who had demanded a job. Mary eventually became a teacher in the Cincinnati school system where she lived after her marriage to George Austin.

Mary was a teacher in an all-Black school district. Given the *de facto* segregation of the schools, she and other Black teachers had to fight for equality and opportunities. Dr. Austin recalled that in her later years her mother became an active member of the Cincinnati Teachers Union, helping to initiate a new ruling that specified that promotion was tied to educational accomplishments.

Although many of her female counterparts were content to stay in place, Mary returned to school to further her education. She was not finished improving her own life:

> And I remember also . . . she went into college after I graduated. I used to help her with her homework. I went to her graduation from the University of Cincinnati. I remember how proud I was to be sitting up in the stands watching my mother get her degree. All of these things meant that she was forever trying to improve upon life's situations for the sake of her self and her family.[63]

Dr. Austin followed in her mother's footsteps and, like her mother, went beyond the "acceptable" career boundaries for women in their respective time periods. She lived by her mother's example, always seeking to improve herself.

Living Outside of the Box

As the preceding and following examples show, African-American Bahá'í women were outside of the "box" normally reserved for Black women. They were unlike other women in their time simply because they chose to do things differently and sometimes against the grain. They were independent thinkers and doers regardless of their social or educational status. Their advocacy of women's equality came almost as second nature, and they were out in the world doing what others merely talked about.

African-American Bahá'í women faced many daunting challenges at a time when women had limited legal rights and few privileges. Basic aspects of everyday life that we take for granted were difficult undertakings at that time. Building a house, for example, was considered man's work in Zenobia Perry's (1914–2004) time. When she discovered that the only way she could live in Wilberforce, Ohio, was to build a house, she had to overcome many barriers to make it a reality. She taught piano theory, composition, counterpoint, and orchestration at Wilberforce University for twenty-seven years beginning in 1943.[64] It was during this time period that she decided to build the house.

> I wanted to build a house because nobody wanted to rent to me. I wasn't AME. I got Mr. Turner to take my money which he would not take until I had Dr. Wesley [my boss] OK it, even though I had the money to buy the lot. I designed the house. Contractors said, we don't build a house like this. I think he would have taken it had I been a man, but I was a woman and he did not want to take my design. . . . Then I tried to find another one who would take it [my design]. I couldn't . . . so I paid Mr. Aarmontrout who was a contractor for cement and that sort of thing to put my basement in. And when he put the sleepers on it, I paid him off and Mr. Steiner, a retired carpenter and I put this house together. I don't think I would have had that trouble if I was a man. It took me three years to build it, but it's what I wanted.[65]

Mrs. Perry was initially caught off guard by the workmen's refusal to cooperate. Even though she was not a financial risk, she still had to have the approval from her male supervisor in order the get the project started. She persisted even though she knew there was great prejudice against women, especially those who were single and those who insisted on doing things their own way.

Lecile Webster (b. 1926) exhibited great perserverance in waiting for many months for an assignment from the Foreign Service before finally receiving an assignment to Tokyo in 1954. She soon became known for her advocacy of women's rights but this did not impress many of her colleagues, as is demonstrated in this story.

> We were invited to the University of Kwangju 'cause Bill was teaching there and the chancellor of the university said he was giving a luncheon for us. Food was very scarce. We must have been about twelve people and they had . . . I imagine it was one chicken. They cut it in little pieces. . . . [W]e all sat on the floor oriental style. And the chancellor gave us a wonderful welcoming speech. He said we're

very honored to have an American lady for the first time visiting our university. Bill Smidt was sitting on one side of me and Bill Maxwell sitting on the other side. And he [the chancellor] said, in honor of the lady we're going to give you the choice piece of chicken—which was the chicken head with the eyes still in it— and they put this on my plate. Bill Smidt then nudged me in the side and said, "OK women's libber [women's liberationist], what are you gonna do about this?" So I made all the polite overtures and I said, "Well, I'm in your country, I honor your traditions and your customs. . . . And I would like to continue some of those traditions in our social [function] and I give my chicken to Bill Smidt." So I put it on his plate. Ha ha! And the professors applauded. They thought it was the greatest thing. Ha ha! Bill Smidt had to eat it. And not only did he have to eat it, but it is tradition to burp afterwards.[66]

Lecile turned the awkward situation to her advantage without having to insult her hosts. Quick thinking earned her points with the Korean university officials and simultaneously put her male counterparts on notice. Her colleague learned that male privilege has its disadvantages.

The final example of living out of the box returns us to Dr. Elsie Austin (JD, 1930). In addition to her accomplishments mentioned in other chapters, she was among the first group of students to integrate the University of Cincinnati. Her class of young African-American women and men entered the university determined to focus on their education, but early on realized that this was not to be the case. The incident began when African-American women were summoned to the dean's office.

[I]t so happened that I was with the first class of young Blacks to enter the University of Cincinnati. And I had some rather interesting experiences there. All the [Black] girls were called into the dean's office. And we were told that we should be as unobtrusive as possible on the campus. That we were members of the subject race, the university did not really want us, but as it was a city university it had to take us. And we left that interview just about in a state of shock because we hadn't been prepared for that chat. And we immediately met with the young [Black] men on campus and told them about it. And we all decided that we're going out for everything. That everybody in that freshman class is gonna come away with some distinction. We didn't burn any buildings down or anything like that. We just decided we were gonna show them. And we all did. Every member of that freshman class had some distinction. And the success of it was that the next year the same official who had spoken to us called us back and apologized. He said, "I made an error and I want you to know that you are a credit to your race."[67]

That the female students immediately involved the male students supports Giddings' theory that African-American women saw themselves as part of a larger whole. Their fight for equal rights was a fight for all African-Americans and not just women. The small victory that Dr. Austin's class achieved opened the door wider for African-American students who followed.

These early African-American Bahá'í women were extraordinary in many ways. Their enrollment in the Bahá'í Faith added another layer of distinction to their already complex lives. Instead of allowing their positions outside of the Black church to marginalize them in relation to the Black community, they continued their activism vigorously and without apology. Documenting Black women's struggles and success in the Bahá'í Faith helps us understand the broad range of African-American history and unleashes, in historian Darlene Clark Hine's words, "our hidden potential."

Spreading the Divine Fragrances: African-American Bahá'ís in the Global Expansion of the Bahá'í Faith, 1937–63

Richard Thomas

The Tablets of the Divine Plan: Guidance for Spreading the Bahá'í Faith Around the World

During the bloodiest period of World War I 'Abdu'l Bahá dictated letters to the Bahá'ís of North America that were part of what he called the "Divine Plan." 'Abdu'l-Bahá explained their purpose as global proclamation of the teachings of Bahá'u'lláh to the whole of humankind. "It is truly breathtaking," one scholar comments, "to contemplate the devising of the Divine Strategy for the redemption of the planet in the midst of the din and destruction of the old order. The transforming vision of 'Abdu'l-Bahá spreads before us the plans for the spiritual conquest of the globe."[1]

Of the fourteen letters that comprise the Tablets of the Divine Plan, four were sent to the American and Canadian Bahá'ís jointly. Eight letters were for the spiritual guidance of the Bahá'ís in specific regions of the United States and two to the Bahá'ís of Canada.[2] In the letters, Bahá'ís in North America were given the responsibility of being the leaders in spreading the Bahá'í faith around the world. "I fervently hope," 'Abdu'l-Bahá wrote in April 1916,

> that in the near future the whole earth may be stirred and shaken by the results of your achievements. The hope, therefore, which 'Abdu'l-Bahá cherishes for you is that the same success which has attended your efforts in America may crown your endeavors in other parts of the world, that through you the fame of the Cause of God may be diffused throughout the East and the West and the advent of the Kingdom of the Lord of Hosts be proclaimed in all the five continents of the globe.[3]

In the Tablets of the Divine Plan, North American Bahá'ís were promised that the moment the message of Bahá'u'lláh was carried by them "from the shores of America and is propagated through the continents of Europe, of Asia, of Africa and Australia, and as far as the islands of the Pacific, this community will find itself securely established upon the throne of an everlasting dominion." At this point, 'Abdu'l-Bahá adds, "Then will all the people of the world witness that this community is spiritually illumined and divinely guided. Then will the whole earth resound with the praise of its majesty and greatness."[4]

The first five letters reached the United States and were published in September 1916 in the early Bahá'í magazine *Star of the West.* Due to the war, the remaining letters were not received until after the war and were "unveiled in befitting ceremonies" on April 26–30, 1919, during a Bahá'í convention at the Hotel McAlpin in New York City.[5] One Bahá'í described this convention as

> a unique event in the history of the Bahá'í Cause and one which will be forever memorable. When one realizes the lapse of time,

weeks and months growing into years, during which communications on the material plane had been interrupted, the absolute joy of receiving the Words of Life, not only in single messages, but literally in a volume of general Tablets and advices, explanations and exhortations will be better understood.[6]

Louis Gregory, one of the early African-American Bahá'ís, was present at the convention and reported on it in *Star of the West*. However, his most moving commentary focused on the impact that the Tablets of the Divine Plan had on the assembled Bahá'ís: "The sources of life, to which the friends looked, were the Tablets of 'Abdu'l-Bahá, unveiled at each session of the Congress, unfolding to the hearts and minds the majestic power and unapproachable eloquence of the Word of God." Gregory was so moved by this event that he went on to write: "It was the conquest of the might of the Covenant of Bahá'o'lláh [sic] over all regions of the earth. Praise be to God, 'who hath awakened us and made us conscious. Verily out of the stones he can raise up children unto Abraham' and out the dust has He chosen instruments for His mention and praise!"[7]

A small group of dedicated Bahá'ís, notably women such as Martha Root and Marion Jack, responding to the call of 'Abdu'l-Bahá, had already begun teaching the faith in various regions of the world.[8] However, the first stage of 'Abdu'l-Bahá's Divine Plan did not begin until 1937, under the guidance of Shoghi Effendi, 'Abdu'l-Bahá's grandson and the appointed Guardian of the Bahá'í Faith. He had the awesome responsibility of implementing the gradual unfoldments of the Divine Plan. Shoghi Effendi envisioned this process of the global expansion of the Bahá'í Faith in terms of epochs and stages.[9]

The first Seven Year Plan (1937–44), which he assigned to the Bahá'ís of North America, represented the first stage of the first epoch. Among the objectives of the first plan was the expansion of the Bahá'í Faith throughout North America and into South America. After its completion, another Seven Year Plan (1946–53) began the second stage of the epoch, in which North American Bahá'ís were given the task of the "spiritual revitalization" of Europe. The third plan executed by Shoghi Effendi was the Ten Year Crusade (1953–63). It was the last stage of the first epoch in which Bahá'ís around the world participated, and the first global plan.[10] Though Shoghi Effendi died in 1957, before the completion of the last plan, the Bahá'í community followed his guidance in achieving the goals laid out before them and subsequently had a pattern which could be used by the Universal House of Justice to create future plans.

The second epoch and succession of plans began in 1964 under the direction and guidance of the Universal House of Justice, which was first elected in 1963. These included: the Nine Year Plan (1964–73), the Five Year Plan (1974–9), the Seven Year Plan (1979–86), the Six Year Plan (1986–92), the Three Year Plan (1993–6), the Four Year Plan (1996–2000), the One Year Plan (2000–1), and a second Five Year Plan (2001–6).[11]

These plans provided the Bahá'ís in North America and elsewhere with a sense of spiritual and historical mission. It offered them an opportunity to participate in a grand spiritual adventure of unprecedented historical significance for the expansion of their Faith around the world. Much of the plan centered on Bahá'ís disseminating to areas where there either were no Bahá'ís or only a few. The type of missionary activity, where Bahá'ís would move to new areas to help establish the Faith there, is called "pioneering."

Bahá'í Teachings on Pioneering

From the very beginning of the Bahá'í Faith, North American Bahá'ís have been commanded to teach their faith far and wide. Bahá'u'lláh's forerunner The Báb called upon the people of the West to "Issue forth from your cities . . . and aid God ere the Day when the Lord of mercy shall come down unto you in the shadow of the clouds with angels circling around Him, exalting His praise and seeking forgiveness for such as have truly believed in Our signs."[12] Bahá'u'lláh repeated this summons to the Bahá'ís of his day and those who followed.

> Center your energies in the propagation of the Faith of God. Whoso is worth of so high a calling, let him arise and promote it. Whoso is unable, it is his duty to appoint him who will, in his stead, proclaim this Revelation, whose power hath caused the foundations of the

mightiest structures to quake, every mountain to be crushed into dust, and every soul to be dumbfounded.[13]

In the Tablets of the Divine Plan, 'Abdu'l-Bahá told teachers of the Faith that they must "continually travel to all parts of the continent, nay, rather, to all parts of the world, but they must travel like 'Abdu'l-Bahá, who journeyed throughout the cities of America. He was sanctified and free from every attachment and in the utmost severance. Just as His Holiness Christ says: Shake off the very dust from your feet."

"Now is the time," 'Abdu'l-Bahá informed North American Bahá'ís, "that you may arise and perform the most great service and become the cause of the guidance of innumerable souls. Thus through this superhuman service the rays of peace and conciliation may illumine and enlighten all the regions and the world of humanity may find peace and composure."[14]

In 1924, Shoghi Effendi reminded the Bahá'ís of their spiritual mission to teach the Faith: "[L]et us arise to teach His Cause with righteousness, conviction, understanding and vigor. Let this be the paramount and most urgent duty of every Bahá'í. Let us make it the dominating passion of our lives. Let us scatter to the uttermost corners of the earth; sacrifice our personal interests, comforts, tastes and pleasures."[15]

Perhaps anticipating the need to advise present and future Bahá'í pioneers on how they should interact with the racially and culturally diverse peoples of the world, Shoghi Effendi outlined some principles for teaching the Faith:

> Let us . . . mingle with the divers kindred and peoples of the world; familiarize ourselves with their manners, traditions, thoughts and customs; arouse, stimulate and maintain universal interest in the Movement, and at the same time endeavor by all means in our power, by concentrated and persistent attention, to enlist the unreserved allegiance and the active support of the more hopeful and receptive among our hearers.[16]

Pioneers did not have to be "highly cultured and intellectual people who can adequately present its Teachings," Shoghi Effendi wrote. Instead, they should be "a number of devoted, sincere and loyal supporters who, in utter disregard of their own weakness and limitations, and with hearts afire with the love of God, forsake their all for the sake of spreading and establishing His Faith."[17] Shoghi Effendi made abundantly clear, "[W]hat is mostly needed nowadays is a Bahá'í pioneer and not so much a Bahá'í philosopher or scholar. For the Cause is not a system of philosophy; it is essentially a way of life, a religious Faith that seeks to unite all people on a common basis of mutual understanding and love, and in a common devotion to God."[18] These words of advice from the Guardian of their Faith clarified the spiritual mission of pioneering and inspired hundreds of ordinary people, men and women, to become Bahá'í pioneers both at home and abroad.

In 1938, as the first Seven Year Plan was just getting underway, Shoghi Effendi sent another message, in which he quotes Bahá'u'lláh's teachings on the spiritual confirmations of pioneering in a distant country.

They that have forsaken their country for the purpose of teaching Our Cause—these shall the Faithful Spirit strengthen through its power. . . . By My Life! No act, however great, can compare with it, except such deeds as have been ordained by God, the All-Powerful, the Most Mighty. Such a service is indeed the prince of all goodly deeds, and the ornament of every goodly act.[19]

Throughout his ministry, Shoghi Effendi encouraged pioneers to rise up and carry the Bahá'í message around the world. He inspired a generation of North American Bahá'ís to take up the challenge of implementing the plans he laid out for them. And when they rose up in response to his appeals, he graciously thanked and praised them. Pioneers were first among the Bahá'ís he mentioned. "To the band of Pioneers," he wrote in April of 1944, "whether settlers or itinerant teachers, who have forsaken their home, who have scattered far and wide, who have willingly sacrificed their comfort, their health and even their lives for the prosecution of this Plan. . . . I myself, as well as the entire Bahá'í world, owe a debt of gratitude that no one can measure or describe."[20] Future generations of Bahá'ís will pay tribute to the sacrifices, courage, fidelity, resourcefulness, discipline and devotion, demonstrated by these pioneers, Shoghi Effendi reminded them.

Shoghi Effendi could not have bestowed a greater honor on pioneers than explaining that their tribute would be "no less ardent and well-deserved that the recognition extended by the present-day builders of the World Order of Bahá'u'lláh to the Dawn-Breakers, whose shining deeds signalized the birth of the Heroic Age of His Faith."[21]

These "Dawn-Breakers" were the thousands of these early believers in the mid-nineteenth century who had accepted martyrdom and endured great suffering in their quest to spread the teaching of the Faith.[22] The Faith's pioneers, therefore, had much to live up to as they embarked on the next stage of the expansion of the Bahá'í Faith.

African-American Pioneers in the First Seven Year Plan (1937–44) and the Second Seven Year Plan (1946–53)

African-American Bahá'ís were actively involved at every stage of the progressive unfoldment of the Divine Plan. They have participated in every plan from the first Seven Year Plan (1937–44) to the most recent Five Year Plan (2001–6). Though leaving home for the purpose of pioneering is rarely easy, it had an added complication for African-American pioneers. Many had to make tough choices between staying at home and contributing to the struggle for racial justice and economic advancement for African-Americans or pioneering to distant lands in support of the Faith's international goals. What sustained them, however, was their firm belief in the teachings of Bahá'u'lláh and the sacred duty of pioneering in the appeals of Shoghi Effendi. Above all, African-American pioneers, like all pioneers, were encouraged by the letters addressed to them by Shoghi Effendi. Having decided to follow the Bahá'í teachings, they were determined to play their part in all the stages of the unfoldment of the Divine Plan.

As already mentioned, Louis G. Gregory reported on the Divine Plan in the *Star of the West*. His presence, and the presence of other African-American Bahá'ís at the unveiling of the Tablets of the Divine Plan in

1919, secured for them a sacred and secure place in the history of the North American Bahá'í community. As the first Seven Year Plan got under way Louis and Louisa Gregory embarked for Haiti on January 14, 1937, on a path of pioneering which other African-American pioneers would follow in the future.[23] They stayed only three months but during that time helped to expose Haitians of all classes to the Bahá'í Faith.[24]

The Gregorys returned to the United States in April 1938, just as the Seven Year Plan was starting to take off. While Louisa went to Belgrade, Yugoslavia, Louis went to the Southern U.S., on a short-term trip to help meet the goals of the plan in that region. He presented talks on the Bahá'í Faith at Tuskegee Institute in Tuskegee, Alabama, and at Arkansas State College, in Pine Bluff, Arkansas. Lydia Martin, the Dean of Women at the latter institution, arranged for Gregory to be invited to the college. She was a Bahá'í and the daughter of two prominent African-American Bahá'ís, Mary and Alexander Martin, who had first heard about the Bahá'í Faith through Gregory at a 1913 talk in Cleveland. Louis spent a month in this short-term pioneering post. After he left, Lydia continued study classes, which Louis had initiated in his time there, for a while, and sent a letter about the Bahá'í teaching activities to Shoghi Effendi.[25]

The reply to Lydia Martin, written on Shoghi Effendi's behalf, was typical of his warm, sensitive, and encouraging attention to the teaching efforts of African-American Bahá'ís throughout all the plans. Always aware of the burden of racism both outside and inside the Bahá'í community which at times discouraged them, he never failed to sense their pain and anguish, as well as their joys in their contributions to the Faith.

> [T]he Guardian's heart [was] immeasurably gladdened at the report of the outstanding teaching achievements which you and Mr. Gregory have been able to accomplish in Pine Bluff during this past year. His heart goes out in deepest gratitude to you both for all the sacrifice, determination & resourceful energy you have displayed all through your teaching work in that center. . . .
>
> [He was] indescribably happy & encouraged to know that as a result the entire Negro population of Pine Bluff has heard about

the Cause, that one of the college students . . . has already declared herself a believer, & that several others are on the point of becoming fully confirmed.[26]

He further praised Lydia Martin for her work among the students at the college and encouraged her to remain there "notwithstanding any opposition, veiled or open, which may be directed against you from certain quarters. . . . [C]onfidently persist in your efforts until you succeed in establishing a strong & united group of confirmed believers, capable of developing eventually into a local assembly."[27] He particularly wanted her to concentrate on teaching the Faith to African-Americans in Pine Bluff, and "thus bring into the Cause this hitherto neglected, though highly promising & spiritually receptive, element of the population in the South States."[28] Unfortunately, due both to the neglect of the Bahá'í community and the opposition in the region, the work of Louis Gregory and Lydia Martin during that short period of the first Seven Year Plan looked bleak. It did, however bear fruit in the years to come.[29] She continued to serve the Faith, and pioneered to Central America in 1950, during the second Seven Year Plan.[30]

Other African-American pioneers of the time included Rosa and John Shaw, who pioneered to Haiti during the first Seven Year Plan, arriving there in 1939. Ellsworth and Ruth Blackwell, an interracial couple, followed the next year and remained until 1943. Ellsworth, an African-American and Ruth, a European-American, spent much of their lives in various pioneering posts pursuing the goals of the various plans.

After three years in Haiti during the first Seven Year Plan, the Blackwells left, returning to Haiti in 1950 during the second Seven Year Plan and again in 1960 during the Ten Year Crusade (1953–63), this time remaining until 1975. Ellsworth was elected chairperson of the first Local Spiritual Assembly formed in Haiti, in the capital, Port-au-Prince, in 1942. When the first Bahá'í National Spiritual Assembly in Haiti was elected in 1961, the Bahá'ís elected Ellsworth chairperson of that institution. He later served as the first member of the Auxiliary Board (an administrative body created to assist the Continental Board of Counsellors) in the Haitian Bahá'í community. He served in that capacity until 1970, after which he was once again elected to the National Spiritual Assembly.[31] Ellsworth's pioneering work covered almost a quarter of a century, from the first Seven Year Plan in 1940 to the Five Year Plan, when he died at his pioneering post in Kananga, Zaire, in 1978.[32]

Throughout their long years in Haiti, the Blackwells received encouraging letters from Shoghi Effendi. At the midpoint of the first Seven Year Plan, in April 1941, soon after they had arrived in Haiti, he wrote to them:

> The work you have done, the sacrifices you have made, the historic mission you have initiated, are highly praiseworthy, meritorious and unforgettable. I will specially pray for you both that in whether field you may labour in the days to come, Bahá'u'lláh may reinforce, guide and bless you and aid you to enrich the record of your pioneer service.[33]

Eight months later, Shoghi Effendi sent the Blackwells another encouraging letter.

> I wish to ensure you in person of my deepest and abiding appreciation of your devoted and indeed historic services. Perseverance will crown your labours with imperishable glory. Rest assured, and relax in your efforts which the rising generation will extol and admire. You are often in my thoughts and prayers. I will always be glad to hear from you, and will pray that your dearest hopes may be speedily and completely realized.[34]

African-American Pioneers in the British Bahá'í Teaching Campaign in Africa (1951–3)

During the later years of the second Seven Year Plan, African-American Bahá'í pioneers began a steady tradition of pioneering to Africa that would later expand during the Ten Year Global Crusade and extend to the Four

Year Plan. Appealing to African-American Bahá'ís to play a role in this campaign, in August 1950, Shoghi Effendi wrote, "I appeal particularly to its [the Bahá'í community's] dearly beloved members belonging to the Negro race to participate in the contemplated project marking a significant milestone in the world-unfoldment of the Faith."[35]

Shoghi Effendi's appeal to African-American Bahá'ís to participate in the pioneering goals in East and West Africa, which were directed mostly at the British Bahá'ís, presented them with great challenges and opportunities to not only pioneer but to connect with their ancestral homeland.

William Foster was the first American Bahá'í who responded to Shoghi Effendi's appeal to American Bahá'ís—and particularly African-American Bahá'ís—to pioneer to Africa in 1950. He wrote to Shoghi Effendi in May 1951 expressing his decision to pioneer in Africa. In September 1951, Foster received an encouraging letter written on Shoghi Effendi's behalf:

> Dear Bahá'í Brother: Your letter of May 2nd was received by our beloved Guardian and brought him great joy. The decision you have taken to go to Africa and teach the Cause is momentous and is worthy of the great race you belong to. The Guardian has been eagerly awaiting a Negro pioneer, and feels that Bahá'u'lláh will surely bless your enterprise and assist you in this work you are planning for His Faith.[36]

It was Ethel Stephens, however, an African-American woman, who would earn the high honor of being the first pioneer from the United States to arrive in Africa. She left for the Gold Coast (now Ghana) via London on October 13, 1951. Two months later, she wrote a letter from Kumais to the African Teaching Committee of the United States National Spiritual Assembly, in which she commented, "I have come into a new consciousness of my relationship to Shoghi Effendi and to the degree to which I draw on this infinite resource my personal and spiritual problems are being resolved to a working and satisfactory basic."[37]

Her arrival in Africa as the first pioneer from the United States and the first African-American pioneer to Africa prompted a predictable response. A letter to the African Teaching Committee from Shoghi Effendi's secretary in January 1952 reported that he "has been most cheered to hear of the arrival of Mrs. Stephens in Africa, and most recently, of Mr. Foster. It is truly remarkable that both of these devoted souls should belong to the Negro race; and we cannot but believe that it is the will of God that has raised up from this race the two first official pioneers from the United States [to Africa]."[38]

A month later, another letter written on Shoghi Effendi's behalf appeared in the *Bahá'í News* that once again clearly expressed the importance he placed on the spiritual primacy of African-American pioneering to Africa and its relationship to 'Abdu'l-Bahá's love for and understanding of African-Americans. Shoghi Effendi's letter said that he "was very pleased to have the first pioneer from American go forth under this organized African campaign; he was doubly happy that it should have been an American Negro who went. This is highly appropriate and surely has delighted the heart of 'Abdu'l-Bahá who watched over that race with particular love, tenderness and understanding. The ever increasing part the colored friends are taking in the pioneer work, gratifies the Guardian immensely."[39]

Pioneering posed harsh challenges to those African-American Bahá'ís who choose to give up family, jobs, and comfort to teach the Faith in foreign lands. While there was an historical and cultural connection between African-American pioneers and the native Africans, there were also hardships to overcome. Although she faced a series of difficulties, including lost luggage, malaria, and restrictions to teaching the Faith upon first arriving in the country, Stephens was able to "build up a reservoir of good will for the Faith in the Gold Coast."[40] No doubt she would have continued in her pioneering post had it not been for a family crisis that necessitated her return to the United States in July 1952. Once home, however, she continued her work in pioneering in Africa through her work on the African Teaching Committee, where she assisted in sending other pioneers to replace her.[41]

Valerie Merriell Wilson also responded to the appeal for African-American Bahá'ís to pioneer to Africa. In 1952, she pioneered to Monrovia, Liberia, where she worked as a physiotherapist while teaching the

Bahá'í Faith, advancing not only the teachings of the Faith, but also able to introduce her field to the local medical establishment. She started a program of nutrition classes for girls and women. President William V. S. Tubman and his wife were among Dr. Wilson's private patients.

Her contributions to the development of the Bahá'í community included service on the Local Spiritual Assembly and helping to establish the National Spiritual Assembly of the Bahá'ís of Liberia. She worked throughout West Africa and was a member of the first regional National Assembly of North West Africa. As was so common for those pioneers, who in obedience to Shoghi Effendi's requests, sacrificed the comforts of home to spread the Bahá'í teachings in distance lands, Dr. Wilson had to endure severe physical hardships and health conditions as she pioneered throughout West Africa. Despite those difficulties, she remained in her pioneering post for twelve years leaving only because of family responsibilities back in the United States.[42]

African-American Pioneers During the Ten Year Crusade (1953–63)

African-American pioneers, both on the home front and abroad, paved the way for the wave of African-American pioneers who would rise up during the Ten Year Crusade. They personified the devotion and sacrifice of the first generation of African-American Bahá'í pioneers. The Ten Year Plan, also called the "World Crusade," was a plan that at the time staggered the imagination of Bahá'ís. The Bahá'í Faith had been somewhat obscured since its birth in Persia in 1844. According to one contemporary observer, it "had grown up in obscurity, painfully and slowly widening its influence in the world, [yet] in one year in 1953–4 [it] overleapt its bounds. . . . Bahá'í crusaders came forth from their homes and normal occupations to claim for their faith the most difficult and remote countries and islands of the planet."[43]

African-American Bahá'ís were among "these spiritual conquerors" and "valiant knights" who made up the vanguard of the pioneers during The World Crusade. Some earned the title "Knight of Bahá'u'lláh," which was bestowed by Shoghi Effendi on those who "opened" (introduced the

Bahá'í Faith to) new territories. Particularly in Africa, African-American Bahá'ís contributed not only to the expansion of the Bahá'í Faith, but the development of a new historical and religious relationship between Africans and African-Americans within the Bahá'í world community. It was the pioneering efforts of African-Americans during the Ten Year Plan that added another chapter to the religious history of the Black Diaspora. Other African-American pioneers went to other places, such as the Far-East. Wherever they went, however, they made their mark by choosing to sacrifice the comforts of families, homes, and jobs to respond to the appeals of Shoghi Effendi.

Matthew W. Bullock (1881–1972) was among the first African-American Bahá'ís who responded to the Guardian's stirring messages. He arose to pioneer during the World Crusade though he was already seventy-two years old. According to an old friend and fellow African-American pioneer, Elsie Austin, he was "an established and prominent citizen of his community, enjoying the fruits of a life of hard work and sacrifice. There was no doubt in his mind about the spiritual service in pioneering."[44] He had overcome "the reservations of his age and those near to him, wrenching himself free from the home community and land."[45]

He had been a Bahá'í since 1940 and was elected to the National Spiritual Assembly in 1952. In 1953, while a member of the Assembly, he was asked to be one of the representatives of that institution attending the first international Bahá'í Conference in Uganda. On his way to the conference he was granted permission to visit the Holy Land for Bahá'í pilgrimage. There he visited the Bahá'í holy places and was given a warm welcome by Shoghi Effendi. As he explained later: "The Guardian has cleared up many things for me. My visit to him and to the Holy Shrines are experiences beyond words. I don't think I will ever be able to express what it meant to me; nor I think that any Bahá'í is the same after being with the Guardian. I wish every Bahá'í could have the bounty which has been mine."[46]

No doubt Bullock's experience in the Holy land and his contact with the Guardian influenced his decision to go pioneering. Yet his trip to the African conference, where he was a "deeply inspired participant" must have also shaped his decision as well. After leaving the conference, he visited the Belgian Congo and Liberia. In Liberia he met President Tubman and the American ambassador and shared the Bahá'í teachings with them. Bullock's discussion of the teachings so impressed the President that he was invited to a special dinner where he presented to a group of distinguished figures from Liberia and other countries. At this dinner Bullock told the guests about the Bahá'í teachings and their application to the problems of humanity and that he was in Africa representing the National Spiritual Assembly of the United States.[47]

When he returned to the United States and attended the Bahá'í national convention, he was ready to go pioneering. He was one of five members of the U.S. National Spiritual Assembly who resigned their positions on that body in order to go pioneering. In 1953, Bullock pioneered to Curaçao, Dutch West Indies, where he helped to establish the first Local Spiritual Assembly there. During this period he traveled throughout the West Indies, teaching people about the Bahá'í Faith and forming and strengthening Local Spiritual Assemblies. Shoghi Effendi named him a Knight of Bahá'u'lláh for his pioneering in the Dutch West Indies. In 1960, due to his advanced age and related disabilities, Matthew Bullock returned to the United States, where he continued to serve the Bahá'í Faith. His illness progressed, however, and he passed on December 17, 1972, in Detroit, Michigan.[48]

One of the greatest sacrifices a pioneer can make is to give her or his life while pioneering. Both Bessie and George Washington made this supreme sacrifice (as would others) while pioneering in Liberia during the World Crusade. An interracial couple, the Washingtons' spiritual journey as pioneers started in 1954 when George wrote to the U.S. African Teaching Committee asking if he and his wife Bessie could "be enlisted in the ranks of the World Crusaders on the continent of Africa." At the time George was sixty years old and Bessie was fifty-five. Both had been active Bahá'ís in Seattle, Washington, for over a decade. George had previously left the Christian ministry after becoming a Bahá'í and worked for a while as an educator and building contractor.[49]

In the spring of 1955, after selling their properties, the Washingtons prepared to pioneer to Liberia with their eight-year-old grandson. Initially,

Hand of the Cause Musa Banani had wanted them to go to the Gambia, but there were problems obtaining a visa, so it was decided that they would first pioneer to Liberia and attempt to resettle later. On July 19, 1955, the Washingtons arrived at their pioneering post in the capital city, Monrovia. After only a few months in Monrovia, George decided to live in the hinterland. So they moved to the village of Gboweta, 137 miles away.[50]

The Washingtons then decided to become Liberian citizens so that they could buy land to leave to the Bahá'í Faith. They were able to accomplish this because "Only citizens could own land there and only people of African descent could become citizens."[51] They purchased four hundred acres on which they built a Bahá'í center and established a school for illiterate Bahá'ís. As a result their land became the first Bahá'í endowment in Liberia and perhaps in West Africa. Like other Bahá'í pioneers, they had many tests and difficulties. But it is reported that the Washingtons "never complained or expressed regret. They courageously and with great steadfastness stood up to all that befell them."[52]

Less than four years after they first arrived in Liberia, the couple both died. After a short illness, Bessie Washington passed on April 23, 1959. She was buried on the property they had donated to the Bahá'í community only a few months earlier. George passed a month later, on May 30, 1959. In a loving testimony, a fellow pioneer wrote: "the name and Banner of Bahá'u'lláh [was] planted on a hill . . . it had cost two precious lives, but it was done and those who follow after will never be able to comprehend how it was done. . . . Bahá'u'lláh can convert all our weaknesses and incapability into immortality."[53]

Some years later, Hand of the Cause 'Amatu'l-Bahá Rúḥíyyih Khánum, the widow of Shoghi Effendi, sent a letter to the Universal House of Justice describing the lasting spiritual impact the Washingtons had on the village.

We spent nights sleeping in the Washingtons' old home; I would have loved to know those two. . . . [T]hey must have been singularly wonderful believers, for in the village where they taught the people have remained firm and devoted and have a great love for those two pioneers. . . . One does not often in any country find a foundation laid like this one.[54]

Among the African-American pioneers who went to places other than Africa were Joy Hill Earl and Adrienne and Dempsey Morgan, who pioneered in the Far East during the Ten Year Plan.

Joy Hill Earl (1912–72) learned about the Bahá'í Faith in the late 1930s, while the first Seven Year Plan was underway. She came into contact with Louis Gregory, who took a special interest in her, and she reciprocated with such love and admiration that soon she was calling him "Uncle Louis." During the 1940s she gave many public talks about the Bahá'í Faith, taught at various Bahá'í summer schools, and served on the Local Spiritual Assemblies of both Detroit and Cleveland. When Louis Gregory passed away in 1951, Joy made all the funeral arrangements, which was a fitting spiritual duty because of their close relationship and his role in her spiritual journey.[55]

She was a living example of a Bahá'í who did not allow physical disabilities to deter her from pioneering. She had been suffering with ill health from childhood, and as her husband, David Earl, explained, she endured "physical pain and successive operations during most of her adult life, for the more than thirty years that she served the Faith." Yet "she was a constant source of inspiration and illumination to all who knew her."[56] Her resolve and courage to go pioneering with her husband was amply demonstrated when, on the eve of their departure to Japan in 1952, Joy had her passport picture taken while she was hospitalized. "But she left on schedule."[57] The Earls then endured "a storm-battered 17-day trip across the pacific" and arrived in Japan on March 14, 1952 in time for the celebration of Naw-Rúz (the Bahá'í New Year) with the Bahá'í community of Tokyo, which "at that time [was] the only Bahá'í community in the entire Far-East."[58]

For thirteen years, in spite of her deteriorating health, Joy never wavered in her pioneering duties and responsibilities. In 1972, there were still active Japanese Bahá'ís who had been taught the Faith by Joy during her first year in Japan. She served on the Local Spiritual Assembly of Tokyo and in the Tokyo Bahá'í center. The responsibility for arranging all the

Bahá'í activities also fell to her, since her husband's job required him to be away for four to six months of each year. Many Japanese became Bahá'ís during Joy's stint at the Bahá'í center, which lasted throughout the duration of the Ten Year Crusade. She also engaged in extensive teaching trips in Japan, Korea, Taiwan, Hong Kong, Macao, and Malaysia. While she never "completely mastered the intricacies of Japanese grammar," she nonetheless "developed an almost flawless accent in speaking the language."[59]

The ideal Bahá'í pioneer does not just focus on the Bahá'í community. The Bahá'í teachings emphasize building loving relationships with all people within and outside of the Faith. In this sense, Joy was a model Bahá'í pioneer. Notwithstanding the countless Bahá'í activities in which she was involved, she found the time to work with many women groups in Japan. As a result she achieved "considerable recognition in Tokyo women's affairs."[60] She was chairman of the Music Workshop, president of the College Women's Association of Japan, president of the Imperial Ball, and a member of the Board of Directors of the Tokyo Women's Club. All the members in these organization knew Joy was a Bahá'í "and respected the Faith because of her."[61]

At the end of the Ten Year Plan in 1963, Joy and David attended the Bahá'í World Congress in London; their pioneering days were not over, however. They pioneered to Korea, where Bahá'ís were just beginning a project to teach the Bahá'í Faith to masses of people, which demanded effort on the part of the Bahá'ís to consolidate those who became Bahá'ís during the mass teaching. She was then honored to be among the first group of Bahá'í pilgrims to the Bahá'í World Center in Haifa, Israel, after the election of the first Universal House of Justice. Struggling with worsening health, the Earls returned to Korea where she spent two years contributing to the development of the Bahá'í Faith in that country. In the summer of 1965, after thirteen years of almost continuous pioneering, Joy and her husband David, returned to the United States.[62]

Even as her health continued to deteriorate, she continued to pioneer on behalf of the Faith she so loved and cherished. In 1972, she and David visited the grave of Shoghi Effendi in London, went on a pilgrimage to Iran to visit Bahá'í historical sites and holy places, and continued on a relentless itinerary. When they reached Malaysia, walking for Joy was becoming impossible. But, as her husband described, "[S]he carried out the itinerary set up for her, with firesides, deepening classes and public meetings for two weeks in Penang, Butterworth, Alor Star and Kuala Lumpur. Her last public talk was given on August 18 at Kuala Lumpur."[63]

She was too sick to continue her itinerary to the Philippines and Taiwan. When she arrived at the Tokyo Bahá'í center on September 3, 1972, she was "surprised and cheered by a massive welcoming party . . . attended by over fifty friends, including some she had known for as long as twenty years."[64] It was most fitting that Joy would end her pioneering and teaching in the place where she first became a pioneer. In November, David brought Joy back to Ann Arbor, Michigan, where she passed on November 27, 1972. In a moving testimony to his wife, and her love for and devotion to her Faith, David wrote, "Throughout her life, Joy had drawn her strength from invisible sources and poured her entire resources into the teaching work: but now her body could not be pushed no further."[65]

In September 1955, Dempsey and Adrienne Morgan joined the Bahá'í Faith while attending a "home coming" event at the Louhelen Bahá'í School in Davison, Michigan. As they listened to the Bahá'í speakers they suddenly realized that "these people are trying to change the world." Little did they know at the time that the Bahá'í world was being swept up in the spirit of the Ten Year World Crusade. Being one of the major centers of Bahá'í social and educational activities, the Louhelen Bahá'í School was probably teeming with excitement two years into this global enterprise.[66]

Before long the Morgans began to realize the historical and spiritual significance of pioneering during this Crusade. The untimely death of Shoghi Effendi on November 4, 1957, also influenced their decision to pioneer. As they wrote later, "It took a little time to truly realize the importance of pioneering, and still more time for the notion to sink in that we should make the effort. But, the Guardian's passing further helped to hammer home the point."[67] By the time calls were made for pioneers at the Bahá'í Conference in Chicago in 1958, the Morgans had already begun to take "definite steps to try and fulfill [their] obligation to Shoghi Effendi's Crusade."[68]

At first the Morgans were planning to go to South America in response to the U.S. National Spiritual Assembly's request for pioneers to that area. When this plan did not work, the Assembly put them into contact with a pioneer in Saigon, Vietnam, who told them they were needed in Cambodia and other areas in Southeast Asia. It was to be the beginning of a long, trying, and spiritually transforming experience for the Morgans.[69]

In July 1958, on their way to Cambodia, the Morgans had to stop off in Saigon and were asked by a Bahá'í pioneer in the city if they would be willing to pioneer in Vietnam instead of Cambodia. The Morgans readily accepted the offer. Because they had entered Vietnam without a visa, though, the Morgans were expected to leave or provide a good reason why they should be permitted to stay. Finally, they were able to receive an extension of their "visit," but the tests and difficulties of pioneering in Vietnam were only beginning. Vietnam's climate took its toll on the Morgans, and Dempsey lost thirty-five pounds.[70]

Flying was the only safe way to travel in Vietnam. Dempsey flew to various centers to meet with Local Spiritual Assemblies and to encourage and train Bahá'ís in Bahá'í administrative procedures. These activities were critical and vital aspects of pioneering necessary for the growth and expansion of the Bahá'í Faith in newly opened areas, particularly at a time when the government harassed the Vietnamese Bahá'ís and had even imprisoned the entire Spiritual Assembly of Saigon. Several months later, the Morgans were forced to leave the country because the government demanded that they have permanent jobs to renew their visas. On March 3, 1959, they left Saigon and arrived in Bangkok, Thailand, with only thirty U.S. dollars.[71]

According to the Morgans, when they arrived in Thailand there were less than twenty Bahá'ís in the entire country. Both of the Morgans were soon elected to the Bangkok Local Spiritual Assembly and assigned the task of investigating the possibility of registering the Bahá'í community as a legally recognized religious organization in Thailand. They drafted the original document and contracted a Thai lawyer who at the time was the legal counsel for the United Nations. He in turn prepared the draft for submission to the Thai government. The Morgans stayed in Bangkok for two and a half years, leaving on July 15, 1961, for Phnom Penh, Cambodia.[72]

Anti-Americanism, the search for work to support themselves while pioneering, and the departure of one of the mainstays of the local Bahá'í community, were among some of the challenges facing the Morgans when they arrived in Phnom Penh. True to form, though, the couple persevered. In October 1961, they traveled to Saigon to see Rúḥíyyih Khánum. Traveling by car from Phnom Penh to Saigon presented the risk of being stopped by Communist guerillas on the Vietnamese side of the border. But, the trip was worth the risk to be with Shoghi Effendi's widow. She provided the Morgans with both inspiration and guidance. "The three days in Saigon with Rúḥíyyih Khánum gave us the spiritual fortitude to renew our efforts to remain in Cambodia," they wrote. "We asked her to pray for our success when she returned to the Shrines. . . . She instructed us to find a place where we could entertain friends in our home. She urged us not to try and persuade the government to allow us to meet; in fact, she said we should have as little as possible to do with the Government, just quietly make friends and teach."[73]

The Morgans returned to Phnom Penh determined to take her advice. They conducted children classes at the Bahá'í center and encouraged local Bahá'ís to fan out and teach the Bahá'í Faith in their goal cities. Because of mounting conflicts between Thailand and Cambodia, the latter accusing the former of planning to attack with U.S. assistance, all unofficial Americans were forced to leave the country. Once again, the Morgans were on the move. They took all they could carry and on November 15, 1961, they moved back to Saigon.[74]

Once back in Saigon, the Morgans began the process of getting settled and seeking employment. Both found jobs and used all their spare time serving the Bahá'í community. Adrienne taught Bahá'í classes and wrote some articles for the local *Bahá'í News*. When he was not working, Dempsey spent his time at the Bahá'í center and on trips to teach the Faith. They wrote of how "the people of Vietnam are very spiritual. They have been waiting for the 'Return.' They have been waiting for the Great Buddha. Bahá'u'lláh is All Things to all people. . . . [Y]ou must find the key that will strike the right note on their spiritual ear. In Vietnam it is

'A-DiDa,' or the Fifth Buddha. In Cambodia, it is 'Siyamytrea,' or the Fifth Buddha again."[75]

The Morgans reported that five thousand people became Bahá'ís in one province through the efforts of Vietnamese Bahá'í teachers. Unfortunately, they were not able to supervise their "deepening" in the basics of the Bahá'í teachings because of the activities of the Viet Cong. The Bahá'í community addressed this problem by bringing the most active new Bahá'ís to Saigon for a week of six-hours-a-day classroom training coupled with much love and fellowship. As the Morgans explained:

> While the believers are with us in Saigon . . . we make every effort to establish the "love of God" in their hearts by personal contacts, showing compassion, warmth, concern and really letting them know that we accept them as Bahá'í brothers. . . . [H]ere they get the teachings and the love of God and return to their assemblies and groups filled and burning with the fire of this love and the teachings of Bahá'u'lláh, 'Abdu'l-Bahá, and Shoghi Effendi.[76]

The year 1963 was of profound historical significance for Bahá'ís throughout the world. The Ten Year Crusade was successfully completed on April 20. The next day the Universal House of Justice was elected for the first time, and on April 28 the first Bahá'í World Congress, the "Most Great Jubilee" was held in London, England, to celebrate the centenary of Bahá'u'lláh's declaration of his station as a Prophet of God. The Morgans were there, and when they returned they left Saigon on July 15, 1963, for Phom Pehn, Cambodia. In 1958, they had joined the ranks of African-American pioneers responding to Shoghi Effendi's call. Now that the Ten Year Crusade was over, the Morgans, like other pioneers, continued their service throughout the duration of other plans, which were now being carried out under the direction of the Universal House of Justice.[77]

In addition to the pioneering posts in Africa and Asia, other African-American Bahá'ís went to Europe during the Ten Year Plan, reflecting the emerging global consciousness of African-American Bahá'ís. Gwili Posey, who became a Bahá'í in Chicago in 1953, pioneered to Switzerland in the late 1950s and remained there for four years. She also pioneered for a year in France, to a suburb of Paris. She returned to the United States in 1965, a year after the beginning of the Nine Year Plan.[78]

In August 1969, Gwili pioneered to Haiti, where she remained for seventeen years. There she followed in the footsteps of a line of African-American pioneers to Haiti beginning with Ellsworth Blackwell and Louis Gregory in the 1930s and Betty Jane Walker and Camillia Love White in the 1960s.

These African-American Bahá'í pioneers, among them Knights of Bahá'u'lláh, demonstrated their dedication to their Faith by making supreme sacrifices of families, friends and comfort, traveling the globe, sharing Bahá'u'lláh's message of love and unity. Although largely unknown by the larger African-American community of religious scholars and laypersons, these brave souls made a major contribution to the history of African-American missionary efforts in the twentieth century and wrote a new chapter in African-American spiritual development that will be felt for centuries the world over.

African-American Bahá'ís Teaching Trips to Africa during the Four Year Plan (1996–2000)

In its 1996 letter regarding the Four Year Plan, the Universal House of Justice made a special appeal to African-American Bahá'ís to arise and support the Bahá'í Faith in Africa. The House of Justice reminded African-American Bahá'ís of the "special responsibility" Shoghi Effendi, the Guardian of the Bahá'í Faith, had assigned them to pioneer to Africa during the Ten Year World Crusade:

We direct the attention of the believers of African descent, so Beloved by the Master ['Abdu'l-Bahá], to the pressing need for pioneers, who will contribute to the further development of the Cause in distant areas, including the continent of Africa for which they were assigned a special responsibility by the Guardian when the first systematic campaign was launched for its spiritual illumination. Although their contributions to all aspects of Bahá'í service on the home front and elsewhere will be of great value, they can be a unique source of encouragement and inspiration to their African brothers and sisters who are now poised on the threshold of great advances for the Faith of Bahá'u'lláh.[79]

As a result of this appeal, the annual Black Men's Gathering, a fellowship meeting for African-American Bahá'í men, became the means for "preparing spiritually for service in Africa" which resulted in annual trips to Africa to teach the Faith.[80] While these teaching trips were not pioneering in the sense used in Shoghi Effendi's letter, the trips were part of the long spiritual tradition of African-American Bahá'ís pioneering activities in Africa.

During these trips the group "collaborated with the Continental Board of Counselors, the Continental Pioneer Committee, and National Spiritual Assemblies in Africa."[81] Soon this teaching project expanded to include Bahá'í men of African descent from other countries. During the first three years of the Four Year Plan, teams of black men spent several weeks traveling and teaching in just one region of Africa. During 2000, the group sent teams to teach the Faith simultaneously to western, central, eastern and southern Africa. As a result of this expansion, "the number of traveling teachers rose from 9 during the first year to 53 in the last year of the Plan."[82]

These travel teaching teams of African-American men resulted in impressive successes, and the African countries that hosted them benefitted from their visits. For example, the groups conducted "deepening" programs, met with prominent Africans and attracted the interest of the media. In addition, they inspired their African coreligionists, particularly the African Bahá'í youth, "and as consequence of this teaching, there were many new enrolments."[83]

African-American women were not about to be outdone by their Bahá'í brothers. In June 1994 a group of nine African-American Bahá'í women visited South Africa inspired by a letter from Bonnie Fitzpatrick-Moore. The women visited Lesotho, where they had tea with teachers, judges, school principals, clergy, and doctors, and shared their reasons for visiting

Africa at their own expense instead of being supported by external funds. As Fitzpatrick-Moore explained:

> Wherever we went on the trip, people could not help but be impressed by the fact that these women were not funded by some big organization, they had made great personal sacrifices to come to see Africa for themselves and to be seen by Africans. This was the first such group to ever have come to southern Africa: unaided, ordinary people who wanted to see with their own eyes and "not through the eyes of others."[84]

In the village of Mofeli in the mountains of Lesotho, the African-American Bahá'í women met with the village elders and were entertained by the children who sang for them. They also said prayers with the Bahá'í Spiritual Assembly of Mofeli. They were invited to speak on two TV talk shows and sang together for a TV program. One of the highlights of the trip was their meeting with the Queen of Lesotho, who had her choir sing for her guests.[85] In Sabie, "one of the most conservative areas in South Africa," the women met with African women, toured the township, and met with representatives of some Bahá'í administrative bodies such as the National Spiritual Assembly, the Continental Board of Counsellors, and the National Teaching Committee.[86]

No doubt, these educated and professional African-American women made a lasting impression on a group of white women in Sabie who were members of a Persian Bahá'í women's garden club and were anxious to meet the visitors. "When the women were told that a group of African-American women were coming to Sabie, all wanted the chance to meet them and associate with them! Many were in tears because they finally recognized the oneness of the 'sisterhood to which all women belong.'"[87] In describing the interaction between the two groups, Fitzpatrick-Moore points out: "Most of these women had never spoken to a black women they consider their equal or above. The tears flowed as the hearts thawed on both sides! The feelings of love, fellowship, and acceptance were palpable."[88]

After this memorable meeting in Sabie, three members of the group flew to Nambia to meet the Bahá'ís there and the rest went to Mmabotho. They spoke at the University of Botswana to a group of nurses which focused on education, social services, chastity among youth and social and medical problems that result "when the standard is not met."[89]

While African-American Bahá'í women and men have been traveling to Africa as missionaries since the early 1950s, some staying for decades, some for life, this most recent group of African-American Bahá'í travel teachers were drawn to Africa by both obedience to the call of their religion and a burning desire to spiritually connect with their African Bahá'í sisters and brothers. This quest for connection, however, went far deeper than a mere diaspora connection to Africa based upon history and culture, although these connections were important. Rather, they were connecting with their Bahá'í sisters and brothers around their shared spiritual mission to spread the divine fragrances of their Faith throughout the world in their mutual effort to transform a divided humanity into one unified family.

6

Unrestrained as the Wind: African-American Women Answer the Call

Gwendolyn Etter-Lewis

Be unrestrained as the wind, while carrying the Message of Him who hath caused the dawn of Divine Guidance to break. Consider how the wind, faithful to that which God hath ordained, bloweth upon all regions of the earth, be they inhabited or desolate. Neither the sight of desolation, nor the evidences of prosperity, can either pain or please it. It bloweth in every direction, as bidden by its Creator.

—BAHÁ'U'LLÁH

African-American women enthusiastically responded to Shoghi Effendi's call to leave the comfort of their homes and teach the Bahá'í Faith in foreign lands. Whether single or married, with or without children, many of these women volunteered for pioneering assignments with little or no hesitation. Although not a single journey or experience was without difficulty, the African-American women who arose to fulfill this goal possessed more than mere spunk or raw religious fervor. They, in fact, saw themselves as serving to a greater cause. According to 'Abdu'l-Bahá,

Again, it is well established in history that where woman has not participated in human affairs the outcomes have never attained a state of completion and perfection. On the other hand, every influential undertaking of the human world wherein woman has been a participant has attained importance.[1]

Through the act of pioneering,[2] Black women claimed a position of honor in the development of the Bahá'í Faith and manifested 'Abdu'l-Bahá's idea that women must participate in all aspects of life. Just as they had taken part in past movements (e.g., the Abolitionist Movement, the Suffragist Movement, the Civil Rights Movement, the Women's Movement), African-American women assumed the challenge of pioneering with equally inspiring courage and fortitude. For many it was a life-changing experience. Elsie Austin, who pioneered to several African countries during the Ten Year Crusade (1953–63) remarked,

I must say that there is no experience like pioneering to deepen you, to make you understand the significance of the history of the Bahá'í Faith. And also to broaden you because you begin to understand how much oneness there is with humanity and how much people in other parts of the world are going through the same experiences that you go through in your homeland.[3]

Finding common ground with people in a variety of international contexts exposed Black women to different or world views and provided them with an opportunity to establish alliances with others who might not otherwise have known an African-American woman or an American Bahá'í. Again, not all African-American women pioneers spoke with the same voice or shared identical points of view; on the contrary, each person was different in the way she decided to pioneer and her approach to teaching the Bahá'í Faith. In the narratives that follow, women describe their experiences and the consequences of being Black women in foreign lands. They construct complex narratives of self-actualization and raise their service to mankind to new levels. Bahá'u'lláh writes, "The day of service is now come. Countless Tablets bear the testimony of the bounties vouchsafed unto thee. Arise for the triumph of My

Cause, and, through the power of thine utterance, subdue the hearts of man."[4]

Prior to the launching of the Ten Year Crusade, Bahá'ís like Hallie Elvera Queen had already begun to teach the Faith to others via international travel. Before becoming a member of the Howard University faculty, Ms. Queen taught English in Aquadilla, Puerto Rico, from 1909 to 1912 and then served as principal teacher in 1912 and 1913.[5] In a 1913 letter to fellow Bahá'ís Joseph and Pauline Hannen, Ms. Queen listed the activities that she carried out to promote the Bahá'í Faith in that part of the world: "During the year 1912–13 I have endeavored to add an 'humble mite' toward the spreading of the Bahá'í Principle in Aquadilla, Puerto Rico, where I was stationed."[6] Hallie enumerated nine specific projects, including sending baskets of fruit to poor women, collecting forty-two dollars for Ohio flood victims, and a first-place prize won by one of her students for an essay on the Bahá'í Faith.[7] She hinted that her efforts represented an initial rather than final attempt at disseminating information about the Faith. Hallie E. Queen is just one example of how the notion of pioneering had begun to take hold among African-American Bahá'ís.

Others sought early pioneering opportunities as well. John and Rosa Shaw, for example, pioneered several places during their lifetime. According to the U.S. National Spiritual Assembly minutes of September 28, 1939, the Shaws left the States to pioneer in Haiti that same year.[8] Later, in 1943 and 1944 Mrs. Shaw also pioneered to Halifax, Nova Scotia.[9] While she was away, Mr. Shaw continued his Bahá'í activities including a talk at Geyersville California Bahá'í Summer School entitled, "The Negro as a World Citizen." The lecture later was printed in a local newspaper, *The People's Advocate*, on 5 January 1944.[10]

Haiti drew other Bahá'í pioneers, including Harriet Gibbs-Marshall. According to the *Washington Tribune*, Mrs. Marshall spent six years with her husband, who was appointed by President Warren G. Harding as attaché to the American Legation at Port-au-Prince beginning in approximately 1922.[11] While in Haiti, Harriet put her educational expertise to work and joined with a friend to found an industrial school. She also wrote a book entitled *The Story of Haiti*.[12] In a January 29, 1937 letter to Harriet, Hand of the Cause Louis Gregory wrote,

You are very much loved among them for the constructive services you have rendered them. "Welcome to Haiti," said one of the officials upon knowing that I had a letter of introduction from you. The Bahá'í seed sown by you is also having effect. So you should be both happy and thankful to the Lord of Might, Bahá'u'lláh, that you have served the establishment of His Kingdom on earth.[13]

Claiming Their Sparkles and Crowns

Each pioneer gave a different reason for arising to serve. Vivian Wesson (1895–1994), felt that this opportunity would be the fulfillment of a long-time dream: "The beginning of my desire to go to Togo or to go to Ghana was because it's where my African ancestors came from and I knew it. So that'll take out whatever sparkle and crowns God might've given me for going."[14] Vivian suspected that her own motives for wanting to go pioneering were not entirely altruistic because she had always dreamed of one day visiting the motherland long before she became a Bahá'í.

Lecile Webster, who became a Bahá'í in Cleveland in 1946, was also inspired by the Ten Year Crusade and decided that she would pioneer. Initially, all of her efforts to acquire an overseas position failed. So along with four other African-American women in her Bahá'í community, she turned to prayer. They organized themselves into a nine-week prayer vigil, "The thought was that whatever we received first, that would be the answer. So I received a notice from the State Department saying they had an opening."[15]

Lecile took the exam and was accepted into the Foreign Service. In 1954, after a six-month wait, she was assigned to Tokyo. This marked the beginning of a long and distinguished career in the Foreign Service. Lecile was able to travel to or live in Korea, Hong Kong, Mexico, Bolivia, Brazil, and Norway.

Like many of her African-American Bahá'í sisters, Zylpha Mapp Robinson (1914–2001) also believed in dreams. A Bahá'í since her youth, she was inspired by a dream to take action in order to fulfill her desire to pioneer:

[Beulah Timmerman] went to Palarimo [Bahá'í conference] with me in '68. She was sitting beside me when I had this experience. And I saw 'Abdu-l-Bahá and I saw an outline of a country in Africa. And I saw the red earth and I saw the waterfalls. And I saw the whole picture of what turned out to be Uganda. And the night before that, I had met [Hand of the Cause George] Olinga. . . . And then he took his hand in mine and he said, "We need you in Uganda." I said, "Oh, well. I always wanted to come to Africa and I will someday." And I just treated it lightly and then the next day I had this vision. I learned after consulting an atlas that what I had seen in my vision was Uganda. So by the time I finished that qualification [post graduate] it [Uganda] became a goal for the United States and I went to Uganda [in 1969]. I was there on and off for nine years.[16]

After Uganda, Zylpha pioneered to Burkina Faso, India, and Botswana. Also, she was able to carry out travel teaching in Barbados, the Turks and Caicos Islands, Jamaica, England, Germany, Italy, Kenya, Liberia, Ethiopia, Ghana, Nigeria, Sierra Leone, The Gambia, Ivory Coast, and Senegal. Her teaching work in Uganda did not go unnoticed. Shoghi Effendi himself acknowledged the importance of activities in that country: "Of all the places in the world where the Bahá'í Faith exists and is spreading, the Guardian is definitely most pleased with Africa, and most proud of Uganda . . . old and staid communities may well learn from, and emulate the example of, the believers in Africa, many of them scarcely a year old in the Cause of God!"[17]

Elsie Austin (1908–2004) viewed pioneering as a natural part of her commitment to the Bahá'í Faith. She was active in the American Bahá'í community and was the first African-American woman to serve on the U.S. National Spiritual Assembly. Though she was a successful attorney, she decided to put her career on hold in order to pioneer:

I had my first pilgrimage in 1953, I think it was. And after that the first International Conference in Kampala, Uganda. And when I came back, I thought, well. . . . I better just make up my mind [about pioneering] and give it the priority it deserves. And at that time I was working with the National Labor Relations Board as a senior attorney. I'd just gotten a raise, moved into a new apartment . . . and I said well . . . the Bahá'ís themselves take this faith around the world and this is a period when all the Bahá'ís are being asked to choose an area which does not know the Bahá'í Faith and introduce it. His name was George Bott, I'll never forget him. He said "I'll give you a year leave of absence for that." So off I went to Tangier, Morocco. I was the first in that area so the beloved Guardian made me a Knight of Bahá'u'lláh. And I stayed in Morocco almost five years.[18]

Elsie became a prominent Foreign Service officer and after Morocco, pioneered to Tangier, Nigeria, Kenya, and the Bahamas. She participated in ten international conferences sponsored by the United States Information Agency and other international organizations.[19]

"O That I Could Travel": Cultivating Difference and Diversity

O that I could travel, even though on foot and in the utmost poverty, to these regions, and, raising the call of Yá Bahá'ul-Abhá [O Thou, the Glory of Glories!] in cities, villages, mountains, deserts and oceans, promote the Divine Teachings! This alas, I cannot do. How intensely I deplore it! Please God, ye may achieve it![20]

The preceding statement of 'Abdu'l-Bahá encouraged many Bahá'ís to pioneer either within their home countries or to foreign lands. The goal of teaching the Faith to others soon became a priority for African-Americans as they grew to understand the vital importance of their role in the Bahá'í Faith. Shoghi Effendi wrote:

The Negroes, though they themselves may not realize it, have a contribution to make to the World Order of Bahá'u'lláh. His teachings and the Society He has come to establish are for every race and every nation, and each one of them has his own part to play and the gift of his own qualities and talents to give to the whole.[21]

Encouraged by support within the Faith, more African-Americans embarked upon pioneering projects in far corners of the world. They had a stake in expanding the Faith, especially in taking it to the homelands of their ancestors. All of the pioneers faced hardships, but for Black women the task was especially challenging given their family responsibilities. The fact that this first generation of African-American women pioneers could arise and accomplish so much moved long time pioneer to South Africa Bonnie Fitzpatrick-Moore to write the following:

> The circumstances endured by the American Black woman in her efforts to raise a family and personally develop, the progress she has thus far achieved can and must be used to inspire and awaken in her African sisters the knowledge of the true and high destiny to which all women have been called by the Revelation of Bahá'u'lláh.[22]

Mrs. Moore regarded the early Black women pioneers as role models, and on the basis of their achievements, encouraged other African-American women to do the same.[23]

The majority of Black women who went pioneering, especially during the Ten Year Crusade, had limited exposure to foreign travel. In fact, most had never been out of the country, so their pioneering experiences were complicated by issues of difference that they could not have anticipated. Their viewpoints of the new worlds they came to occupy as well as their perceptions of self in the context of another culture were insightful. Lecile Webster, for example, perceived that the Japanese people in her community were fascinated by her height:

> I learned enough [Japanese] to get around and I could hear their reaction to me without them knowing that I understood. And the first reaction was that I was so large. "Isn't she tall?" [they would

say]. But I never heard any mention of my color, it was always my size. And then when I would respond in Japanese to them, to their remark, then they would just turn hand springs and practically give me half of the store.[24]

Lecile also discovered that her fluency in Japanese provided many opportunities to tell others about the Bahá'í Faith directly, without the assistance of a translator. She recalled that she was able to make friends with Japanese colleagues and soon after arriving spent more time with them than her American counterparts.

Zylpha Mapp Robinson, on the other hand, had very pressing decisions to make in her pioneering post. Uganda was in turmoil and civil war seemed a certainty. However, this did not deter her from carrying out her intended work of teaching the Bahá'í Faith in the country.

Different things happened in Uganda. For example when Idi Amin took over the country he began doing a lot of crazy things. And finally [he] insulted the ambassador's wife so America pulled out of Uganda. And then the American embassy gave me 48 hours notice to leave the country. And I refused. I said, "I am here as a pioneer, it's too bad." I'll have to protect myself with God's help. And I wouldn't leave the country. A couple of others [pioneers], Velma Ferguson [for example] did the same thing. No. Why should we leave? We went there to pioneer. We didn't go to care whether there's no diplomatic immunity or what have you. So that's the way things were.[25]

Elsie Austin experienced another difficulty: traveling alone as a single woman. While her situation would not have seemed unusual in the US, the same was not true in other countries where women had fewer rights. She recalled that

It was a tremendous experience for me as it is for any pioneer. Particularly if you've never been out of the country before, and if you're going to a place where you have no contacts, no people that you know. Your sole reliance must be upon God because you have nothing else. And for me it was even more I think because I was Black, I was a woman, I was alone in a far Eastern culture where women were very suppressed. The idea of an unattached single woman entering a country [like this] must have raised many eyebrows. But I must say that Bahá'u'lláh's protection was with me because never during the whole four years that I was in Morocco, did I ever have an unpleasant experience as a woman. Nobody assaulted me, nobody said unkind things to me and from the very moment that I entered the country it seemed as if unseen hands and unseen power arranged contacts that were helpful, educational and very wonderful to me.[26]

Being a Black woman alone in a foreign country could have been a very uncomfortable situation for even the most daring of women. However, for Elsie Austin, it was reliance on God that made her pioneering experiences positive.

Africa and the Diaspora

It is significant to ponder that the first, the opening of this halfway point of the World Crusade was chosen by him for the heart of Africa, and that the last, the closing Conference, was set midway in the Pacific-Asian region. He did not thus honor the old world and the new. No, he chose the Black people and the brown people for this distinction. He visualized the African and the Pacific peoples vying with each other in the spread of the Faith.[27]

Even though many African-American pioneers volunteered to live in non-African parts of the world, the majority expressed a desire to reside in an African country. For those who left the U.S. for their posts during the Ten Year Crusade, there was a keen interest in the motherland coupled with 'Abdu'l-Bahá's emphasis on the role of people of African descent in advancing the Bahá'í Faith. However, this does not suggest that African-

Americans romanticized going to Africa as "going home" to ancestral roots, but rather a longing to be connected to the continent in spiritual ways that the legacy of slavery had almost completely erased. Bonnie Fitzpatrick-Moore explicitly pointed out that African-American suffering could be turned into a positive force:

> As I look around the world, I am struck by the fact that Negroes are a unique race of people. They are perceived by so many of the Black races of the world as a people who have overcome many great hardships and succeeded against all odds. They are an inspiration to the Black peoples of the world.[28]

African-American participation in the dissemination of the Bahá'í Faith was of great importance on several levels. Mrs. Moore's observation that Black people are an inspiration to other Black people in the world reinforces the importance of the involvement in the Faith of all "Black races."

Finally, the emphasis on Africa was intended a reciprocal endeavor. That is, the idea was not that the people of Africa had so much to learn, but that they had so much to give. Shoghi Effendi indicated that "Africa is truly awakening and finding herself, and she undoubtedly has a great message to give, and a great contribution to make to the advancement of world civilization."[29] Thus, as the following biographical sketches reveal, African-American pioneers who taught the Faith in Africa were part of spiritual movement that not only raised the continent of Africa to a new level of respect and distinction, but also had the potential to revolutionize the world.[30]

West Africa: Vivian Dunlap Wesson

Vivian Dunlap Wesson became a Bahá'í in 1921 and served the Faith for more than thirty years in the Chicago area before she answered the call for pioneers to Africa during the Ten Year Crusade. However, she went to Africa in spite of any misgivings and was named a Knight of Bahá'u'lláh by Shoghi Effendi for her services in pioneering to French Togoland (now

Togo).[31] In 1954, at the age of fifty-nine Vivian and Mavis Nymon, a young student who also wanted to pioneer in Africa, were asked to relocate to French Togoland:

> So this, I came to the conclusion, this is what you get when you offer to do something for God because *you* want to do something for yourself at the same time. . . . So we both got what God wanted us to do, was to be together. She was young and white . . . from North Dakota . . . I was from the deep South. . . . We had all the things that . . . that didn't make sense for the two [us] people being together.[32]

Because of the great geographical distance between them and the short amount of time to prepare for the trip, Vivian and Mavis did not meet until a few days before their ship left for Africa.

> [W]e found that the ship was gonna sail that evening and that was very good. . . . But our miracles began then. The miracles of being taken over and being taken care of through the will of God. We had no idea of the complications that were going to stand in our way. We had *no* idea. We'd never traveled that far before. Never been out of the United States. . . . So we talked to each other and had wonderful times [on] the ship. . . . It took us sixteen days I think.[33]

Mrs. Wesson explained that after a stop in Liberia the cargo ship that they traveled on landed in Ghana. From there they had planned to take a taxi to their pioneering post in the neighboring country of French Togoland. They had twenty-four hours to get there in order to establish a Local Spiritual Assembly before the deadline:

> We went into the customs house and identified our luggage and signed all the papers we had to sign. And then we asked the customs man if he could tell us where we could find a taxi. And he looked at us and he says, "You haven't been here before have you?" I said, "No

we haven't." He said, "You can't go anywhere today. Today is Sunday and it's a holiday. No taxis run and there's no traveling."[34]

Mrs. Wesson remembers that she and Mavis were stunned by the news. Not knowing what to do, they proceeded to exit the customs house where they stood by the gate and looked around the town:

> [W]hile I was standing there, and we were pondering what to do, we both closed our eyes and started to pray, not out loud, but to ourselves. We just stood there with our hands folded and started to pray because we could see this was [a] serious thing for us . . . and we heard people passing . . . and I heard in the speech of the people passing my grandmother, my great-grandmother, who was an African woman. That's where I got my blood; I heard her voice. I heard her accents. Certain words the man would say in his own tongue would sound *just* like my grandmother.[35]

When they finished praying, Vivian explained, a young man who had been watching them came over, introduced himself and offered to help. She said that Mavis told him of their plight and although he doubted that he could assist them in getting to their destination, he invited them to go with him to meet a professor he was waiting for at a nearby hotel. The professor, it turns out, had a brother-in-law who drove them to Togoland. It was one of many miracles that Vivian recalls occurred during her years as a pioneer.

After four months in French Togoland, the pair were told by authorities that due to the country's conflict with France, their visas would not be renewed. So they moved to Monrovia, the capital city of Liberia, on the advice of the National Spiritual Assembly of that country. From there, they moved on to a small Liberian mining town. They had left behind a Bahá'í community in Togoland and helped form a new community in Liberia. Even though Mavis returned to the U.S. to complete her education after two years, Mrs. Wesson stayed in Liberia for eleven years.

"Well, we left a pretty good sized [Bahá'í] community behind us because we stayed there so long a time. . . . And we had literacy classes.

. . . We felt that this was the need that we could care for."[36] Vivian explains that they had so much interest in the project that they asked permission from the president of Liberia to open a school for adults. The president granted their request and they began classes immediately: "We invited all the people who wanted to learn to read and write to come to our school. We would open it twice a day. We'd have day school and a night school for them. So what we got was the most beautiful collection of people, up into their seventies . . . wanting to get in."[37]

Mavis's departure meant that the school lost one of its teachers, and that left the work to be done by Mrs. Wesson. She struggled to maintain the literacy project without adequate help:

> So when Mavis had to go . . . it was hard for me to get along without somebody because I wasn't prepared. I couldn't do everything that needed to be done. So I got a smart boy who had been through seventh grade in school and when he went through eighth grade, I told him I was gonna send him away to one of the colleges in Liberia so that he could get an industrial education if he wanted one. He jumped at it. So this was my next project, was to find ways to help this boy get through school. I did, God helped me. Put him through. He graduated from one of Liberia's schools and he helped me after Mavis left. He was a great help to me.[38]

Despite the loss of Mavis, the school became very successful, though Vivian did not take credit for this contribution to the community. Instead, she pointed out how others have come before her. "Why were we sent to that place in that particular time when we got to Liberia? Why? Because somebody had [already] been in Monrovia teaching the Faith: William Foster, Valerie Wilson and a lot of other pioneers from other places met in Monrovia."[39]

As with the school, Vivian was philosophical about her role in the many successful projects she facilitated in Liberia:

> What to do? What to do when God takes hold of you? What can you do? You just try to be a vessel that will hold whatever it is that

God has given you and let as much of it spill out as God will allow to spill. So that's all I did. And I was the most amazed person in the whole world that it turned out as well as it did 'cause so many things went turned out wrong, but this turned out alright.[40]

After Liberia, "Ma Wesson," as she, became known, pioneered to Sierra Leone where she stayed until 1977.[41] In all, she was a pioneer in Africa for more than twenty-three years.

East Africa: Zylpha Mapp Robinson

Zylpha Mapp Robinson combined her love of education with service to the Bahá'í Faith. Initially trained as a social worker, she went back to school in order to better serve the Faith, and at the age of 78 earned her Ph.D. in education and curriculum planning. When describing the history of her life long pursuit of education, she remarked

I finished my qualification in guidance and counseling. And that's how I got a lovely job in Uganda having gotten qualification just in time because three months after I got there I was offered a director of guidance [position] at the school. So you know, you really ought to study with Bahá'í needs in your mind.[42]

With her education firmly in place, Robinson pioneered to Uganda in the 1970s, and in 1976 she was elected to that country's National Spiritual Assembly. She remained in Uganda for nine years. Robinson recalls that teaching the Faith there was a very rewarding experience:

Now that's the most glorious experience of my life. The people are so receptive. . . . John [my interpreter] would always accompany me when I went to the villages . . . And we would go out almost every Sunday. And when I had been in Kampala before going up country, I had found the names and addresses of many Bahá'ís within a twenty-mile radius of where I was. And so I went in search of them. And that is how we began to get our teaching work done every weekend. John eventually became a Bahá'í through the youth who came to my place at the school.[43]

Uganda remained close to Robinson's heart throughout the years, and she returned to the country at the age of eighty-six to organize an Institute for the Advancement of Women in Kampala. During that time she had to return to New York for medical treatment, where she passed away in 2001. Her passion for teaching the Bahá'í Faith took her to different parts of the world. After Uganda she pioneered to Burkina Faso, India, and Botswana. She also conducted travel teaching in Barbados, the Turks and Caicos Islands, Jamaica, England, Germany, Italy, Kenya, Liberia, Ethiopia, Ghana, Ivory Coast, The Gambia, and Senegal.[44]

North Africa: Elsie Austin

In addition to Elsie Austin's extensive service on Bahá'í institutions in the United States, she pioneered to Tangier, Nigeria, Kenya, and the Bahámas.[45] Her first experiences as a pioneer to Tangier, Morocco, were filled with both tests and blessings: "I sailed to Morocco on a steamship. . . . I did not know it, but at the same time there were four other Bahá'ís [on the ship] going pioneering. . . . John and Earlita Flemming, Louella McKay and her small son, and Alice Jansen, a widow. . . . Alice was white and the Flemmings and McKays were all Black."[46]

Eventually, Elsie and the other pioneers went their separate ways. After getting settled she tried to make contacts right away. She thought she was going to a foreign country where she knew no one, but was pleasantly surprised that this was not the case.

The next thing I did as a pioneer and I was very grateful, was to try to get acquainted with social services in the city and at the school, educational services. . . . And when I got to the American school, I went to the principal's office and introduced myself. He said, "I know you." And my eyes widened. He said, "Yes, were you not connected with the Delta Sigma Theta Sorority?" I said yes. I was at one time their national president. He said, "Well, you set up a chapter at a University in Louisiana when I was president there and I wrote you. I remember your name." And then with the utmost grace, he called in several of his teachers, introduced me to them and told them to show me around. . . . They became very dear friends. This was unheard of because I knew nobody in Morocco.[47]

Unpredictable connections characterized much of Elsie's first year in Morocco. Another issue was how she would go about teaching the Faith as an English speaker in an Arabic speaking country.

I began to worry about how I could begin teaching the Faith because I found that so few people spoke English. They spoke French, they spoke Arabic, and some Italian, but not much English. So I guess about the third day that I had been in the hotel, I was sitting in my room in the early evening. There was a knock at my door. I opened it and the porter said a man is downstairs asking for you. . . . I went downstairs and here was a Persian gentleman. He said hello and then I discovered that he spoke no English at all. . . . He came back the next day with another dear Persian friend who spoke English, Persian, and Arabic. And from this encounter I learned that . . . there would be five more Persians [Bahá'ís] who would come and this was wonderful too because we would not be alone.[48]

Joining together with the other Bahá'í pioneers, Elsie found that the teaching work soon resulted in the establishment of a Local Spiritual Assembly.

In time that Tangier community of pioneers grew to Assembly status. We had one native Moroccan believer who became a Bahá'í who was an artist, then a Spanish-Moroccan accepted the faith. . . . So it was an extremely interesting atmosphere. I was there from 1953 to 1957.[49]

The inauguration of the Local Spiritual Assembly was a major accomplishment, and it was no small feat considering sociopolitical conditions in the country.

> Teaching the faith in that area of the world was extremely difficult because the country . . . had a state religion—Islam. It tolerated the Christians and tolerated the Jews but the Bahá'ís [were a different issue]. . . . We proceeded mainly by building up friendly contacts around the city. . . . We had a great many picnics and teas in which we would entertain. We would go to the homes of people that we met and be entertained. . . . And in that way a family of Moroccans joined the faith and became very devoted Bahá'ís.[50]

At other times the pioneers met with resistance. Some of the indigenous people were not necessarily pleased with the Bahá'ís.

> When our Bahá'í activities extended into other areas than Tangier, we met serious pressure. . . . In fact, one of the great tragedies of the Faith occurred in Morocco, when Bahá'ís who were mainly Moroccans, were put into prison. And there had to be much effort on the part of the Bahá'í communities outside of Morocco and around the world through the United Nations . . . to do something about that. And after about a year or so, they were released but many of them forfeited their jobs, their pension rights. For instance, one of the Moroccan believers lost her husband. And the government said because he was a Bahá'í they didn't owe him anything [as a pension]. . . . So there were grave tests for them and for us too.[51]

In spite of these perilous difficulties, the Bahá'ís were able to persevere and establish strong communities. Elsie Austin was named as Knight of Bahá'u'lláh for Morrocco after being the first to bring the Faith to the country, during the Ten Year World Crusade. Elsie said, "When I left in 1957 there were assemblies in Casablanca, Tatwan, Larachee, Tangier. So that was four assemblies in all. In fact, all of them were new."[52]

Far East: Lecile Webster

Lecile Webster (b. 1926) became a Bahá'í in 1946 in Cleveland, Ohio, where she attended Cleveland College. She applied for a position with the American Foreign Service Agency and later discovered that there were just sixty African-Americans in the service at that time. Mrs. Webster recalls her excitement about the prospect of being able to combine pioneering with professional work.

> [W]hen I got the appointment here at the State Department I came up and took an examination in a separate room. I was the only Black in that recruitment in 1954 and I don't really think today they knew that I was Black until I got there. Then of course they had to accept me and I was kept here [Washington, DC] for almost six months before I was given an assignment. . . . And I was then assigned to Tokyo which was one of the largest and better posts. And then I got my ticket and all my travel arrangements. And I was amazed because I was traveling first class.[53]

Guided by instructions from the Asian Teaching Committee, a subcommittee of the U.S. National Spiritual Assembly, Lecile was directed to work with Japanese women and try to interest them in the Bahá'í Faith. The Japanese Bahá'ís who had previously enrolled in the Faith gave her a warm welcome. "But the third day I was there, the Japanese Bahá'ís got in touch with me and took me to the Bahá'í center. Right away I had a nice, small group of friends."[54]

Within the context of her work environment, Lecile found no overt discrimination, but rather a cool, "hands off" attitude: "On weekends you were left on your own so had it not been for the Japanese friends, I would have been a very unhappy, lonely person."[55] Mrs. Webster's friendship with Japanese women deepened as they immersed her in their culture. She was never at a loss for something to do. Bahá'í and other social activities were plentiful:

> They invited me to join their pottery class and their flowering class. And they would take me to all the quaint inns around Tokyo and

shopping. I had firesides then in my apartment and I had about twenty Japanese professors coming to the firesides. And about five Japanese came into the Faith. So you see on one hand it was the best thing not to be caught up in the social thing at work. The primary thing was to teach the Faith. That was the priority.[56]

Lecile lived in Japan for about a year and half. During that time she met with other Bahá'ís who were also pioneering in the area. She said that they had received specific advice from Shoghi Effendi:

The beloved Guardian [Shoghi Effendi] told us that we must serve as a regional National Assembly for Japan, Korea, Hong Kong, and Macau. And the Guardian wrote us in his own handwriting the instructions, what we were to do to hold our community together. We had on our Local Assembly at that time Persian, Chinese, Japanese, and American [people] and we had to have a Local Assembly meeting in four languages.[57]

After leaving Tokyo, Lecile went to Seoul, Korea, which was still devastated by war, "When I got off the plane and looked as far as the eye could see, there was no tree, no blade of grass, nothing."[58] The Asian Teaching Committee instructed her to

Look for one Bahá'í that they thought was in Seoul. . . . the committee said he is a Korean, his name is Kim. He lives on a hill; he has dark hair and brown eyes. Well, Kim in Korea is like Jones or Smith here. . . . And I was to work with the ladies. As far as I knew when I landed, I was the only Bahá'í in Seoul. . . . I know I was the first woman pioneer in Korea and certainly the first Black pioneer except for Bill Maxwell.[59]

Bill Maxwell, a Bahá'í pioneer who was in Kwangju, traveled to Seoul so that he and Lecile could consult about how to find Kim: "His thought was, we must find this Kim and we need him for translation. And I said, well, I'm sort of restricted here to my career. It was different than Tokyo.

In Korea I had to live in a compound which was heavily guarded. We were not to associate with Koreans without permission."[60]

Lecile's work constraints hampered them from coming up with a viable plan at that time. After weeks of prayer, Lecile found that another Bahá'í pioneer, Bill Smidt, had arrived in Korea. Together with Smidt, she formulated another plan to find Kim: "[Smidt] said, alright, we'll find him. So I said, I think the best thing to do is to go to all the tea houses because that's where all the Koreans would congregate to keep warm. So we must have drank umpteen cups of tea."[61] Finally they found Kim at a tea house and began holding firesides in his home as well as starting groups for people to study the Bahá'í writings. As a result, several Koreans became Bahá'ís, which soon lead to the formation of Korean Spiritual Assemblies, in 1956, with one in Seoul and another in Kwangju.

Lecile had been in Korea for almost a year at this point. According to State Department regulations during her tenure, those enlisted in the Foreign Service had to take at least two months of vacation every two years. Lecile used her time to travel to Hong Kong, Macau, Rangoon, Thailand, New Delhi, and Malaysia on trips to teach the Bahá'í Faith.

Lecile's next assignment was in a very different part of the world: Mexico. She had to adjust once again to a new culture, but remarked that this became her favorite location: "I was on the Local Assembly there in Mexico [City]. . . . We had many firesides. And I'd have like forty or fifty people in my apartment. . . . Then I went down to [La Paz,] Bolivia and was immediately put on the Local Assembly there."[62]

In 1959 she left Bolivia for Rio de Janeiro, Brazil, where she also served on a Local Spiritual Assembly. She then took several months leave in Washington, DC. After her leave was up, she traveled to Norway, where she served on yet another Local Spiritual Assembly, as well as Norway's National Spiritual Assembly. "I was elected as chair [of the National Assembly] for two consecutive years. And then we were invited by the Hands [of the Cause of God] to go to Haifa for the election of the first House of Justice. I tell you, that was an experience."[63]

Lecile was a pioneer in Norway from 1961 to 1964, then moved to France, where she served on a Local Spiritual Assembly in a small town outside of Paris. She retired shortly after that, and came back to the U.S. Of all her Bahá'í activities, She was especially proud of the work she carried out for the Universal House of Justice. During a three-day visit to the Bahá'í World Center in Haifa, Israel, in the late 1970s she was asked to stay longer and organize files and other aspects of the office administration:

> I drew up staffing patterns and plans and job descriptions, all kinds of things that you do when you organize an office . . . and the House studies this and they called me in. . . . So the first organizational plan for the administration of the office of the House of Justice was done by a woman and a Black woman, yours truly.[64]

A diligent worker for the Faith, Lecile continued her work on the homefront. Retirement simply meant that she entered a new phase of activities, but always with a focus on serving the Bahá'í Faith.

Conclusion

The preceding snapshots of African-American women pioneers indicate that Black women indeed helped fulfill the Faith's focus on African-American participation in all activities at home and abroad. Through their teaching efforts and leadership, many Bahá'í communities were established throughout the world. Furthermore, their sense of moral responsibility prompted them to make meaningful contributions to the local areas where they lived and worked, which resulted in many educational and social programs, specifically for the indigenous people, many of whom became Bahá'ís. A letter written on behalf of Shoghi Effendi remarked that, "It has been a great step forward in the Cause's development in America to have Negro pioneers go forth, and their work has been of the greatest help and very productive of results."[65]

The first generation of African-American pioneers inspired other African-Americans to pioneer, single women and men as well as entire families. They include the following list of believers from all parts of the U.S.

Earlita and John Flemming pioneered shortly after Earlita attended the dedication of the Bahá'í House of Worship in Wilmette, Illinois, in 1953. She was inspired by the call for pioneers and though newly married consulted with her husband, a new Bahá'í, and together they decided on Africa.

So naturally we wanted to choose a place in Africa. So we got this map of the world and we got down on the floor, and we would choose a place. And then we would write to national and we'd say we'd like to go to this place and they would write back and say someone has already chosen that place. . . . And finally we saw this little dot on the map. It's the northern most point of Africa, and right across from the Gibraltar Strait, the southern coast of Spain, this little place called Seenta.[66]

Both were later named Knights of Bahá'u'lláh for Spanish Morocco. Earlita and her family had learned about the Faith from their African-American neighbors Rosa and John Shaw. As previously mentioned, Rosa pioneered to Nova Scotia and did extensive travel teaching in Jamaica.

Other pioneers during this early period included Valerie Wilson (d. 1993), who pioneered to Monrovia, Liberia in 1952. She worked as a physical therapist and counted among her patients the president of the country and his wife, President and Mrs. Tubman. She was a member of the first Regional National Assembly of North and West Africa as well as on the local spiritual assembly of Monrovia. She experienced severe physical hardships, but remained in Liberia for twelve years.[67]

Luella McKay (1918–95), also a Knight of Bahá'u'lláh for Spanish Morocco, pioneered to that country with her young son Nicholas. She was the first Bahá'í to set foot in that country. She stayed there for six years.

Eulalia Bobo Taylor, a tireless Bahá'í teacher noted for her all night firesides, spent a year in Africa. She was the sister of the great heavyweight boxing champion, Joe Louis. Helen Hornby (d. 1992) retired early to pioneer to Columbia and Ecuador.

These are just a few of the many African-American women who made tremendous sacrifices in order to pioneer. Bahá'u'lláh has assured all those who leave their homes to live in a foreign country in order to teach the Faith that pioneering is, "Such a service is, indeed, the prince of all goodly deeds, and the ornament of every goodly act."[68]

7

Black Roses in Canada's Mosaic: Four Decades of Black History

Will C. van den Hoonaard and Lynn Echevarria

Introduction

The Bahá'í Faith took hold among Blacks in North America not only in the United States but also in Canada. There were significant differences in the development and organization of the two countries. Research on the Canadian Bahá'í community is just beginning.[1] Given the small number of Blacks in the early days of the Bahá'í community, it is difficult to make generalizations about the Black Bahá'í community as a whole. More importantly, there is a dearth of reliable primary sources from which potentially useful information could be drawn. Hence the situation of Black Bahá'ís in Canada must be explored through the eyewitness accounts of a small number of still-surviving early believers, both Black and White.

Brief Survey of Blacks in Canada

The earliest "unobserved"[2] presence of Blacks in Canada dates back more than 350 years. Perhaps the earliest Black in Canada was Matthew Da

Costa (d. 1607), a member and interpreter of the Poutrincourt expedition of Champlain, the "father of Canada."[3] During those 350 years, the Blacks in Canada have come from a wide variety of geographical areas, depending sometimes upon the region settled in Canada. Blacks in Eastern Canada constitute perhaps the largest influx, approximately 3,000 Loyalists (those who were loyal to the British Empire) and 1,500 slaves[4] who came with the white Loyalists after the American Revolutionary War in 1783. Canada's Black population also included a sizeable number of slaves (including those from the other British colonies) and freemen who were living in relative isolation in Canada "well into the twentieth century."[5] The 1812 war between the United States and England resulted in another 2,000 Black refugees coming to Canada's Eastern Shores.

In Central Canada, which includes Montréal in Quebec, and Ontario, the Black population was largely derived from West Indian immigrants or descendants of those who had fled north by way of the "Underground Railroad," in addition to those who had arrived earlier with the French.[6] In British Columbia, one finds descendants of Blacks who ventured from America's West coast as gold diggers.

During these three-and-a-half centuries, a "parallel society" took shape[7] and separate schools and churches were still the social norm in the 1960s. Institutional racism meant that Blacks were excluded from cemeteries, theatres, residential areas, schools, and unions. One Black describing his memories of the absence of Blacks in visible jobs in the 1920s and 1930s states, "I never once saw a Black nurse, secretary, politician, teacher, policeman, fireman, civil servant, clerk in a department store, trade union or business leader."[8] This anti-Black feeling and the smallness of the Black population maintained the Black communities' isolation and effectively curbed them from acquiring any economical or political strength.[9] Yet despite the commonality of discrimination which both Canadian and American Blacks share, there are several important differences which set the Canadians apart from the Americans.

First, the Canadian Black population consists primarily of those of West-Indian and Loyalist origin, in addition to those who fled slavery.

Second, there is no national Canadian organization which would have united the Blacks, who are extremely diverse in social and historical makeup. As a consequence, Black leadership in Canada seems to consist of local leaders, rather than national ones.

Third, within that parallel society social differentiation among Blacks was based upon ethnicity, class, and shades of color. Depending upon the diversity of Black settlement within a city it was possible to find, as in the case of Toronto in the 1930s: Black migrants from Nova Scotia established "old line" families who had been settled since the mid 1800s and had intermarried with white families,[10] West Indian immigrant families of domestics or immigrant families of West Indian school teachers, and American Blacks.

The old Black families had an economic and social status different than the more recent, darker Blacks. It has been noted that the lighter skinned Blacks were among the established prominent people in the community.[11] Class differences kept poor and working-class Blacks separate from the Blacks with better jobs, usually those who worked on the railway as porters. These men were considered middle class because they had the best paying jobs and subsequently were able to afford better housing and better education for their children when it became available.[12]

American Blacks in Toronto were considered more aggressive and able to integrate more fully into city life as they had more experience in a dominant white environment. The West Indians, who had come from a large community of Blacks, were more race conscious, and kept their national pride by staying separate as a group. They were critical of the Toronto-born Blacks who had not progressed as far as they had occupationally, socially, and economically.[13] The Nova Scotian migrants (aside from sons of clergymen) were described as being "socially disorganized and disoriented."[14]

Fourth, prejudice was uninstitutionalized and unorganized which made the struggle against prejudice more elusive and difficult. Braithwaite quotes a Black from Toronto:

In Canada we have not had to fight Jim Crow, poll tax and other evils that replaced the 8 year democracy after the Civil War. But we have had to fight, and are still fighting for the right to education, to choose the work we are fitted for, to get *any* work until recently, to get proper homes to live in, health and recreations with other young people, social and civil rights.[15]

Finally, the Blacks in Canada have had a longer period of legal freedom. However, there is evidence which shows that slaves were being auctioned on the block in Nova Scotia. For example, Hamilton speaks of a time when "Black female slaves were called upon to do more than simple domestic chores for their masters."[16] There were also Black "freemen" who having come with the white Loyalists, "bore the euphemistic title 'servant for life.'" Both of these groups joined the small number of Black slaves already present in Nova Scotia.[17]

World War II was the beginning of great change for the Black community. The war opened up more economic opportunities. Those industries and offices undergoing labor shortages began to hire Blacks. "The job ceiling was broken in semi-skilled work and there was a slight filtering into clerical work."[18] The number of people in the skilled and professional classes increased. Both war and Fair Employment legislation facilitated the interaction of the races.[19]

Since the 1960s, however, the number of Blacks in Canada has seen a vast increase, partly due to the arrival, as immigrants, of those from the Caribbean. The total Black population in Canada in 1986 was 170,340, or 0.68 percent of the total Canadian population.

An initial perusal of the material on hand shows that the major concentration of Black Bahá'í history can be traced through the activities of Bahá'ís in Montréal, the Yukon, Atlantic Canada, and Toronto. Cross-cutting regional variations are temporal ones. During the years 1920–65, sixteen Blacks enrolled in the Bahá'í Faith (see table). The earliest period (1920–42) saw the declaration of four Blacks; between 1943 and 1946, we see eight new adherents; and between 1947 and 1965, we have five names on record. There are, however, Black Bahá'í connections in Canada that have been recorded elsewhere. Gwen Etter-Lewis, for example, mentions Harriet Gibbs-Marshall, the second African-American woman in the United States to have embraced the new religion, in 1912, who was born on Vancouver Island in 1870.[20]

List of Early Black-Canadian Bahá'ís, 1921–1960s

Name	Place	Declaration Date	Occupation
Mr. Eddie Elliott	Montréal	before Nov. 1921	Electrician
Mrs. Dora Bray	Dawson	1922	Teacher
Mr. Ralph Laltoo	Halifax	20 Oct. 1940	Student
Miss Lucille Giscome	Ottawa	1942	Journalist
Mrs. Inez Ifill-Hayes	Toronto	1943	Domestic
Miss Esther Hayes	Toronto	1943*	Secretary
Mrs. Sarah Downes	Toronto	1945	
Mr. John Hayes	Toronto	23 May 1945	Porter
Miss Ferne C. Harrison	Hamilton	7 Oct. 1945	
Mrs. Rita (Elaine) Marshall	Halifax	19 June 1946	
Mr. Ernest Marshall	Halifax	Nov. 1946	Printer/taxi driver
Mr. Fred Lorne Izzard	Halifax	7 Aug. 1953	Shipyard worker
Mr. Donald Carty	Toronto	11 June 1955	Postman
Mr. Raymond Flournoy	Montréal	9 Jan. 1962	Interior architect
Mrs. Violet Grant States	Verdun	8 Jan. 1963	Music teacher
Mr. Clyde Carty	Toronto	21 April 1965	

* formally enrolled on 6 April 1951

Early Black Bahá'ís of Montréal

The first contact between the Bahá'ís and a Black church occurred during 'Abdu'l-Bahá's visit to Montréal in September 1912, when he was asked by the church to speak to its congregation. 'Abdu'l-Bahá had to decline the invitation on account of a very busy schedule.[21] An account by Amine De Mille states that Eddie Elliot was the "only member of his race to become a Bahá'í during His ['Abdu'l-Bahá's] lifetime."[22] We shall turn to Eddie Elliot later. In any event, 'Abdu'l-Bahá provided an essential example through which May Maxwell, known by Bahá'ís as the "Spiritual Mother of Canada," felt inspired to conduct work, both philanthropic and Bahá'í, among the Blacks in Montréal.

Though the Maxwells were white, their home was completely free of any racial prejudice. It was through the diligence and intense interest in racial harmony of May Maxwell and the spiritual thirst of the individuals involved that the first few Blacks entered the Bahá'í community in Canada. The magnet which drew these early believers to the Bahá'í Faith was the profound hospitality of the Maxwell home and the remarkable attitude of her daughter Mary Maxwell.[23]

There is a telling account about May Maxwell regarding one visit to her home:

> [T]he first day that Miss X. went to visit before she was a Bahá'í, she went to visit May Maxwell at her invitation. And when she arrived, the maid came bustling down the stairs and said she really didn't think Mrs. Maxwell could be disturbed today, she was terribly sorry, and then Mrs. Maxwell herself came down the stairs and apologized profusely but she said that she had a woman upstairs giving birth to a baby because she was Black and none of the hospitals would take her. So she was bringing in her own doctor and having this baby be born right in her house and would Miss X. mind coming back another day.[24]

May Maxwell was also involved in the social and philanthropic work of the city. In 1927, for example, she became the honorary president of the Negro Club of Montréal.[25] The club aided the poor and provided clothing to newly arrived West Indian immigrants. It operated soup kitchens for the unemployed and burial plots for those who could not afford any. Its members also volunteered as visiting mothers and mothers' aides.[26]

The visit of Louis Gregory to the city during the summer of 1924[27] likely had an important bearing in reinforcing May Maxwell's work in the area of race relations. The life of Blacks in Montréal, who numbered at least 1,200, was "dwarfed to an unhealthy extent." Facilities were practically negligible, according to a report of the Montréal Council of Welfare Agencies, except for pool rooms and flats.[28]

By 1927, the Bahá'í community of North America had reached a propitious point in improving its racial climate. It is reported that when the nineteenth National Convention of the North American Bahá'í Community was held in Montréal in April 1927, race "was discussed at length and with unprecedented frankness."[29] One of the early contacts made by May Maxwell was with Rev. Charles H. Este, pastor of Montréal's only Black church, the Union United Church which was formally organized in 1907.[30] This church was initially the first of all agencies to concern itself with the recreational, cultural, and educational activity for Blacks in the city.

Rev. Este was a personal friend of Mary Maxwell and visited the Maxwell home on many occasions. He also visited with her at the 1963 Bahá'í World Congress in London, England. He became a close friend of the Bahá'ís, although he never joined the Bahá'í Faith. Rev. Este received numerous awards for his contributions to religious, social, and community affairs.[31]

The following account, taken from the memoirs of Rowland Estall, an early Montréal Bahá'í, illustrates May Maxwell's work among the Blacks in Montréal, and her neighbors' response to that work:

> The [Maxwell] house was full of people, the Bahá'ís and many members of the Negro United Church of which Reverend Charles Este was pastor. Mrs. Maxwell had addressed Reverend Este's congregation the previous Sunday and had invited the congregation to visit her the following Thursday, or so. During the course of the evening, I was sitting beside Mrs. Maxwell in Mr. Maxwell's study and a maid came and said that Mrs. Maxwell was wanted at the front door. A policeman had arrived in response to a complaint from a next-door neighbour that there was some disturbance in the neighbourhood. Mrs. Maxwell said she was simply entertaining guests and invited the policeman to see for himself. Somewhat embarrassed and obviously taken aback by Mrs. Maxwell's charm and graciousness in inviting him to come in, he demurred and departed. This was one incident which demonstrates the hostility of some of the neighbours in that exclusive residential district at the time and to Mrs. Maxwell's unconcern for the prejudices of her neighbours.[32]

A number of people from Rev. Este's church on Atwater Street became Bahá'ís, including Eddie Elliot, Canada's first Black Bahá'í, and Mrs.

Blackburn (a white woman who married a Black) and her two daughters, the latter two being members of the youth group of Montréal.[33]

Edward "Eddie" Elliot (1902–53) was the first member of his race to accept the Bahá'í Faith in Canada. He was a member of Reverend Este's church. His mother had been a maid in May Maxwell's household, and he and her daughter Mary were close childhood friends and remained friends until his death in July 1953. Mr. Estall's account speaks further about Elliot's involvement in the Bahá'í community:

> [A]s a youth, he [Elliot] was both part of the Bahá'í youth group and of a social club organized by Ruhíyyih Khánum called the "Fratority Club." By this word, Ruhíyyih Khánum meant to put together the words "fraternity" and "sorority" and had invited to belong to it people, mostly young students at McGill [University], who would otherwise not have been able to find membership in the exclusive fraternities and sororities around the campus.[34]

In later years, Eddie Elliot was often elected as chairman of the Local Spiritual Assembly of Montréal, although he remained a member of the Negro Church (retaining membership in one's church was not an uncommon practice among Bahá'ís during those early years).[35] In an effort not to arouse suspicion among May Maxwell's neighbors, Eddie would arrive in the Maxwell home after dark:

> He [Eddie] was tops [in his field]. But because he was Black, they [electric power company] gave him nothing, nothin', no credit. But they had him teach everyone else how to get up there and fix those currents. . . . [I asked,] "When are you coming to my fireside?" He said, "After dark, you know I wouldn't come when its light." So nine o'clock he show up and it was time to go home. These are the sad things about those days.[36]

Elliot was a singer in addition to his occupation of electrician, in which his company never allowed him to advance, but always asked him to train others.[37] According to Rowland Estall,[38] he would often be asked to sing at the Maxwell home. He participated, as a representative of the Canadian National Spiritual Assembly, in the African Intercontinental Teaching Conference held in Kampala, Uganda, in February 1953.[39]

His sudden death soon thereafter, in July 1953, while working on a high-voltage transformer for the Montréal power utility, left the Canadian Bahá'í community bereft of the only member of his race to have embraced the Bahá'í Faith in Canada at that time.[40] He is buried in the Mount Royal Cemetery in Montréal. Estall describes him as a "very pure and distinguished soul," having "warmth and strength." He served as the "first bridge between Black and White communities in Montréal."[41] At one time he was member of the Inter-Racial Board[42] and the Committee of Management of the Negro Community Centre.[43] According to Amine De Mille, "He distinguished himself by his loyal services, his honorable character, and his beautiful singing voice."[44]

Another Black who became a member of Mary Maxwell's Fratority Club in those early days of the Bahá'í community of Montréal, although not a Bahá'í, was Dr. Phil Edwards (1907–71),[45] who also attended firesides in the Maxwell home.[46] Edwards was an Olympic champion runner who participated in three Olympic Games (1928, 1932, 1936) and in the 1934 British Empire Games, winning increasingly greater honors.[47] He was also apparently the first Black West Indian to graduate as a medical student from McGill University, Montréal.[48]

It was eight years before another Black Canadian, Violet Grant States, enrolled in the Bahá'í community. States was the organist in Rev. Este's church and was the last one to have joined the Bahá'í community from that congregation. She enrolled on January 8, 1961[49] in Verdun, near Montréal, and has been a member of the Local Spiritual Assembly there since that time, having served for many years as its secretary.

She heard of the Bahá'í Faith through Eddie Elliot when she was in her early teens, when he showed the children at Sunday School the letter from Mary Maxwell (who was then living in Haifa, Palestine, at the Faith's international headquarters) inviting him to the dedication of the House of Worship in Kampala, Uganda. She asked the minister's wife about the Bahá'í Faith, and she said, "Nice people, but never join them because they don't believe in Jesus." Then Violet saw an ad in a newspaper for a gathering to mark the birthday of Bahá'u'lláh at the Montréal Bahá'í Shrine on Pine Avenue West and began attending informal meetings in 1953. She became an accomplished musician, at one time giving a performance at Carnegie Hall.[50]

The interest of the Bahá'í community in reaching Blacks was not confined only to Montréal. African-American Hand of the Cause Louis Gregory undertook a trip to Vancouver to speak at five meetings in the early 1920s.[51] Little is as yet known about the context or the results of these meetings. While a Black woman enrolled in the Yukon Territory, the attention of the Bahá'í community was concentrated primarily on Canada's east coast, and in Toronto itself.

To Yukon goes the distinction of having enrolled the first Black Canadian woman into the Bahá'í community, Dora Bray of Dawson. Between 1922 and 1937 there were sporadic visits to this area by Bahá'ís, including by Orcella Rexford in 1922, who spoke to an audience of 550 at a public meeting in Dawson.[52] It was during this time that Bray enrolled.[53] A school teacher, she subsequently moved to Washington State.[54] She eventually became, in 1971, the oldest living Bahá'í in the world, aged 105.[55]

Activities in Atlantic Canada

Our attention now turns to Canada's eastern seaboard, where the settlement of Blacks had been an ongoing feature of the social landscape there. An early Bahá'í contact with a Black community took place in Saint John, New Brunswick, where a Dorothy Beecher, known as "Mother" Beecher, had tried in vain to speak at a number of churches in the city on a teaching trip to the area in 1919. Even the "church of the coloured people" in Saint John refused Mother Beecher's request to speak to them in November or December.[56] It was not until four years later, during the 1923–4 winter, that a more opportune time arose and a new pastor of the Black church, Rev. Stewart, "a wide awake, radiant soul," "gladly consented" to Bahá'ís' speaking to his congregation.[57] Dr. Edna McKinney of Philadelphia spoke five times and Miss Jack gave an exhibition of her paintings. This was the first church in the East coast of Canada ever to open its doors to the Bahá'í Faith.[58] There was even an interest in starting a group "among the colored children" in that church.[59]

Little is known of the results of what must have been exhilarating meetings, and we can but speculate that some forty years later, during the late 1960s, the Bahá'í community of Saint John must have met the spiritual children from those early years. The Saint John Bahá'ís provided viable and memorable children's classes which included a large number of Black children. Such a service spilled out into the relationship of the Bahá'í community to the larger Black community of that port city.

Further east, the settlement of Bahá'í "pioneers" in Halifax, Nova Scotia, attracted a few Black adherents. Our narrative, so far, has omitted mention of the fourth Black to have declared in Canada, Ralph Laltoo, a student from Trinidad and son of a United Church minister. He had come to Halifax and was among the first to enroll in the Bahá'í Faith in that city, in October 1940,[60] after its having been opened by Beulah Proctor in the previous year.[61] Little is known of Mr. Laltoo, except that he introduced the Bahá'í Faith to a number of other students.[62]

Significantly, Halifax attracted a Black pioneer in her seventies, Rosa Shaw from San Francisco, to strengthen the work in that city which had the highest concentration of Blacks in Canada at that time.[63] She became the first Black member of the Halifax Spiritual Assembly and chose to live in the Black slum area of the city, where she stayed for about a year.[64] Before she moved into the slum area, Shaw spent some time living with a Bahá'í couple, one of whom relates the following incident:

> We had Rosa Shaw come up from the States and she was going to stay with a coloured family and they didn't have room for her at the time. So my husband said, "Oh, she can come and sleep on our couch." He said, "Everybody else does." And everybody said, "Well we really couldn't take her because she coloured you know. People talk around." Fred said, "Well, let them talk. You're a Bahá'í." He said, "She'll come and stay with us." So we had the Collector of Customs down below and we had the American Customs Agency across the way and my husband used to proudly take her out for a walk and nobody said a thing.[65]

In 1946 Rita (Elaine) and Ernest Marshall of the Leeward and Windward Islands declared in Halifax, Rita on 19 June and Ernest in November of that year.[66] According to Audrey Rayne, who herself declared as a Bahá'í in Nova Scotia in 1943, the couple attended every Bahá'í function. They are described as a "well-off" Black family who managed to put all their children through university; the daughter became a dentist and the son a doctor.[67] They were members of the local Spiritual Assembly of Halifax until 1959,[68] before Ernest retired, and the family moved to a Toronto suburb.

One Bahá'í, Lloyd Gardner,[69] recalls another Black Bahá'í who came to Halifax, Reginald G. Barrow, who was still a practicing bishop of the African Orthodox Church in Halifax. Gardner is not quite sure even how it happened that he maintained this ecclesiastical post, but he thinks that some communication he had from Shoghi Effendi permitted him to carry on his ministry for a time. Reginald G. Barrow, Jr.—the son of Reginal Barrow—confirmed that Shoghi Effendi "had said that he could continue in the church as it was his profession and he had a family to support."[70] Gardner states:

> But he was a very confirmed believer in Bahá'u'lláh and he would preach direct sermons on the [Bahá'í] Faith. And he loved to have the Bahá'ís come and his role in that church; they were his flock and he was their leader. It was that kind of a relationship, he had no sense of being daring in doing this, he felt quite confident. But he would deliver addresses, straight Bahá'í talks related to scripture. And he loved to have the Bahá'ís come and he not only liked to have us come, but if he saw us in the audience he would ask us to come and sit behind him, behind the pulpit while he delivered his sermon. But there was no questioning his belief in the [Bahá'í] Faith.

Another early Black believer in the Halifax area was Fred Lorne Izzard from Preston, Nova Scotia. He was a shipyard worker. He was taught the Bahá'í Faith by Bill Halfyard and enrolled in the Bahá'í Faith in August 1953.[71] He eventually moved to Bridgewater, south of Halifax.[72]

Although the Local Spiritual Assembly of Halifax never formed a committee to teach the Bahá'í Faith to Blacks, a lot of work was undertaken in the Black community.[73] To the discouragement of the Bahá'ís, there were no obvious or immediate results of this work until well into the 1960s when Paul and Sylvia Norton—an interracial couple—lived in Beechville, a Black area outside of Halifax. Through their efforts, a Black family, the Carveries, entered the Bahá'í Faith.

While the seeds of the Bahá'í Faith had been quietly sown in Montréal, New Brunswick, and Nova Scotia, where a small handful of Blacks had declared their allegiance to the Bahá'í Faith, other parts of Canada still had not witnessed the entry of Black people into the Bahá'í communities. Some Bahá'ís, such as those in Edmonton, Alberta, had attempted to acquaint Blacks in that city with the Faith,[74] though without apparent success. Even Ontario, which had a sizeable community of Blacks, had to wait until the 1940s before the first adherents of the Black race entered the Bahá'í Faith. The first of this group was Lucille Giscome. A native of North Bay, Ontario, Lucille "excelled in the secretarial and journalistic fields."[75] At the time of her enrollment in 1942 as the first Bahá'í in Ottawa, she worked for the Dominion Bureau of Statistics and wrote articles for one of the local Ottawa newspapers. She had outspoken views which met with disapproval by various officials. She left for Toronto, and after unsuccessful attempts to find work as a journalist, travelled to England, after which she settled in Czechoslovakia. In that country, speaking fluent Czech, she found new friends and was able to work as a journalist. In later years she fell ill and wanted to return to Canada but was refused entry on a legal technicality. She died in Czechoslovakia. Lucille's sister-in-law, Icsolene Giscombe, desribes her as someone with a "passion for reading" which was "unmeasurable."[76]

Toronto

Inez Atheline Ifill-Hayes was another among the first to have declared herself a Bahá'í in Ontario. Through the account of Inez's daughter, Esther, and her wealth of archival materials, we are able to present a more in-depth picture of the early Toronto Bahá'ís.

Inez Hayes was born in Barbados, West Indies, on November 28, 1896. She journeyed to Canada in 1915 to join her mother, Mary Ifill, who had moved to Canada several years before. The young Inez spent her girlhood years growing up in Toronto and met and married her husband, Nathaniel Hayes, in that city. Mr. Hayes was also a West Indian. Born in Grenada, he left his homeland to take up work on the building of the Panama Canal. When his work term ended, he headed north to Canada and worked in the Nova Scotia mines for a time. He then moved on to Toronto. Nathaniel and Inez had a family of five children, Esther, Eleanor, Roland, Wilfred, and Harold.

When Inez visited the Anglican Church with the purpose of joining, the church would not accept her, so, she took her children down the road to the Beverley Baptist Church. She raised her children in that church, but her religious path of discovery continued. In the course of her work as a domestic, Inez answered an ad to do homemaking for a young couple with four children. Here, in the words of her employer, is the story of that meeting: "The doorbell rang and Audrey [my wife] went and was a little surprised but thrilled to see a smiling, attractive-looking Black person standing there; but before coming in she looked at Audrey and said, 'You wouldn't object to my color, would you?' Audrey really wanted to welcome her with open arms."[77]

Of the applicants who came to apply for the part-time job of housekeeping, Inez was the unanimous choice. The couple were Audrey Robarts and her husband, John, who was later appointed as a Hand of the Cause of God. John wrote,

> Inez brought something new in the way of a loving spirit, joy, and happiness to all of us, and I remember often leaving my office a little earlier on those Thursday afternoons and coming home and finding Inez ironing and Audrey sitting on the stool reading the words of Bahá'u'lláh from the *Hidden Words*. They went straight to Inez' hearts and how she loved them.[78]

Inez loved the way the Robarts brought up their children. She would share her experiences of working at the Robarts house with her own children when she returned home from work. She did not know what religion the Robarts were; she thought they might be Jewish. Audrey sat with Inez at lunchtimes, which was something unheard of in those days. One day, Audrey did not eat, and she explained to Inez that she was a Bahá'í and she was fasting.[79] She invited Inez to come to a Bahá'í meeting and learn more about the Bahá'í Faith.

Inez went to her first Bahá'í meeting in 1943 at the home of a prominent Bahá'í, Laura Davis, in Rosedale, Toronto. Inez did not want to go alone, so she took her daughter Esther with her. In those days Black women did not go to Rosedale, an exclusive white neighborhood, to visit, but rather to work as domestics. Davis's house was packed that night. There were many people from different places, but they were all White except for Inez and Esther Hayes. Dorothy Baker, a Bahá'í teacher greatly loved by the Bahá'ís was the speaker for the evening. From that night forward, both Inez and Esther considered themselves Bahá'ís. Inez formally enrolled, but Esther carried her belief in her heart until many years later. According to Esther, "My mother didn't have a great deal of education, nor did she read as much as her children, but she had a sense about the [Bahá'í] Faith."[80]

Inez deepened her belief through regular attendance at meetings and summer schools. She also had daily contact with many Bahá'í women; May Pallister, Doris Richardson, Ethel Priestly, and Laura Davis all used to call Inez on a daily basis.

Her becoming a Bahá'í did not adversely affect the rest of her family. She never forced her Bahá'í beliefs on the children, but went about her activities in her own quiet way. She had always been a religious woman, and this dedication carried through in her devotion to the Bahá'í Faith.

She spoke to all her Black friends about the Bahá'í Faith and to anyone else she could. The fewness of Black people in the Bahá'í community affected her profoundly. She was hurt when her Black friends would ask her what was she was doing with these people. Nevertheless, Inez continually gave the news about the Bahá'í Faith to all her friends and anyone new she met.

She was delighted to meet Black Bahá'ís such as Rosa Lewis and Laura Jackson from the United States at summer schools. Once Elsie Austin and her mother came up from the United States to a summer school at Rice Lake, and Inez and Esther were pleased to meet them. Esther Hayes said that when her mother met another Black person, "she just took onto them!"

Inez taught many people about the Bahá'í Faith and a few became Bahá'ís during her lifetime. Sarah Downes (d. 1960), Inez's closest girlhood friend, learned of the Bahá'í Faith through her and became a Bahá'í in 1945. Downes was foster mother to Lincoln Alexander who later became Canada's first Black to sit in the House of Commons and the first Black lieutenant-governor. Her son, Wray Downes, although never officially declaring a belief in the new Faith, was an active participant at Bahá'í meetings, especially in Britain, where he studied classical music.

John Hayes, cousin to Nathaniel Hayes and longtime friend of Lincoln Alexander's father and boarder with the Downes family, also became a Bahá'í through Inez. John was a porter with Canadian National Railways and traveled continually, so he did not have the chance to attend Bahá'í meetings or summer schools. His acceptance of the Bahá'í Faith was based on a strong foundation of personal study, and commitment to the understanding of the truth of Bahá'u'lláh's teachings to which he gave testimony in his diary in 1945, on 23 May (the date that Bahá'ís celebrate the Báb's declaration of his message), asking God to "help him to remain steadfast for the rest of his life."[81]

Another person who was connected to the Downes/Alexander family and became a Bahá'í was Ferne C. Harrison, a sister of Lincoln Alexander's wife. She lived in Hamilton and became a Bahá'í on 7 October 1945.[82] She had a talent for singing and often graced Bahá'í meetings and events with her voice. Inez and Esther met Ferne occasionally at summer schools and conventions, though she later resigned from the Bahá'í Faith.

Inez always kept her home open to travelers and "seekers"—those who were interested in the Bahá'í teachings. She gave a warm reception to anyone traveling through Toronto, and featured many guest speakers at meetings in her home to introduce the Faith. When Inez moved to Thornhill Avenue in York, a suburb of Toronto, she invited all the people in the neighborhood to an open house. Her neighbors (who were all White) went to the minister of their church to discuss whether they should go or not. No one came. Several years later, after a large, racially diverse gathering in Inez's home, a neighbor remarked to Inez, "Well, I must say your family has lived up to our expections!" According to Esther, these comments and attitudes never held Inez back. "She had a big heart and plenty of love in it for everyone." She kept up a large correspondence with friends who were interested in the Bahá'í Faith, and encouraged those who were not.[83]

Another area of service in Inez's life was her work for the administrative institutions of the Bahá'í Faith. Inez, who had never served on a committee in her life, was elected to the Local Spiritual Assembly of the Bahá'ís of Toronto in 1948; she also served in later years on the Local Spiritual Assembly of the Bahá'ís of York.

In 1957 Inez went back to Barbados to visit her family and to tell her friends about the Bahá'í Faith. There were no Bahá'ís in Barbados when Inez set off on her trip, but several weeks after her arrival she received a letter from the Western Hemisphere Teaching Committee in the United States informing her that some weeks prior to Inez's arrival a gentleman, Winfield Small, had gone to Barbados from Bahamas as a Bahá'í pioneer. Their paths did not cross, but she saved that letter for years after, probably as a memento of her precious times and memories in her homeland. Inez also traveled to Grenada to visit her relations there.

After her return from Barbados, she wrote many letters to friends answering questions about the Bahá'í Faith. Every year, Inez would send a Christian calendar with a personal message and a Bahá'í pamphlet to the acquaintances and friends she had met. Her daughter has kept up this tradition to this day, thirty-one years later.

Inez also took a trip to visit her dear friend Doris Richardson in Grand Manan, and traveled there teaching the Bahá'í Faith. Inez's style of teaching the Faith was to just talk to everybody. When she got on a bus she would talk to her fellow passengers and to the bus driver, too. Doris wrote to Inez's family, "Everyone was attracted to Inez—she took the island by storm."[84]

Her services were countless and she is remembered by many people. After her passing at the age of seventy-seven, on October 20, 1974, many testimonials were written about her unique character. Older Bahá'ís who had served the Bahá'í Faith for many years said that Inez had inspired and given them the courage to carry on with their work. Inez was described as "a spiritual Rock of Gibraltar with a rich sense of humour."[85] She was very active socially in the Black community of Toronto. Her steadfastness and sublime faith in God was an inspiration to many. She had "great common-sense and a down-to-earth appreciation of human suffering, having suffered much herself."[86] The National Spiritual Assembly of the Bahá'ís of Canada praised her untiring service to humanity.[87]

The story[88] of Esther P. Hayes, Inez's daughter, provides a keen insight into the circumstances of the earlier Black adherents of the Bahá'í Faith in Canada. Esther was born in Toronto in 1922. She grew up with her sister and three brothers in the Toronto area. Raised in the Baptist Church, she began, in her early teens, a lifelong commitment to fight racism. She was a quiet and reserved person, whose creative ability expresses itself through inventive ideas and whose strength of mind showed in her determination and perseverance to carry these ideas through. She was a founding member of the Negro Youth Council, and an active member of other Black organizations. Esther has found many ways to support and help the Black community.

In 1943 Esther was twenty-one when she accompanied her mother to that first Bahá'í meeting. The speaker, Dorothy Baker, affected her deeply. Her talk was about the meaning of creation. Esther said she pictured that the mother of Christ would be "like Dorothy Baker." From that night on she carried the belief in her heart that, "this message of Bahá'u'lláh was God's will for the world." Esther felt she "didn't need to join the Bahá'í Faith—it already included me—it included everyone!"

Esther began to attend Bahá'í meetings regularly and read the Bahá'í literature. She said, "It was good being with people that accepted you, had no objections to you, and were relaxed with you." There were Bahá'ís who were interested in Black history. Some of them, however, had never had any contact with Blacks before. The Hayes' realized that "many were ignorant of other races, and asked embarrassing and often rude questions." Esther described this attitude as an "ignorance born out of innocence."

Esther's mother never discussed the new religion with her when she was younger, but left books for Esther to read if she wished. Mother and daughter would attend meetings, summer schools, and Bahá'í social events together. One day, Laura Davis gave *The Promised Day Is Come* (a letter by Shoghi Effendi published as a book) to Inez. She thought Esther would be interested in reading it. After reading the book, Esther decided it was necessary that she formally join the Bahá'í Faith. Eight years after her initial contact with the Bahá'ís, she wrote a letter to the local Spiritual Assembly of Toronto saying she wished to enroll.

"In those days," Esther said, "you had to write a letter of intent to the local Spiritual Assembly, stating you believed in the central figures of the Faith [the Báb, Bahá'u'lláh, and 'Abdu'l-Bahá] and that you had read *Bahá'u'lláh and the New Era* [by J. E. Esslemont], and the Will and Testament of 'Abdu'l-Bahá." When Esther met the committee of the Assembly, they talked with her and then asked her to step out into the hall while they discussed her acceptance. Esther said she knew that whether they accepted her or not, she was a Bahá'í—the Bahá'í Faith belonged to everyone. "Why be formal about it?" Esther thought, "They couldn't keep me out, so why bring me in? It was my right." The Bahá'ís welcomed Esther into the community.

Esther helped her mother with the firesides and meetings held at their house, and also took on new avenues of service. She became known for her devotion, reliability, efficiency, and attention to detail. Because of these attributes, she was asked to serve on many committees in the Bahá'í administration, such as the Regional Teaching Committee, the Icelandic Conference Committee, the Ontario Youth Committee, the Community Counselling Committee, and others. Esther also served on the Local Spiritual Assembly of the Bahá'ís of York. She worked at the Bahá'í National Centre in Toronto for eight years, the job she enjoyed most in her life.

Esther always loved children and was asked in 1959 to teach Bahá'í children's classes, a service she performed for two years with great enjoyment. Esther said she enjoyed many hours of preparation of material for the classes as well as teaching the children themselves.

In those early days, Esther and her mother were the only Black Bahá'ís in Ontario, and greatly valued contact with other Black Bahá'ís. Esther met Violet Grant States, of Montréal, at Geneva Park summer school in

1953. The two became firm friends and although they could not see each other often because Violet lived in Montréal, and Esther in Toronto, they kept in constant touch through letters and phone calls.

One of the examples of Esther's ability to combine her dedication to serve and support the Black community with her desire to spread the message of Bahá'u'lláh, was the production of the *Negro Directory,* which she founded in 1965. The *Directory* was a brochure listing businesses and services offered by the Black community in Canada. It also included educational articles of interest and assistance, particularly to Black people. Aside from these articles, Esther would include one page devoted to the principles and teachings of the Bahá'í Faith. The *Directory* was financed by Esther, and the Hayes family helped out with the production. Eleanor, Esther's sister, collated the information, Esther edited and typed, and brother Harold and her mother helped to copy it with the aid of an old nonelectric Gestetner machine. This booklet was produced for eighteen years as a service to the Black community.

When Bahá'ís are asked to describe Esther's character, the description they give is of a person who is "compassionate, determined, thoughtful, committed, and dedicated" and one who "is a survivor through thick and thin." Esther was very active in her service to the Bahá'í Faith, and the Black community, as well.

Esther reached out to the local Black community where she met Donald Carty at one of the Black organizations. Carty, a nineteen-year-old, was becoming disillusioned with the Black associations, as they "did not provide healing answers." He was very concerned with the social and racial problems of the day, and was doing what he could for his community through involvement with the scouting movement, music, and the YMCA. Esther told him about the transforming power of the Bahá'í Faith. He began to attend meetings and he declared himself a Bahá'í on June 11, 1955.[89] Don Carty belonged to the Anglican Church at that time and was, in fact, being prepared to become a lay preacher. When the minister heard that he was investigating the Bahá'í teachings, he warned the congregation to stay away from him. A special service was even set up for Carty, on the subject of the Antichrist;[90] his volunteer services for the Cubs in the church's basement were no longer needed.

The reaction of the Black community was no less difficult: The feeling I got from the Black community was of noncommital acceptance of inter-racial associations or involvement, and of course if you are going with a white girl or vice versa, it was always a topical thing. I became known [within the Black community] as "Don the Bahá'í." I found [my involvement] quite often evoked conversations, and the determination to convince me that I was on the wrong path. I would emphatically point out to them that there were lots of points of difference, but, "let's dwell on our similarities."[91]

Carty remembers Esther's gentle persuasion and support over the years, as she taught him about the Bahá'í Faith. In his words, he "embraced what Esther had told [him] with a curiosity and with an intense suspicion, because [he] had identified with groups who came on very beautifully, but after awhile the realities began to dilute the illusion."[92] Behavior, not words, was the keystone to his accepting the Bahá'í Faith:

The real turning point came when I was out to a function and a young woman, whom I had known by sight, gave a grand hello and how are you, said, "I have something to do, will you hold my purse for a minute?" I thought she would be gone for a minute or so, but there I was tagging this purse around an hour later! I thought, not only was there the open show of affection, it was supported with trust. More than just words it was manifested in conduct. And I thought, yes, I think I would like to be a part of these people.[93]

Don's brother, Clyde, became a Bahá'í in Scarborough, near Toronto, on April 21, 1965.[94]

The gradual attraction of Blacks to the Bahá'í Faith was slow. However, any new adherents themselves became the center of service and activity in the Bahá'í community. No area of service was closed, whether of an administrative, social, or teaching nature.

In recent decades the Bahá'í community has given serious attention to focusing the teaching work in the Black community. Nowhere is this more evident than in Eastern Canada. In Saint John, New Brunswick, the site of the first church to open its doors to the Bahá'í Faith, the Bahá'í community regularly held children's classes where attendance of non-Bahá'í Black children was a very happy common occurrence. The Bahá'í community of Saint John established intimate connections with the Blacks of the city.

The other major center for this work was Nova Scotia, which has a total Black population of 20,000. Much of the enthusiasm among the Bahá'ís in the teaching the Faith was generated through teaching the Black community, a number of whom enrolled. However, the teaching work was not only confined to the city. Certain towns and very isolated spots in the province known for their concentration of Blacks, were visited by Bahá'í teachers. In particular, Guysboro District[95] in eastern Nova Scotia, which can be reached only by tertiary roads, has the unique position of being the first—and only—all-Black Local Spiritual Assembly in Canada, elected for the first time in 1977.[96]

The Canadian "Black rose" defies the tiles laid out by dominant society. Not only is the Canadian "mosaic" arranged vertically,[97] but it speaks only to those ethnic communities which conform to a particular pattern of organization and culture. The cracks in the mosaic show that despite attempts to favor only particular ethnic communities, the ethnic reality of Canada may be giving way to an ethnic "garden." The Black community comprises the strong and resilient flowers who, despite the wide open opportunities favored to others and denied to themselves, have labored to push on and up, and have become increasingly recognized for their contributions to the rest of the garden—the Canadian cultural heritage and society. In such a garden, all cultures can flourish and add to each others' attractiveness, and contribute to the whole.

II

Creative and Social Commentaries, Letters, and Family Histories

Introduction

Part II is intended to give readers some ideas about how some influential African-American Bahá'ís perceived themselves and the larger communities in which they lived. Their writings reveal a keen sense of justice as well as an acute awareness of their own responsibilities as African-American Bahá'ís living at a time when race prejudice and gender discrimination were rampant, a situation complicated by the struggle of their new Faith to create a unified community in direct opposition to American separate and unequal social policies. The documents contained in this section represent a diversity of thought and approaches to the social ills of the time.

The first group of essays entitled "Creative and Social Commentaries" contains works written and published between 1900–30. Some authors explicitly name Bahá'í principles, while others do not. They all attempted to give voice to some aspect of Black life and/or the Bahá'í Faith that would be meaningful to the public, but especially to African-Americans. Coralie Cook, for example, wrote a short story about the long-term effects of slavery and a very short nonfiction piece on women's right to vote. Elsie Austin and Louis Gregory discuss the relevance of the Bahá'í Faith to African Americans and challenge ideologies of race separation. John Shaw and Hallie E. Queen make connections, respectively, between the status of oppressed groups such as African-Americans and Puerto Ricans and notions of citizenship.

The second grouping of documents, "Letters Across Time," contains two letters that are generations apart, but which both address issues central to the role of the African Americans in the Bahá'í Faith. Audiences for the letters were different, but the sentiments of both authors are very much comparable. Coralie Cook wrote directly to 'Abdu'l-Bahá and filled her letter with historical references that argued against racist myths popular at that time. Her main objective was to describe the status of race relations in the U.S. and to challenge Bahá'ís to be more active in the elimination of prejudice. Bonnie Fitzpatrick-Moore wrote to African-Americans and shared her pioneering experiences in South Africa as a means of inviting and challenging African-Americans to become pioneers themselves.

The third and last section, "Family Histories and the Growth of the Faith," includes narratives of four Black families who were active in the development of the Faith during its earliest formation in the U.S. Several of the histories have been passed down within the family for several generations, particularly those of the Mapp, Ellis, and Martin families. Each of these histories identifies the first person in the family to become a Bahá'í, the impact of the Faith on the family, and significant accomplishments and acts of service by individual family members.

Many of the documents in this section are previsouly unpublished. Written from a first person point of view, they preserve a little-known history that expands our notions of African-American religious traditions.

CHAPTER 8

The Bahá'í Faith
and Problems of Color, Class,
and Creed

Elsie Austin

This essay was originally published in volume nine of
The Bahá'í World (1940–4).

In some future age when history is no longer written to advance the
prestige and power of particular groups and nations, perhaps historians
will be able to state frankly how much of the tragedy and chaos of our
world has been due to the efforts of men and women who distorted
civilization and humanity by deliberately provoking animosity and
division over the outward differences of men.

This age has brought us certainly to the peak of disunity and bitterness
over the colors of men's skins, their types of work and their paths to
God. It is as if the whole human race has been agitated and forced to a
showdown over the retention of old ideas of division and the adoption
of new ideas of unity and cooperation.

The terrific pressure of conflicting social forces are making it increasingly difficult today for white or colored peoples to avoid the extremes of

social reaction. The swollen hatreds and fanatic efforts of those who champion the old ways have, indeed, forced many to bitter acceptance of hate and division as the chief instrumentalities which must govern the development and power of peoples. For colored and white, the importance of rejecting decisively such an idea is superseded only by the urgency of finding and using the kind of faith and effort which are needed for the individual and social victories for enlightenment so essential to this period.

It is not that colored peoples need this, or that white peoples need that. It is rather that all men, all races, all classes, all creeds, and all nations are in need of new balance and new direction for this day.

There are many established and familiar causes and purposes at work today attempting through various types of programs to meet this need for balance and direction. They have taken the best of the old knowledge and techniques and are attempting a revised use of them on either the inner life or the outer life of men. Some are making a bona fide effort to teach the efficacy of the ageless spiritual standards of brotherhood, justice and cooperation, but their efforts are weakened, first, by their failure to meet the complex needs of a complex period, and second, by their fatally compromising use of "accepted patterns of action" which in themselves accent the long embroidered differences of race, creed, and class among men.

Others have discarded the spiritual and are concerned mainly with the correction of outer practices of prejudice and division. Their stress is upon the practice of brotherhood and cooperation which come as a matter of law and enforced compliance. The practice of brotherhood, however, is something more than a matter of law. It involves the use of inner discipline which uproot and destroy the hidden jealousies, the secret fears, inner suspicions, greeds, and enmities of men. For it is these inner motives which, if undestroyed, sooner or later find a way to make mockery of law and social compliance.

There is in the world today, however, a new Faith which is meeting the desperate need of all peoples for balance and direction. It is the Bahá'í World Faith, now barely one hundred years old, but already spanning the continents of the world with a membership which embraces all the known races, classes, and creeds of humanity. Bahá'u'lláh, Founder of this Faith, in a matchless revelation of spiritual teachings and laws, gives through religion the desired balance for humanity. It is religion which trains man inwardly and outwardly. In giving the foundations of the Bahá'í Faith, Bahá'u'lláh, without compromise, goes to the heart of the ills and needs of this age . . . the disunity and hatred among men. He clears away the tawdry, vicious, false bases which have been used to make differences in men the cause for animosity and strife.

The Bahá'í Faith gives mankind a new and creative concept of unity. It is the understanding that all men, whatever their outward differences may be, share in common the divine gift of the higher self and its creative urge for expression, development and fruitfulness. True civilization, then, has never been and can never be the special project or property of any particular group of humanity. It is indeed the best contributions of all men.

The Oneness of Mankind as Bahá'u'lláh sets it forth, and as Bahá'ís all over the world are learning it, is something more than the usual argument and gestures which imply wishful thinking and future possibility. Bahá'u'lláh has made it an element of belief in God. Its expression is therefore an operating principle of worship, and worship is not a ceremony. It is the act of living, of translating one's beliefs into the experiences of life. The Bahá'ís have no rituals, or ceremonies, or select group whereby worship may become a formal gesture. Their way of expression of belief is their constant endeavor to work it into the patterns, the standards, the customs of life.

It is in terms of this Oneness of Mankind that the Bahá'í world functions with entirely new patterns of effort and achievement for the creative ability and capacity of its individuals. There are no special groups. There is only mankind. Therefore Bahá'ís do not work and achieve and live in terms of the old hatreds, greeds, and conceits. An individual who accepts the mighty standard of responsibility which Bahá'u'lláh has established cannot preserve the old jealousies and prides. "All men have been created to carry forward an ever-advancing civilization."[1] Each man, then, whatever his background and his measure of capacity, has both a destiny and a mission in life which taxes his best. He must prepare to express that best and to give it with full understanding that it is related to the best of every other man.

There are great differences of religious background among the followers of Bahá'u'lláh, but there is also difference of perspective in interpreting those differences and living with them. The great faiths of the past are not destroyed or belittled. They are connected and unified and those interpretive elements in them which have been the source of conflict and dissension are exposed in their imaginative and superstitious falsity. There is unqualified recognition of the unity of God's Divine Messengers who have come at various ages of mankind with an ever increasing measure of Truth for the enlightenment and progress of men. In concentrating upon the ever growing measure of Truth and the unity of its Bringers, men achieve true spiritual maturity, for they lift faith and worship above the realm of contentions and confusions over the outward names, forms and systems of religion.

Upon the subject of racial differences the Bahá'ís have achieved a balance which deserves the study and attention of all peoples. The age-old tensions, superstitions, and cultivated enmities in terms of racial differences are certainly not easy to lose. They have been worked into all the experiences of men with such elaborate detail that they come out unconsciously in thought and action patterns. But these scars and wounds of the past are somehow removed and healed by the loving power in the Revelation of Bahá'u'lláh. That recognition and concentration upon Oneness captures the heart and clears the mind. The common destiny of men, their potentialities for development as given by Bahá'u'lláh call forth such inspiration and ambition among His followers that, in setting themselves to another goal, they pass by and forget the old emphases. In the Bahá'í community racial differences become normal differences. They are no more a cause for strife, fear, and separation than the color of eyes and hair. In the effort and training for better character, better minds and better achievement each man forgets his skin color and that of his neighbor. The Bahá'í pattern is indeed a new and tremendously potential guide for group relationships of men. There is no strained and obvious effort to love white people or colored people. There are only people who are learning together the courtesy, cooperation and regard required for an enlightened and progressive society of human beings. Humanity is one soul in many bodies. It is one thing to say this philosophically. It is another to feel it as a heart experience and as a necessary law of life.

Colored or white, we need the sort of belief that gives every man the power to give his neighbor deserved faith and credit. Bahá'u'lláh's searching analysis deserves careful thought and unreserved acceptance. Said He, "The well-being of mankind, its peace and security, are unattainable unless and until its unity is firmly established. . . . So powerful is the light of unity that it can illuminate the whole earth."[2]

Colored or white, the world faith of Bahá'u'lláh offers us the needed purpose and direction for our times. In its creative Truth lies the one path wherein we all may find understanding and will to pass by and be done with the outmoded fallacies, the consuming greed, the shameful injustices and accumulated vengeance which have corrupted our past and crippled us all.

9

Racial Amity in America: An Historical Review

Louis Gregory

This essay was originally published in volume seven of
The Bahá'í World (1936–8).

The Sun of Truth, the Orb of Revelation that is Bahá'u'lláh, appears in the realm of being. Nothing is hid from the penetration and light of His rays; no soil of human hearts is neglected in cultivation; no veils of error need dim the sight of the sincere; no problem that has hitherto foiled even the wise now needs remain to vex and perplex. Simplicity, purity, potency, wisdom, concentration, guidance, harmony, unity, universality—all attributes and signs—are in the Creative Word which brought the world into being and it is that selfsame Word that now speaks with a new culture and laws. It also gives forth directions for its own application to human needs. Bahá'u'lláh by the might of both His teachings and life removed the causes of difference in the Orient. He also revealed His Great Tablet to the Americas, illustrating His Providence of freedom for all nations. It was during the days of His Covenant, however, that His Faith began to attract adherents in America, and 'Abdu'l-Bahá, its Center,

175

began to apply the healing and gladsome light of a new revelation to the great continent of the West.

Among the early American pilgrims to the Holy Land was Robert Turner, a Negro, who accompanied the party of Mrs. Phoebe Hearst. It was thus that the Master[1] had His first personal touch with the American race problem and His keen and kindly interest begun, continued to the end. He gave many instructions both public and private. He showed most impressively to pilgrims of all races His universal love. During His American tour He addressed a number of gatherings of the colored people and seemed happiest when He saw the two races in cooperation. He wisely interpreted one group to the other and with the utmost love and kindness pointed to the time when all discord would cease and all superficial differences vanish. This divine outpouring of knowledge, although expressing but one reality, as mortals classify knowledge, may fall into three categories, the scientific, the social, and the mystic.

This wisdom inspires deeper knowledge of physics and a clearer grasp of all the phenomena of nature. Does it not become evident that skin color is a slow but constant variant even in an individual as it is among the masses of people? It may be duly admired, but not overprized. Color is not inherent in surfaces but in light. Pure light contains all colors. Dark surfaces receive the light, a fact well known to the photographer and to that Great One Who made the pupil of the eye. Light surfaces refuse the light, reflecting it back to us, and we attribute to the surface what is the innate quality of the light. Make the lens blue and all the surfaces appear blue. Withdraw the light and all the surfaces lose their color. People as a rule grow darker as they become older, thus being able to receive more light. The pallor of death followed soon by the decoloration of the tomb comes at length for each and all. As no one chooses his own color at birth, whence either pride or shame over a semblance that is fleeting? Among the various peoples scattered over the earth the amount of pigment lessens in higher altitudes and grows in lower. Where is the merit or demerit of all this? Certainly not in the creatures who did not cause such a spectacle. Color collapses as a test of both ability and character. If ever a test of racial differences it must be extremely and conveniently elastic to serve the world! A blonde and a brunette are often found in children of the same parentage. They are nonetheless sisters. Have not groups large or small the same right to be varied? Shall we make an optical illusion the cause of widespread disturbance and ruin? Welcome the vision of basic oneness to free our souls from all such trammels. Sameness is dull. Variety lends charm. The Pure One stresses the color of service!

'Abdu'l-Bahá envisioned a new sociology for the world in general and America in particular. He invites the attention of social workers to the oases rather than the deserts of their environments and helps them to extend the boundaries; He is able to make all places fruitful. His is a wonderful culture of hearts and minds. As a preliminary to the study of His teachings, it may be fitting to observe that the close contact of two groups divided from each other by either racial, religious, or national traditions has rarely, if ever, been happy. It has resulted often in conquest, slavery, even extermination of one by the other. The Tasmanians have completely disappeared. So have the American Indians once in Haiti. The Ainu of Japan are near extinction, showing what may happen in ordinary human processes to a white group who may contact a more powerful yellow group. The Maori of New Zealand, although regarded ethnically as of the same stock as their Aryan neighbors from Europe, have been reduced, according to a statement reported by K[eith] R[ansom] Kehler, from a million to sixty-five thousand. Glimpses of the known continents during the last thousands of years show continuous fermentation and upheavals with no end in sight which does not involve a change of human nature.

The American Negro, in striking contrast to all this, has increased his numbers three-fold during the seventy years of his freedom, and his wealth, culture and influence in far greater proportions. This amazing progress indicates not only capacity and striving on his own part but the aid and cooperation of friendly whites. Yet despite all the good that has been done as proving merit on the part of both races, in the nation's internal development there is no more lurid and tragic chapter than that of race relations. It is to this, therefore, the 'Abdu'l-Bahá directs His great thought, turning His searchlight upon the national disease and prescribing with marvellous wisdom the remedy. It is thus that He summarizes the problem: "The blacks hate the whites and the whites distrust the blacks.

You must overcome this by showing that you make no distinction. The end will be very unfortunate for both if the differences are not removed."[2]

This diseased state of the body politic brings from Him repeated warnings, and He lays the responsibility for its removal upon both races. As the colored people were forcefully expatriated and brought to America, the situation arising imposes upon their abductors the obligation to be fair and just. Responsibility rightly goes with power. Kindness and generosity are its ornaments. While the colored people as a minority have less strength, they are not, thereby, freed from the duty of striving to heal the breaches of humanity. The plumb line suspended near a mountain is attracted out of its plumb; but the plumb also attracts, however imperceptibly, the mountain. Smaller social groups can influence larger ones, especially if they use their talents in ways prompted by Guidance.

The gravity of all the worlds is love, and whoever learns to love and praise people for whatever tokens of the Creator they show has discovered an impregnable fortress of strength. The Master's gentle injunction to the colored race is to remember the heroic sacrifices of the whites in the Civil War which led to the freedom of the colored people and to accord due praise for a service which was so great an incentive to freedom throughout the world. He has also mentioned the fact that the colored race in America enjoy educational advantages denied those in Africa, resulting in the progress of the former and the backwardness of the latter. Subtle and powerful is the effect of praise. It is acceptable to God and it gladdens the heart of man. The praise mentioned here is, of course, not flattery, which has a bad motive and selfish foundation. But praise of the good in man is in reality praise of God, since all good comes from the one Source. Sincerely and wisely used it favorably influences all human relations inspiring movement to a higher plane.

'Abdu'l-Bahá teaches that "Colors are phenomenal; while the realities of men are essence. When there exists unity of the essence, what power has the phenomenal? When the Light of Reality is shining, what power has the darkness of the unreal?"

He is the first to enlighten us as to the many points of agreement between the races which outweigh so greatly the one point of difference, color, which is relatively unimportant and which assuredly cannot always be a cause of estrangement.

Among His more mystical teachings is the explanation of the creation of man in the divine image and likeness as a station which refers to the virtues of his inner and true being. His annulment of superficial barriers and promise that the confirmations of the Holy Spirit will aid all those who labor for conciliation of the races give a bedrock of assurance.

'Abdu'l-Bahá outpoured His great love and wisdom, with race amity in view, upon various gatherings. He told the story of the wonderful fidelity, heroism, and courage of Isfandíyár, the colored friend who served Bahá'u'lláh under the most perilous conditions. This meeting was in the home of white friends and was largely attended by the colored. At another meeting in a colored home largely attended by whites He compared the colored to rubies and sapphires and the whites to diamonds and pearls, showing how their harmony would adorn humanity and elevate the nation.[3] He explained, at a meeting of the Bethel Literary and Historical Society, the divine nature of science and how it might be used for the unity of the world. Other occasions favored by Him were at Hull House in Chicago, founded by Jane Addams, and the National Association for the Advancement of the Colored People at their fourth annual gathering held in the same city. In these meetings He received most enthusiastic responses and made His audiences divinely happy. But perhaps the most powerful and impressive of all His utterances on race relations was that at Howard University, Washington, DC, the premier institution for the higher education of the colored, although by its charter open to all races. On this extraordinary occasion its chapel was filled with faculty, students, and a large number of visitors, both races mingling. The Master on this occasion went to the heart of the race problem. It was a talk which combined simplicity, beautiful imagery, noble idealism, and practical applications with a spiritual atmosphere which raised His hearers to a pitch of joyous enthusiasm. The applause which followed was so long continued that this marvelous speaker felt moved to speak briefly a second time, assuring that a time would eventually come when all differences would fade. It appeared to be His wish that the problem of the races in

America should be worked out along lines stated in this address and in view of its extreme importance it should not only be read but studied.

First Convention

It was following His return to the Holy Land, however, and after the World War that 'Abdu'l-Bahá set in motion a plan that was to bring the races together, attract the attention of the country, enlist the aid of famous and influential people and have a far-reaching effect upon the destiny of the nation itself. This was the first convention for amity between the races, and He placed its responsibility entirely in the hands of one of his most devoted American followers, Mrs. Agnes S. Parsons, whom He lovingly called His daughter. Her instructions were quite brief. The details she was free to work out with people of her selection to aid. Nothing daunted through her faith by the magnitude of this task, this heroine of God who had high rank in the social life of Washington returned from her pilgrimage and went prayerfully to work. She took as consultants the local Spiritual Assembly and a few personal friends, gradually widening the circle. Howard University responded in a way that showed the fruitage of seed sown by the Master nine years before. There were flowers and beautiful songs, the best musicians of the city lending their skill. The publicity was of the best with Martha Root at the helm.

The North and the South, Orient and Occident, colored and white mingled in a picturesque setting of five sessions over a period of three days. The First Congregational Church which in past years had welcomed so many liberal and progressive groups opened its doors for all sessions. Among the distinguished people who aided this endeavor were Rev. Dr. Jason Noble Pierce; Hon. Moses E. Clapp, former Senator from Nebraska; Senator Samuel Shortridge of California; C. Lee Cooke, famous southern business man; Dr. Alain Locke; Hon. Martin B. Madden, Congressman from Illinois; Alfred W. Martin, president of the Ethical Culture Society; William H. Randall; Albert Vail; Prof. George W. Cook; Mrs. Coralie Franklin Cook; Howard MacNutt; Mountfort Mills; Roy C. Wilhelm; Jináb-i-Fádil-i-Mazindarání of Iran; and Lieutenant General Nelson A. Miles, commanding the American Army. Certainly not less important was that little band of silent workers whose deeds were so apparent and whose names are doubtless better known in Higher Worlds.

The specific purpose of this initial convention was race understanding; but it also served to convey the Bahá'í teachings to the nation's capital and many interests centered there and radiating there from. Eloquent addresses, large audiences, responding not only to the wide press notices but the circulation of nineteen thousand programs, ideal weather, and an atmosphere that was spiritual and heavenly could have but an extraordinary effect. The workers had unusual experiences, and the spirit of reconciliation seemed to sweep the city. This convention had the fervent approval of the President of the United States although officially he took no part in it. The gratitude of the chief executive may be well understood when it is recalled that but a short time before, that historic city had been violently disturbed by a race riot fatal to many. Now the cleansing and purifying power of the Holy Spirit was at work bringing harmony and peace to those who had passed through the shadows of death. This esoteric bower of the Bahá'í Faith was thus illustrated. It enabled a few devoted believers to perform a herculean task.

This convention for sustained and interesting features seemed to make a unique record. But what was by far its most impressive event was the delivery of the message of 'Abdu'l-Bahá, which He had intrusted to Mountfort Mills, a recent pilgrim to Haifa and by whom it was conveyed with admirable wisdom and tact. It was as follows:

Say to this convention that never since the beginning of time has one more important been held. This convention stands for the oneness of humanity; it will become the cause of the enlightenment of America. It will, if wisely managed and continued, check the deadly struggle between these races which otherwise will inevitably break out.

The importance thus attached to this great movement by such an authority shows the vast potentialities of the race amity work and the vital need of its continuance. The Words of Bahá'u'lláh and of 'Abdu'l-Bahá appearing upon the program, the Bahá'í speakers, the humanitarian ideals expressed by eminent speakers who came to aid, the singing of the Bahá'í hymn, "Great Day of God," the assembling and cooperating of two groups traditionally separated and the sublime *Faith* and courage shown by the sponsor and her cohort of workers lifted the matter of race relations to a plane never before contemplated by those who had hitherto felt its burdens.

Under the leadership and through the sacrifices of the Bahá'ís of Washington three other amity conventions in after years were held. The Mount Pleasant Congregational Church opened its doors for two of these conferences and the Play-house in whole or part for the other. Christians, Jews, Bahá'ís, and people of various races mingled in joyous and serviceable array and the reality of religion shone forth. In this way, as Bahá'u'lláh reveals: "In truth, religion is a radiant light and an impregnable stronghold for the protection and welfare of the peoples of the world."[4]

Also as 'Abdu'l-Bahá says: "There is only one love which is unlimited and divine, and that is the love which comes with the breath of the Holy Spirit—the love of God—which breaks all barriers and sweeps all before it."

Eventually the Washington friends continued their race amity work in another form by organizing an interracial discussion group which continued for many years and did a very distinctive service, both by its activities and its fame as the incarnation of a bright ray of hope amid scenes where racial antagonism was traditionally rife. Stanwood Cobb, Mariam Haney, Coralie F. Cook, and Agnes S. Parsons were active leaders in this work. An interesting after effect of the first amity convention was the stimulus it gave to orthodox people, who started the organization of interracial committees very soon thereafter.

Springfield

The second city to respond to the urgent call of the Master was Springfield, Massachusetts, where at the time there were but three Bahá'ís, one of whom was an itinerant teacher. They consulted, and first of all communicated by cable, with 'Abdu'l-Bahá, telling their wish to hold a convention for amity. They were assured that God would confirm their labor of love. These friends were Roy Williams, Olive Kretz, and Grace Decker. Going to the aid of them were three more experienced Bahá'ís, William H. Randall and Alfred E. Lunt of Boston and Dr. Zia M. Bagdádí of Chicago. The local workers who cooperated included three clergymen, a rabbi, the mayor of Springfield and another public man of prominence. The *Springfield Republican*, one of the most powerful newspapers of New England, gave the best publicity. The date of the two sessions was December 5 and 6, 1921, and the city high school auditorium was well filled with those who received both instruction and entertainment. The work left a sweet spirit in Springfield. Perhaps this was best expressed by Rev. Neil McPherson, a venerable clergyman who with Dr. W. N. DeBerry and Rev. A. L. Boulden took part, and a year or more afterward said, "The Bahá'í teachings are all love!"

New York

The next city to undertake this important service was the metropolis of the country, New York. The date of this public conference devoted to interracial harmony was the period March 28 to 30, 1924. The Spiritual Assembly unobtrusively led with the following participating groups: the Community Church; the National Association for the Advancement of Colored People; the National Urban League; the Committee on International Cooperation of the League of Women Voters; and the organization known as America in the Making. The speakers were Mountfort Mills, Rabbi Stephen S. Wise, Dr. Alain Locke, James Weldon Johnson, Ruth Morgan, John Finley, Dr. John Herman Randall, Lucius Porter, Jane Addams, and Stephen P. Duggan. The plan was to attract people of other races as well as the colored and white. One of the best features of the program was the address of Dr. Franz Boas of Columbia University, who by scientific deductions appeared to lay waste the foundations of race prejudice. Quotations from the Words of Bahá'u'lláh and 'Abdu'l-Bahá were creative and impressive. This praiseworthy effort showed the possibilities of the work and led to a brilliant succession of similar conferences, interracial dinners, and fellowship meetings through the years, under the Banner of the Greatest Name and connecting Harlem,

Manhattan and Brooklyn, sections of New York. The names of Mary
Hanford Ford, Ludmila Bechtold, Saffa Kinney, Mr. and Mrs. E. R.
Mathews, Annie K. Lewis, Wandeyne LaFarge, W. E. B. DuBois, A. Philip
Randolph, Samuel Allan, James H. Hubert, Juliet Thompson, Harlan F.
Ober, Dr. Genevieve Coy, Horace Holley, Hopper Harris, Elsa Russell,
Hubert Dulany and others appear in these various plans with the added
inspiration of beautiful music. Especially outstanding for teaching and
nationalizing the fame and light of the Faith was the dinner given by the
National Race Amity Committee through the generosity of Mr. and Mrs.
E. R. Mathews, to the leaders of the New York Urban League and the
National Association for the Advancement of Colored People. This gala
event assembled about one hundred and fifty prominent people in the
banquet hall of one of the large hotels. The Bahá'í service, fine repast,
unique musical program, joint chairmanship of a white with a colored
teacher, number of addresses limited to a few minutes, wide publicity,
genial wit and humor, and what seemed the special favor of the Almighty
made this occasion one of great significance. All who attended seemed
grateful and happy. It harmonized some who had long been discordant,
even though in organizations working for a common end. Truly those
who serve reality obtain results.

Philadelphia

Philadelphia was the fourth city to respond to the idea. The Society of
Friends, popularly better known by the derisive title of Quakers, applied
to them centuries ago because of their opposition to warfare, gave hearty
cooperation to the Bahá'í community, which made great sacrifices to
present its ideals. The Bahá'ís on their part did a greater service for the
Friends. This convention was the first to indicate by announcement that
it was wholly under Bahá'í auspices. An appeal to the public read in part
as follows:

> All humanity should reflect the love of God for all His children.
> Hatred between races must be removed if we are to follow God's
> Word. A movement to fulfill the greatest law of Christ as well as to

follow the Light of Knowledge revealed in our day is the convention for amity between the white and colored races, Witherspoon Hall, October 22 to 23, 1924. The aim is to remove the gloom of conflict by the Light of spirituality. For only Divine Teachings can create harmony where human traditions have long established discord.

It had so happened that the Bahá'ís and the Society of Friends, at the same time, as moved by one Spirit, had planned interracial conferences. As the dates selected were contiguous but not conflicting, each agreed to boost the spiritual enterprise of the other as well as its own. The result was phenomenal success for both. The Bahá'í conference illustrated happily, as announced on the program, that thrilling statement of 'Abdu'l-Bahá: "This is a new cycle of human power. All the horizons of the world are luminous. . . . It is the hour of the unity of the sons of men and the drawing together of all races and all classes."[5]

Two large and exceptionally fine audiences attended and among those listed as speakers and workers, besides the local community, were Louise D. Boyle, Horace Holley, Dr. Herbert E. Benton of the Universalist Church, Agnes L. Tierney of the Society of Friends, Leslie Pinckney Hill, Albert Vail, Dr. Zia M. Bagdádí, Dr. John M. Henderson of the African M. E. Church, Dr. Alain Locke, Judge John M. Patterson and Hooper Harris. The goal of amity was nobly won. Philadelphia Bahá'ís improved Friendship Week to hold their second amity conference February 14, 1930, with the subjects, "How to Improve Race Relations," "New Proofs of the Oneness of Mankind," "A Brotherhood Which is Eternal," "A New Universal Brotherhood" and "God's Wonderful Plan for Humanity," and speakers among those who had served previous conferences.

Dayton

Dayton, Ohio, the "Gem City," was the fifth to express the need of an amity conference and to set itself a task which seemed far out of proportion to the strength of its two resident Bahá'ís. This was during that memorable year for amity congresses, 1927. Joined by two traveling [Bahá'í] teachers, the little group improved the momentum of a scheduled world unity conference to append an amity conference as its first session. Several liberal organizations were rallied to their support and Wilberforce University, a few miles distant at Xenia, gave the services of its highly trained Glee Club. This meeting was successful in promoting good will, spreading the fame of the Faith and seed sowing in very promising soil, as students are aspiring and have a future. The home of Xenia of Mrs. Ada M. Young, widow of the late Col. Charles Young, US Army, from this time became a center for Bahá'í activities in that section, with many interracial meetings and addresses at Wilberforce University to follow. The Dayton Bahá'ís, recruited in numbers, held a second amity conference April 12, 1929, using the services of Prof. M. N. Chatterjee of Antioch College and a Bahá'í speaker, with Josef McCoy, versatile and accomplished, as both entertainer and chairman. The names of Frances Fales, Helen McVey, Josef and Helen McCoy, Ada M. Young and Sylvia Margolis will be inseparably linked with the early evolution of the Bahá'í Faith in Dayton, which now has the blessing of a Spiritual Assembly.

Green Acre

Race amity conferences at Green Acre, the summer colony of the Bahá'ís in Maine, cover the decade beginning 1927. More than by any other great event since the passing of the Master, they were called into being by the moving eloquence of Shoghi Effendi, Guardian of the Bahá'í Faith, in his letter of April 12, 1927, to the National Spiritual Assembly. This letter came not long after the pilgrimage of a colored Bahá'í, Mrs. S. E. J. Oglesby of Boston, to the Holy Shrines at 'Akká and Haifa, she being the third of that race to make the pilgrimage. Like those preceding her, she received a warm welcome, meeting Shoghi Effendi and other members of the Holy Household. The letter of the Guardian mentions with approval the activities of the newly appointed National Racial Amity Committee and is a powerful portrayal of the needs of the work. The conferences began at this historic spot under most favorable conditions, having in addition to the seasoned workers of other conferences, the aid of Ruhí Effendi Afnán, a grandson of 'Abdu'l-Bahá, visiting America.

Among others were Devere Allen, editor of *The World Tomorrow,* Dr. Samuel McComb, founder of the Emanuel Movement, Rev. William Stafford Jones, Unitarian clergyman and Mesdames Edwina Powell and S. E. J. Oglesby, recent pilgrims to 'Akká. Some themes in conferences during the decade follow: "The New White Man;" "The New Negro;" "A New Vision of Human Oneness;" "Superior Men: The Lovers of Mankind;" "The Message of the Orient;" "Welcome!;" "The Message of the Negro Spiritual;" "The Practice of the Heavenly Virtues;" "The Temple of God: Its Light of Unity;" "The Oneness of Humanity;" "How the Supreme World Illumines This World;" "Making the World Better;" "Progress toward Racial Understanding;" "The Negro's Gift to Civilization;" "Youth's Amity Forum;" "Race Prejudice and Modern Civilization;" "Better Race Relations;" "Scientific and Spiritual Proofs of Human Oneness;" "Negro Civilization in Ancient Africa;" "How to Improve Race Relations;" "The Spirit's Fire of Attraction;" "The Great American Liberator;" "Economics and Race Relations;" "Negro Scientists Overcome Prejudice;" "Racial Amity and World Peace;" "A World Community;" "The Psychology of Prejudice."

Among the workers and speakers of this fruitful period may be mentioned: William H. Randall; Alfred E. Lunt; Dr. Leslie Pinckney Hill; Horce Holley; Juliet Thompson; Dr. Glenn A. Shook; F. St. George Spendlove; Hon. F. W. Hartford; Dr. Albert D. Heist; Doris McKay; James H. Hubert; May Maxwell; Paul Haney; Samuel A. Allen; Reginald G. Barrow; Albert Vail; Robert W. Bagnall; Agnes S. Parsons; Louie A. Mathews; Ludmila Bechtold; Rev. H. B. Harris; Prof. William Leo Hansberry; Dr. Walter B. Guy; Rev. Harry B. Taylor; Zylpha O. Mapp; Annie K. Lewis; Louise N. Thompson; Philip A. Marangella; Keith Ransom-Kehler; Harlan F. Ober; Grace Ober; Saffa Kinney; Orcella Rexford; Mary Hanford Ford; Elizabeth Greenleaf; Max Yergan; Stanwood Cobb; Judge Edward H. Adams; Siegfried Schopflocher; Carl Cartwright; Prof. J. S. Carter Troop; Mynta B. Trotman; Dr. T. E. A. McCurdy; Dorothy Richardson; Maxwell Miller; Mary Coristine; Sherley Graham; Dr. Genevieve Coy; George W. Goodman; Howard and Mabel Ives and Rúḥíyyih Khánum. It is with admiration and gratitude that this mention is made of but a few of those who have shared their treasures of mind and heart to bring about racial harmony and peace. A special tribute seems due to the last mentioned, Rúḥíyyih Khánum, née Mary Maxwell, now the consort of our noble Guardian. She was an amity worker from her earliest years, being without race consciousness in the selection of her friends and showing a maturity rarely found in one so young. She seemed always to grasp so subtle and profound a principle as the oneness of humanity with all its implications. While her frank, courageous and winsome influence will be missed in the West by young and old, let us hope that her prayers at the Holy Shrines in our behalf will be even more effective in shaping the destiny of the work she loves.

Praise belongs also the spiritual communities of Eliot and Portsmouth, to Boston friends and to Mrs. Lorol Schopflocher for their continued and delightful hospitality during the years, a pleasing and impressive feature of the amity work at Green Acre. These conferences have been cherished by the friends and have always ranked high among the season's attractions, pouring out their scientific and spiritual knowledge, beaming hope, cultivating talents, broadening horizons, overcoming prejudices, diffusing through the descent of bounty the divine fragrances and heralding the great message of the Manifestation of God.

Chicago

Chicago gave setting to a brilliant amity conference under the date of January 22, 1928. Its purpose was stated as improvement of race relations and strengthening friendships. This great city compared its own location to the center of the continent and its heart. The invitation was thus extended to cooperating friends to purify the heart that love and kindness might happily flow through it to all the arteries of the American continent. The response to this invitation filled, with an exceptionally fine audience, the large auditorium of Masonic Temple. Music and Bahá'í prayers brought a spiritual atmosphere to the gathering over which Albert Vail presided in his usually eloquent way. Following a prayer by Rev. Harold Kingsley of the Liberty Congregational Church were three addresses.

Prof. A. Eustace Haydon, teacher of Comparative Religions at the University of Chicago, said that men must be real friends, not on the basis of words but deeds. He advocated a reorganization of the social structure and a unity based upon loyalty to common ideals. He held that loyalty on a spiritual plane enriches and beautifies.

The second speaker, a representative of the colored race, presented some of the Bahá'í teachings on the overcoming of prejudices. As ignorance caused men to be narrow, those influences which had a tendency to broaden the horizons should be carefully noted. Travel, trade and commerce, and education are playing their part in the expansion of men's minds through a better acquaintance. But the only power that will completely make a conquest of prejudice is the reality of religion. This led us to the great flood of Light through the Revelation of Bahá'u'lláh.

Rabbi Louis Mann of Sinai Temple and also a professor at the University of Chicago, made a brilliant address frequently interrupted by applause, on the Oneness of Mankind. He declared that God in His Holy Book speaks of man, not of races, colors of nationalities, not of Jews or Christians. He deplored the fact that religious people so often allow business people to be far cleverer, in that the latter ignore racial and class limitations when looking for trade. Shall we do less when trying to serve God? Love and virtues have at times brought Jew and Christian together and will establish the unity of mankind. He expressed admiration for the Bahá'ís and his willingness to serve them at any time. The chairman told an interesting story of how a colored boy to whom white boys were hostile during the race riot had won them to friendliness by telling them the teaching wherein the Master had compared the different races to the varied flowers growing side by side in the same garden. The spirit won!

Chicago's amity activities continued over a number of years with monthly meetings resulting in a series of brilliant reports. The guidance of the Spiritual Assembly and the loving service put into the work by Rachel O. North, Fanny Lesch, Shelley N. Parker, Philip R. Savilles, Vivian Wesson and others is truly worthy of great admiration and praise.

Montréal

The Bahá'ís of Montréal, Canada, amplified their record of service to humanity by their amity convention of February 11 and 12, 1928. They expressed the hope that their stand in this regard would be emulated by all the cities of America. The artistic program bore quotations from the Words of Moses, Jesus, Bahá'u'lláh, and 'Abdu'l-Bahá. The Young Men's Christian Association, Channing Hall and the Union Congregational Church, colored, gave their cooperation. Hon. Agnes MacPhail, the first and only woman member of the Canadian Parliament and a strong advocate of peace, was the first speaker. She seemed much pleased with the Bahá'í Writings, demonstrating a most friendly spirit. Other contributors were Mr. and Mrs. W. S. Maxwell, Rev. Laurence Clare, Rev. Charles Este, Dr. E. M. Best and F. St. George Spendlove. The three meetings had appreciative audiences, a sign of the growing consciousness of unity. It is interesting to note that the only colored church of that great city and which had a part in this conference is made up of people of various denominations drawn together and that two of its successive pastors have been taught the Bahá'í Faith by that center. The contacts of the Bahá'ís with the students of McGill University are also a bright sign of promise. One of them, Miss Mathews of Louisville, Kentucky, after her return home was instrumental in arranging for a Bahá'í lecture which was the means of giving the message to many hundreds of students. The ardent Bahá'í love and understanding which these friends put into service has far-reaching results.

Urbana

Urbana, seat of the great University of Illinois, is a fine strategic center for Bahá'í activity. Over a period of many years it has been active and successful in amity work, touching the lives of many groups within range. While such work is continuous, a special amity conference was arranged for May 6, 1928. The music was planned by Mrs. F. M. Leslie and drew upon Negro spirituals largely. Edwin W. Mattoon served as chairman. Dr. W. Russell Tylor of the university's department of sociology was the principal speaker and went elaborately into a scientific study of humanity in races, giving proofs of its essential unity but recommending a wise approach to so complicated a problem. This was followed by another speaker with the Bahá'í teachings. The place of meeting, Lincoln Hall of the university, gave a classic setting to this conference and its spirit was most refreshing. This Bahá'í community, which is quite influential, has arranged both within and without the university many meetings for visiting Bahá'í teachers.

Wilmette

The Bahá'í center of Wilmette has the bounty of close proximity to the Mashriqu'l-Adhkár which some of its members serve. They perform a valued aid for racial amity by their charming courtesy and kindness to visitors of all races. Outstanding and distinguished were the services of their fellow member, Dr. Zia M. Bagdádí, an associate for many years. The son of Mustafá Bagdádí, one of the most renowned and useful of the Oriental friends, he was the sole Bahá'í of the Occident whose life touched successively three great leaders of the Faith. As a child of three in the Holy Presence of Bahá'u'lláh he was given by Him his name, Zia, meaning "light." As a student at Beirut he went through perilous days of devotion and was sent to America by 'Abdu'l-Bahá, Whom he knew so well and loved so devotedly. His loyalty to the administrative order created by the Will,[6] his great personal love for Shoghi Effendi are jewels of memory to those who knew him. His courage was leonine in demonstrating the oneness of humanity. He met his fellow beings on the basis of merit and attraction to the Faith and this ideal he lived in his business, social and professional life, whether East or West, whether he labored in Chicago or the far South. Ever remembered will be his cool courage in going to the rescue of the colored Bahá'ís during the race riot when such an undertaking, through the tying up of traffic, meant great expense to one of modest means and journeying to another section of the city incurred the peril of almost sure death. His passing in the fullness of his powers fills his friends with grief; but his many virtues are an ornament to the world which leave a fadeless mark. Under this intrepid leadership, the Bahá'ís of Wilmette arranged a succession of gatherings in the home of Dr. and Mrs. Bagdádí, the Bourgeois studio and in the foundation of the Temple. They also aided and inspired similar efforts in the neighboring city of Evanston, carrying the campaign of divine education into the Northwestern University through the class in Comparative Religions and elsewhere stimulating such interest as resulted in a race amity meeting addressed by the mayor of the city, the former Vice-President of the United States, Gen. Charles Dawes, and other notables. The meeting of those of different races, colors, and social ranks was the means of confirmation and power to the workers.

Various Cities

The year 1927 saw the genial fires of racial amity cheering and heartening various cities. Geneva, New York, in the dead of winter and despite the accident of meeting in a hall that was not heated, where heavy wraps were necessary to comfort, carried through a meeting for this noble purpose which all present enjoyed, divine enthusiasm entering hearts warmed by the Fires of God and minds illumined by the signs of reality. At Portsmouth, New Hampshire, the friends gave glad welcome to Mabel Ives who traveled a long distance to sound the note of interracial accord in the friendly atmosphere of the Women's Club and with the association of beautiful music. Rochester, New York, a city famous for its traditions of freedom, held a conference that was highly successful under the banner of the Greatest Name. Doris McKay, thoroughly alive to the idea, made an impressive chairman. A remarkable address was made by Rev. Raymond Prior Sanford, executive pastor of the Brick Church. It was a stirring account of the melting pot of racial antipathies during the period following the world war and a most powerful plea for the brotherhood that is real. This was followed by a Bahá'í address in which both scientific and spiritual proofs were given. This conference inspired a column's report in the leading journal of that city, the *Rochester Democrat and Chronicle*. It was most friendly and favorable to the Cause.

Boston

Boston, among the early cities to become active, inaugurated meetings which were to be extended over a period of years with a brilliant gathering during November, 1927. Dorothy Richardson, contralto, and George A. Fernandez, tenor, gave a festival of song. Dr. John Herman Randall spoke most eloquently upon "The Growing Appreciation between Races." A second address was delivered by William Stanley Braithwaite, famous colored poet, literary critic, and anthologist, who said that he felt moved by a high sense of duty to be present on such an occasion. The educational and spiritual value of this and the series of meetings that followed was to make the Boston friends wish entirely to forget color as a sign separating mortals. A. Philip Randolph, industrial leader, was one of the most polished and brilliant speakers at other meetings, all of which had unusual value.

Detroit

The friends in Detroit under the rallying cry, "New Views on an Old, but Unsolved Human Problem," raised the standard of unity in a conference March 14, 1929, using the auditorium of the Federation of Women's Clubs. Mrs. Philomene Altman, representing the Bahá'ís, presided and the speakers were Rabbi Leon Fram, Rev. Frank Adams, and Rev. Augustus P. Record. Their subjects were respectively, "The Search for Brotherhood," "The Chief Obstacle to World Unity," and "The New Internationalism." These religious leaders represented progressive schools, and their brief and eloquent addresses indicated a search for reality. Under the caption, "Vision of the New Age," their attention and that of the audience was focused upon the ideals and message of the Bahá'í teachings. It proved a profitable and enjoyable evening for each and all. Other efforts of a like nature were made during the years following, to have the races know each other; this in cooperation with the National Racial Amity Committee. The services of these friends are unforgettable.

Atlantic City

One of the most remarkable of the racial amity conferences was that of Atlantic City, New Jersey, in that it had but one active Bahá'í worker on the field and was opposed by the orthodox among the clergy, an attitude which unfavorably affected the press. The date of this conference was April 19, 1931, and not less than twelve organizations of the island city were brought into cooperation in furtherance of its object. These were: the Society of Friends, the Young Men's and Young Women's Christian Associations, four churches, two schools, the Colored Board of Trade, the Unity Truth Center and the Jewish Community Center. The thought of the conference was directed into Bahá'í channels and the Bahá'ís of Philadelphia cooperated by coming and giving the message. A high note was struck in fellowship in a way to impress many of the noblest people of the city, about four hundred of whom attended. It was said to be by far the best meeting of its kind ever there attempted and it came at a time when race relations were much disturbed with blows struck at economic values. Other interracial committees had mustered but a feeble response. There was an outpouring of love and good will in the utterances of noble speakers from both groups, one of the most eloquent of whom was a former southern judge. Those who had heard the teachings of old and those to whom the good news came for the first time were alike charmed by the spell of the hour. The printed program carried lines composed by two friends:

> O Temple of the living Word
> Through Whom the universe is stirred!
> Eternal Presence hid from sight
> By countless veils of dazzling Light,
> Yet viewed by those in every clime
> Who penetrate the clouds of time,
> Prepared with inner eye and ear
> The PROMISED ONE to see and hear:
> Let Thy sweet concord fill man's heart
> And all the din of strife depart!
> Deign Thou our peaceful aims to bless;
> Make real our vision; grant success!
> Creative Source of ancient Power
> Let brotherhood adorn this hour!

The place of meeting was the great auditorium and convention hall on the boardwalk and the program carried Words of Bahá'u'lláh: "Peace be to those who follow Guidance;" also those of 'Abdu'l-Bahá: "The lovers of mankind, these are the superior men of whatever race, class, or color they may be."

Pittsburgh

Pittsburgh, Pennsylvania, one of the great cities visited by 'Abdu'l-Bahá, arranged a conference October 25 to 27, 1931, with three sessions. The Central Young Men's Christian Association and the Oakland Methodist Church cooperated with the plan by giving the use of their auditoriums and helping the attendance. The other place of meeting was the Frick Training School. A Bahá'í chairman and speaker served each session. Other workers were a rabbi, five clergymen, and two social workers. An impressive link with the past was Mrs. Walter S. Buchanan, whose distinguished father, the late Dr. W. H. Councill of Alabama, as president of its Normal School for colored students had a vision of interracial friendliness and cooperation and had been its eloquent advocate at a time when few believed it possible. He did not live to hear the Bahá'í message, but it seemed a blessing to his memory that his daughter and son-in-law should, hearing it, have become confirmed believers and have a part in this conference.

The program was attractive in its artistic beauty and statement of the Golden Rule from many religions and Bahá'í quotations. As Pittsburgh is known to be one of the most conservative of American cities in religious matters, the small community of Bahá'ís showed great courage in taking this stand for the essential unity. Those who met them shared light and hope. Their work was like a breeze from the Eternal Garden of Roses.

The Far West

News has reached us from time to time of the interracial dinners arranged by the friends in Denver, Colorado, high up among the Rocky Mountains; of the great esteem in which the Bahá'ís are held by Fritz Cansler of the Young Men's Christian Association Branch and of the faithful cooperation he gives whenever called to serve. Happy indeed have been those who partook of such heavenly treasures enriching both mind and spirit. Those who have been fortunate enough to see in action the Bahá'ís in the Bay Cities, Portland and Seattle, know that racial amity is one of their spontaneous habits, whether or not formally expressed. They are mindful of the needs of the Day of God. Most inspiring, however, have been the reports that have come from Los Angeles, where special success was attained under the brilliant leadership of Sara E. Witt, who developed a genius for this work. She succeeded with the cooperation of the Spiritual Assembly in widening the circle of racial amity activities so as to include not only the white and colored, but the red Indians, aborigines of America, also the Chinese and Japanese, who are found in such numbers in that region. A number of meetings taking the form of banquets appeared to give to those who shared them a foretaste of Heaven. As a sample of this work, the dinner of February 27, 1932, may be mentioned. Nellie S. French, a member of the National Spiritual Assembly, presided with grace, kept the meeting in motion and made all feel cordially welcome. A number of Indians under the leadership of Chief Standing Bear and decorated with their feathers and paint were in attendance. It was of this race that 'Abdu'l-Bahá indicated a bright future when they would become imbued with the Spirit of the Bahá'í Faith. Robert Theiss voiced the Oneness of Humanity in behalf of the spiritual assembly. The Indian Chief then prayed and with eloquent voice praised peace as the covenant among all races. Among other speakers Joseph R. Scherer dwelt upon the unity which would come with the adoption of a universal tongue. Emmett R. Smith, colored, made a plea for the world court and peace. J. Kam Machida, president of the Chinese Club, who lives internationally by being the wife of a Japanese, made her spirit of conciliation felt. W. J. Clarendon, president of the Japan-American Club, and his wife extended cordial greetings. On this occasion their presence expressed a heroic resolve, as on that very afternoon of this conference dinner Mr. Clarendon had met with a painful and dangerous accident, which he refused to let enforce his absence from so notable a gathering. Nipo Strongheart, who let it be known that he was himself partly of Indian blood, spoke impressively for justice between the races. The program was further varied by an Indian tribal dance. Near the end of this fascinating program and after many distinguished guests had been made known, Williard P. Hatch was called upon to speak for the Bahá'ís. He was first of all overcome by the Spirit, a Presence which all seemed to feel. Then recovering his composure, he found his voice and all were melted into unity by the great Message and its wonderful ideals. The Bahá'í Benediction played by Shahnaz Waite, who composed it, closed a meeting memorable and of great joy.

Cincinnati

Among the last amity conferences of which there is a record is that of Cincinnati, one of the most interesting and influential of all. The Bahá'ís of the Crescent City having with one mind and heart decided upon such an undertaking, under the guidance of their Spiritual Assembly, proceeded to work the matter out in the most methodical and scientific way. Besides their own organization, they succeeded in laying under the tribute of service some sixteen others noted for welfare and progress. Among these were centers of culture, such as Wilberforce University, the University of Cincinnati, the Cincinnati School of Music, Hebrew Union College and the Sherman School, Churches both liberal and orthodox, the Bahá'í Center of Lima and the National Race Amity Committee. They touched the heart of the city, evoking high praise through twenty-two press articles, only two of which were paid advertisements. Due to ceaseless rains over the period of three days, the attendance was small; but results should in nowise be measured by this. As according to the law of creation, "All life begins in water," rain is one of the signs of bounty. The rain of bounty within the auditorium of the YWCA, graciously given for all sessions, seemed even more generous than the falling weather without. Such was the marshalling of gifted speakers that no imaginable phase of the constructive side of the American race problem appeared to be left untouched. The printed programs also reached wide areas of progressive thinkers through the courtesy of the local peace society which lent its mailing list of about nine hundred names.

Dorothy Baker, as chairman, opened the conference, voicing its purposes with golden phrases and spiritual attraction. Among other distinguished speakers was Rabbi Samuel Wohl, who but the summer before had visited the Holy Shrines on Mount Carmel and felt oneness with the Bahá'ís. John W. Scott, the scholarly principal of a colored school, nobly gave utterance to the spirit of interracial cooperation, using figures of speech drawn from the curious workmanship of nature. Prof. Gustave G. Carlson, visiting Professor at the University of Cincinnati, gave a curiously interesting study of race prejudices, exposing their fallacies. Other inspiring speakers were Rev. E. H. Oxley and Rev. C. Baker Pearl, pastors of colored churches. The Bahá'í ideals were set forth by chairmen and visiting Bahá'ís. The music was of an exceptionally fine quality. On Sunday afternoon following the conference, a reception was held at the home of Mr. and Mrs. Joseph Stauss; it was especially helpful to those newly interested and diffused much happiness.

Interracial Journeys

One of the most unusual and interesting forms of amity activities was that of interracial cooperative journeys by white and colored Bahá'ís into the heart of the South. There were three such trips, all inspired by a line from the Holy Land expressing the wish on the part of the Guardian, that two teachers whom he mentioned should campaign in the South together. Consultation with Dr. Will W. Alexander of the Southern Interracial Commission also brought assurances that the parties to such a plan, white and colored, would meet with many agreeable surprises. Thus the Holy Land and good old Georgia were animated by one spirit in an age of marvels.

During the autumn of 1931, Philip A. Marangella, an Italo-American Bahá'í, and Chauncey Northern, a famous musician of the colored race, journeyed South to give the Bahá'í message. Setting out from New York by motor, they visited Washington, Richmond, Hampton, Enfield, North Carolina, Orangeburg and Columbia, South Carolina, and found wonderful opportunities in schools and colleges for their entertainment of poesy, song and spiritual illumination. They met many who had previously heard of the Bahá'í teachings gladly and were now pleased to renew their interest in so artistic a setting. Others were hearing the call of the Kingdom for the first time, but, almost without exception, they found attracted souls in those they sought to reach. The journal of their work is beautiful and thrills with the joy of life. One of the most interesting discoveries of their trip was to find the same interest at the University of South Carolina, for whites, as at Allan University and Benedict College, located in the same City of Columbia, for colored.

During the spring of 1932, Willard McKay of Pittsburgh, a former instructor in the University of Texas, and Louis G. Gregory, racial amity worker, met by agreement at Atlanta, Georgia, where they started a Bahá'í study class and conveyed the teachings to various educational and religious organizations. They later went to Tuskegee Institute and the two State Normal Schools of Alabama for colored at Montgomery and Normal, in all of which they were honored and welcomed and given wonderful opportunities for service. As they made use of the ordinary method of travel by omnibus and sometimes found it necessary to room together, their work caused a sensation and evoked inquiries wherever they went as to an interest which could make representatives of two races so happily united in service. Later they went to Fisk University, Nashville, Tennessee, and had many opportunities to speak, also addressing the city High School. At Cincinnati they served meetings arranged by Bahá'ís and were luncheon guests of Prof. W. O. Brown of the University of Cincinnati, a southerner whom they met through an Atlanta connection and the professor's keen interest in better race relations. Their trip ended with work at Columbus, Ohio, in meetings with the friends. The detailed report of this itinerary written by Mr. McKay consists of about two thousand words and is unusually interesting.

During the winter of 1933, Charles A. Wragg, a Bahá'í and native of Australia, and the writer took a business trip together into the South and improved it for teaching. Starting from Portsmouth, New Hampshire, they visited nine cities, six of which were in Virginia, their most notable work being in Petersburg, Norfolk, Charlottesville and Roanoke. They used a motor car and no friction arose as a result of their travels together, although so much at variance with custom.

Racial amity suffers a grievous loss by the departure from this mortal plane of our distinguished brother, Alfred E. Lunt, August 12, 1937. His sacrifices and devotion in many lines of service were extraordinary. He took a deep and special interest in the improvement of race relations, exemplifying the oneness of humanity as a principle of life. He served as chairman and speaker at various amity conferences and it was upon his motion as a member of the National Spiritual Assembly, that the series of amity conferences that gave such light and happiness to Green Acre was set in motion. In the pursuit of this ideal he had the united cooperation of his talented family. Highly trained and very able, he was strong, proficient and faithful to the end, with spiritual attraction and personal charm.

"The bravest are the tenderest, the loving are the daring!" Like an aroma of heavenly incense is the fragrance of so glorious a life.

In ending what is but a crude and fragmentary sketch of this one phase of Bahá'í work during the years, mention must be made of the letters and reports by the national and local committees, beautiful in expression, absorbing in interest, stimulating effort and raising high our hopes. Appreciation also goes to those devoted friends who have compiled the teachings which have a special bearing upon this subject and to one who, in addition, has marshaled the thoughts of contemporary men of genius whose discoveries in sociology reflect the great Light of Unity appearing in this marvelous age. Grateful acknowledgments must also be made to the Administrative Order which in letter and spirit has promulgated this vital use of the new civilization and to each and all who to any extent and in any way have aided these endeavors.

Since the passing of 'Abdu'l-Bahá, the guiding wisdom of Shoghi Effendi has been the greatest blessing. At all times he clearly discerns the needs; discloses the state of the world; encourages the workers; opens new vistas of duty; clarifies methods; reconciles conflicting viewpoints and applies the teachings with consummate skill to the capacities of the day. He also keeps before his spiritual army the vision of a united world, that goal toward which all progress wends. His is a continuous motion which inspires others to move.

Considering the present state of mankind, finite strength seems directed in this spiritual enterprise toward a superhuman task; but divine promises assure victory. Observe the little ball thrown into the fountain. Buffeted by the water it dances without ceasing upon its uneven, moving floor, air current forming invisible walls for its tenuous home. It is light, elastic and rotund, traits which augment its adaptability and power to please. But that moment the flow ceases its house collapses; gravity resumes its sway and the dull earth reclaims its own. Racial amity, peace, brotherhood, with all they imply of new alignments in the human world, are now ordained of God. Those who prize them will try to keep in motion, relying upon the Source of all good. Zephyrs of Heaven are wafted; streams of knowledge are gushing forth; the Orb of Truth is gloriously ascendant. The transformation of the world of being, on the plane of reality, is already an accomplished fact.

---

1 0

Social Basis of World Unity
Elsie Austin

This essay was originally published in volume 4 of
The Bahá'í World, pp. 694–8.

Today, people who seek to stress the spiritual basis of peace and justice among men, or who dare to accent the necessity for the regeneration of human hearts and characters as the first step to needed social change, are usually rebuffed by those who immediately cry out, "Oh, you must be practical and realistic."

This is because so many folk think that the only practical approach to human problems is one which deals immediately with outward evidences of what is desirable. They do not see human needs beyond the specific projects devised for education and security. Outwardly these matters do represent the things which separate the "Haves" from the "Have Nots" in human society, and if you look at them in this light, they may seem to be the sole issues which have all along produced restlessness, division and strife among men.

However, any social program which is to operate for true world betterment must of necessity go beyond outward evidences, if it is to be really practical. The best plans for social cooperation and peace are always limited by the kind of human beings who must use and apply them. There is no more realistic force in the world today than the Bahá'í Faith. In its teachings and its social program there are profoundly realistic approaches to the fundamental social changes which must be the basis of any real and lasting unity for mankind.

The Bahá'í Faith is first of all a Faith which harmonizes the inward incentives and outward procedures to unity. Outward procedures give the means for unity, and inward incentives give the heart for unity. There is great difference between folk who have the means for unity and the folk who have the heart for unity.

Legislation and the interplay of conflicting social interests may furnish a kind of means for unity and even a certain state of outward compliance. However, legislation and the pressures of expediency have never been able to get at the inward fears, jealousies, greeds and animosities of men. And it is these which furnish the vicious inner motives which can browbeat the intelligence of men and make mockery of outward social compliance. Nearly every day we see tragic instances of failure where social change depends upon means alone. Instances where people nullify and obstruct legislation, where they sabotage social effort or fail to produce and support the kind of courageous policies and action needed for the patterns and standards consistent with just and enlightened ideals. The means for unity is there, but legislation is killed or evaded; communities lose their moral integrity in compromise with policies of hatred and division, and people excuse themselves from honest upright action by saying, "Law is not the way to do this." "The time is not ripe" or "This is the right policy, but we must work up to it gradually." Now, all such people are really saying is, "I have not the heart to do this thing" or "The people whose opinion I fear have not the heart for forthright action about this, and I do not know how to reach them."

The religion of Bahá'u'lláh, founder of the Bahá'í Faith, begins with that essential spiritual regeneration of the human being which creates a heart for brotherhood and impels action for the unity of mankind. Bahá'u'lláh has made it very plain that the test of Faith is its social force. Principle and social planning are useless until they are rendered dynamic by the stamina and will of men to enforce and apply spiritual ethics to human affairs.

The second great realism of the Bahá'í Faith is that it provides new patterns for the application of spiritual principle to the social problems of humanity.

When Bahá'u'lláh first proclaimed some eighty years ago, "This is the hour of the coming together of all the races and nations and classes. This is the hour of unity among the sons of men," the prophecy was a far-fetched ideal to the world of jealous politics and cultural isolation which received it. But the unity of mankind today is no mere social necessity.

It is not surprising then to see that human unity is an increasingly popular subject for liberal thought and action. Nor is it surprising that programs to foster unity are being launched on every hand. Yet so many of the bona fide efforts for unity are being fatally compromised because they must be launched through the established social patterns which preserve old disunities. Do people learn brotherhood and the spiritual attitudes and social cooperation which brotherhood involves by lectures or hesitant compromising ventures, which leave untouched and un-changed the separate education, separate worship, separate security, separate social planning which shape every phase of their community living—embittering separations made in terms of differences of race, creed, culture and nationality? Any social pattern which elaborately preserves and accents these outward differences and their resultant inward animosities must of necessity crucify the objective of social unity.

The Bahá'í Teachings not only destroy without equivocation the fallacies which have nourished social strife and disunity, but they provide new patterns of social living and development through which men learn brotherhood by performance.

And what realistic way is there, you may ask, to deal with the ancient bitter diversities of race, religion and culture? What can be done with the changing pressures of unstable economics and the conflicting education of the world's peoples?

The Bahá'í Faith provides for the diversities of religion, that long needed centers of reconciliation, which can produce harmonious under-standing of its varying prophets and systems. Bahá'u'lláh has shown us in the Bahá'í Revelation that the great revealed religions of the world are like lamps which carry the pure light of Divine Truth providing social teaching and discipline for humanity. But as that lamp is borne by human hands, there are periods when conflicting interpretations of the Divine Word, dogmas and superstitions, alienate and divide men. Periods when the temptations of material power pervert religion into an instrument for the exploitation and suppression of human development. It is because of this that new lamps have always come and will always come. Each of the great lamps tests the social force of the others. In this men should find source for progress, not reason for strife. God in His mercy has provided in the Divine Faiths a continuous and successive renewal of Universal Spiritual Truth.

The Bahá'í learns the relation and ordered unfoldment of Truth in all Divine Religions thus Spiritual Faith is lifted above the period differences of its various names and systems. Is it unrealistic that in a world so in need of spiritual regeneration, Jews, Christians, Moslems and Believers of all Divine Faiths should be given that which will relate their spiritual purposes and development and thus enable them to travel harmoniously a wide free path to greater social demonstration and understanding of the Truth? Is this not a more effective way to create the heart for unity than the elaborate separations and the jealous fencing off of Religious paths? Today men so preserve and concentrate upon their symbolic differences that the common goal is lost in confusion and animosity.

There are really no diversities of race to those who truly accept the fact that all mankind is God's creation. Yet the outward differences of color, physiognomy and culture have annoyed and divided us. When members of the human family meet each other who have striking differences in appearance and manners, they resort very naturally to reactions of fear, distaste and derision, which grow out of the human complex for conformity and the fear of strangeness. Unity of mankind is not only a basic principle in the Bahá'í Faith, but it is also the basis of a new social pattern in terms of which Bahá'ís worship, work, educate themselves and contribute to their capacities to civilization. Living in a Bahá'í community is a matter of learning differences, appreciating them and achieving with them great loyalties to human welfare, which are above the narrow confinements of race, creed and class, color and temperament. The most practical knowledge in the world is the knowledge that the world can never become what so many people like to believe; a world in which we make other people look, act, and understand in terms of that with which we are familiar. That kind of world is neither possible nor desirable. What we really want is a world of harmonized differences, where a man can make his contribution with other men for the good of all mankind. This is the world of the Bahá'í Community, a community covering seventy-eight national backgrounds and thirty-one racial origins and Heaven knows how many temperaments and cultural backgrounds in this first one hundred years. A growing Community which operates with every possible human difference to take into consideration, yet its members through practicing and perfecting their practice of the Bahá'í Teachings, have achieved a unity of objectives through which entirely new social patterns, standards and virtues are being evolved.

People do not like to mention religion and economics in the same breath. The problem is that of the economically disinherited who in bitter restless upsurge change periodically the pressures and controls of this world's unstable economics. It is practical to talk of trade policies, of commerce regulations and spheres of influence, now. However, the world must soon face the fact that economic instability and the bitter struggle and suffering which go on because of it, have a question of human motives, human development, behind them. Motives behind the failure to use opportunity, or the use of it to selfishly acquire and control wealth, goods, and services, constitute the real factors causing the unhealthy inequalities, the exploitation and suppression in human society. Bahá'u'lláh stressed the need of a spiritual basis as the first step in the development of stable world economics. The extremes of poverty and vast wealth are not only matters of material opportunity and education, they are also matters of greed and slothfulness in human characters.

Material education and spiritual enlightenment must be applied to bring the kind of economic adjustments which will make possible responsible efforts for all people and insure a just distribution of wealth, goods and services for all people.

Until then, we are all, regardless of our skins, creeds and countries, caught economically between the evil extremes which are produced by the Jeeter Lesters and those masters of selfish financial genius, who, like a cancerous growth, feed upon and weaken the earth's human and material resources.

Nothing but the wholesome regeneration of human hearts and establishment of new social objectives for the efforts and acquisitions of men, will in the final analysis remedy these ills.

The great realisms of the Bahá'í Faith lie in its new spiritual teachings and in the new social patterns which they provide for needed development of mankind; a development which will turn men from the beliefs and superstitions which are destructive to human solidarity and create in them the heart to initiate and perfect new standards, new morals and new undertakings for a great new era of civilization.

These achievements are possible when man is afforded that perfect combination of Human and Spiritual Unity. 'Abdu'l-Bahá, the great expounder of the Bahá'í Teachings, has described it in these words:

> Human Unity or solidarity may be likened to the body, whereas unity from the breaths of the Holy Spirit is the spirit animating the body. This is a perfect unity. It creates such a condition in mankind that each one will make sacrifices for the other and the utmost desire will be to forfeit life and all that pertains to it in behalf of another's good. It is in the unity which through the influence of the Divine Spirit is permeating the Bahá'ís, so that each offers his life for the other and strives with all sincerity to attain His good pleasure. This is the unity that caused twenty thousand people in Iran to give their lives in love and devotion to it. It made the Báb the target of a thousand arrows and caused Bahá'u'lláh to suffer exile and imprisonment for forty years. This unity is the very spirit of the body of the world.[1]

Racial Amity

Louis Gregory

This report of an address given at the First Convention for Amity
between the White and Colored Races, held in Washington, DC,
was originally published in *Bahá'í Year Book*, 1925–6.

All races, tribes, sects and classes share equally
in the bounty of their Heavenly Father.
The only real difference lies in the degree of faithfulness, of obedience to
the laws of God. There are some who are as lighted torches; there are others
who shine as stars in the sky of humanity. The lovers of mankind, these
are the superior men, of whatever nation, creed or color they may be.
—'ABDU'L-BAHÁ

The new springtime is the spiritual springtime, with the flow of the light
and the love of God, the Divine Unity, into the hearts of mankind.
When the springtime comes, the winter, with its decay, degradation,
and death, has passed away, and we find the sun shines with brilliancy
and splendor, and that clouds of mercy shower their drops upon
humankind. We feel these zephyrs of divine providence waft upon all.
The light of reality gleams. The human heart becomes more tender and

sympathetic to the needs of its fellow beings, and all these vibrations of love that are transmitted from the Kingdom of God have their play in the hearts of men and make more certain and real this thought of brotherhood. We have our problems to solve in this country, but let us not become despondent over them, realizing that today the whole world is having its problems and difficulties. There is no country in the world today that has not difficulties equaling, if not surpassing, our own. I do not say this with the suggestion that misery loves company, but in order that we may not be despondent and think that these difficulties are hindrances. The divine springtime has appeared and the great enlightened principles, which are the light and progress of the whole world of humanity, are set in motion. These relate to the great peace, the universality of truth, to the great law that humanity is one, even as God is one, to the elevation of the station of woman, who must no longer be confined to a limited life but be everywhere recognized as the equal and helpmeet of man. These pertain to the universality of education, to the oneness of language, to the solution of this economic problem which has vexed the greatest minds of the world and its noblest hearts, and to that supreme dynamic power, the Holy Spirit of God, whose outpouring upon the whole world of flesh will make this a world of light, of joy, and of triumph. "In His Name," as the Herald[1] proclaimed, "In the name of God, the victor of the most victorious, proclaim! God will assist all those who arise to serve Him. No one is able to deprive Him of His majesty, His dominion, His sovereignty; for in the Heavens and the earth, and in all the realms of God, He is the victorious and the conqueror!" If we follow the Creator in all His marvelous work, we shall find that it is characterized by infinite diversity and variety. Wherever the human eye moves in creation we see variegated forms. In the mineral kingdom if you should bring together a number of jewels, the diamond, the emerald, the ruby, the sapphire, the pearl, you will find that their combined beauty is greater than any single element. They enhance each other's value. Traveling through the far western country one may see thousands of sheep gathered together in a peaceful fold, one shepherd and one fold. The fact that some of these sheep are black and others are white does not make the slightest difference in that community of interest, for they know each other not by their color but by their kind, and they love each other in response to that spirit of God which vibrates in all creation. One star differs from another in magnitude, but each and all of these stars contribute to the brilliancy of the heavens. We have heard the wonderful harmony of an orchestra. We have heard those rich strains. Have you ever stopped to consider that in an orchestra the words, the music, the voices, the instruments may be different; and yet exquisite harmony, under the guidance of a great master, may come from that orchestra? The world has had a note of discord for many thousand years, and it must impress itself upon every reasonable man that war, force, and violence are the greatest calamities that afflict the world of mankind. But now we are striving for the note of harmony. The thought of harmony, itself, is a happy thought, something that makes the hearts of men joyful, something that makes their minds flash with the gems of reality. For our own peace, safety, and salvation, we should make every effort to bring harmony out of these discordant notes that have been struck for time and ages throughout the world.

The races living side by side need each other. If even two communities which are near each other cooperate, it works to the commercial development and the happiness of both. We know the advantage and benefit which comes through cooperation when it affects two great nations, even though their ideals and principles and self-interest differ in every stage of their growth; but, today we need a harmony which is so universal that it will bind together the hearts of all these struggling elements which make up creation. Let us follow the guidance and the wisdom of God! Have you stopped to observe that the clouds of His mercy shower upon all the world of humanity; that the air we breathe is not confined to one church, or one synagogue, or one mosque, but the universal bounty of God supports all life and creation? The sunshine, with its great splendor, is not limited to this class or that class, or this race or that race, or one nation or another, but it beautifies and glorifies the whole realm of existence. God's is the universal bounty and He loves all of His children. He has provided for them out of that great love. Shall men, therefore, reverse the purposes of God? Shall we reject the divine wisdom and initiate a different plan? If the divine plan is one of light, shall we make ours one of darkness? If the divine plan is one of providence, shall we devise a plan of greed? If the divine plan is one of altruism, shall we make ours the plan of selfishness? If the divine plan is universal tolerance, shall we inaugurate a plan of prejudice and pride? How can man escape disaster and humiliation if he is so self-centered and so self-satisfied that he attempts to reverse the principles of God?

The races living side by side have a common origin and a common destiny. From God we came and to Him we return, and we have many things in common. We live in the same favored land; we are warmed by the same sunshine; we strive for those same virtues and ideals which adorn and beautify the home; we have the same virtue of patriotism (and may this embrace the world!); we speak the same language; and, most significant of all, we profess the same religion. If we but put our religion into practice, and do not quarrel about its form, this alone would be sufficient to solve any human problem. But there is more than this to consider. In the past the white people of America have done a very noble service to the colored people of our land, and this is something we should stop to consider. About the time of the civil war you fought each other for our freedom. That is one thing which we should not wish to forget. The eloquent Senator has referred to the progress made by the colored people in America as distinguished from their backward condition in Africa. This, too, is a service which has come to us through you, from contact with your civilization. This is something that we should appreciate. This is something that all thoughtful people must appreciate. On the other hand, if you stop to consider the other side of the question you may find that there are some services which are valuable which the black people of America have rendered the white people. Lest I, who am outwardly identified with one racial group should be thought to be claiming too much for my own, I wish to quote to you the ideas of two distinguished southerners: Passing through the city of Atlanta a few months ago, I saw the statue to the Hon. Henry W. Grady, a statesman of the New South, and one of its most brilliant advocates, now passed away. It was this enlightened statesman and friend of men who declared that one of the greatest mistakes ever made was that this country did not erect a monument to commemorate the loyalty and fidelity of black men and women during that awful period of the civil war. About a year ago it was my pleasure to listen to an ex-confederate soldier, Doctor Boags of Florida, a man bowed by the weight of 80 years, who had come from his home in Florida, leaving a sick bed, and had taken a journey to Washington to speak upon this very question. The subject which he selected was the golden rule applied to the race question, and the eloquent speech which he delivered was a vibration of love. He said more for us, that ex-confederate veteran, than we are willing, in our most sanguine moments, to claim for ourselves. So I say to you that these enlightened souls saw the relationships of these races to each other. It is only by cooperation, mutual appreciation, and good will that we can get anywhere in the solution of these problems that vex us. If this room were filled with darkness, we could not remove that darkness by intensifying the darkness, nor can we remove discord from the face of the earth by increasing discord. Darkness has no reality. Darkness is only the absence of light. When the light comes in, darkness disappears of its own motion. So all the turmoil, and distress, and hatred in the world are only the absence of this divine, perfect love.

Therefore, let us shed the light of divine love, a real love, upon all of our fellow beings, a love for the sake of God, a love which has no limits, no boundaries of race, or country, or clime, or creed, but is a universal reality of the Sun of Truth shining from the very Throne of God. Such a love will remove all these questions from the world and will make us realize our relations to each other as we realize first of all our relations to God. Without knowing the divine bounty and the divine love, a man cannot know even himself. I believe that under the providence of God this Nation of ours has a bright destiny—it may reach it through sorrow, I hope it may achieve it through joy—and that is, as has been so eloquently expressed by our noble friend, the nations of the whole earth are looking to America for peace, for the example of ideal brotherhood. If they are asking us for bread, shall we give them a stone? I believe that America, under the inspiration of divine Guidance, will fulfill the high ideal of this noble destiny by fusing with the fire of love, into one harmonious brotherhood all the variegated elements of which this world is composed, and it is incumbent upon each individual, just in so far as he can, to contribute to this ideal brotherhood; and not only theorize about such a condition, but put his thoughts into action; for the wise man today is the man who makes his knowledge practical.

Speaking about the interrelations between the white and colored people; some months ago, traveling through the city of Monroe I met a friend who travels much and uses his eyes. He told me one of his impressions. He said that, if traveling through a section of the South, he came into a community and in this community saw nothing but white people, he could immediately form a correct impression by their general bearing and manners about the habits of their colored neighbors. But if, on the other hand, he saw nothing but colored people of the community, he could also form a very vivid and correct impression of the habits and manners of the white people. Now this may seem somewhat far-fetched, but you can see that it is the logical condition with regard to these civilizations so closely associated for centuries, that one should be but the reflex of the other. Therefore, instead of being critical toward our fellow beings, we can most happily occupy our time by considering what contribution we can ourselves make to the spirit of peace and brotherhood throughout the world. If our thoughts, and our aims, and our ideals are constructive, they will be supported in this day by divine confirmation and will bring this light of peace and brotherhood to all the people of the world. Let us not for a moment be despondent, for the glorious Sun of Reality has dawned and the light of that Sun now illumines the whole world. It is only for us to discover what a great bounty God has provided for us. "To the state of holiness He calls us!" To the exalted state of peace and ideal brotherhood he summons us! If we bring the best treasures of our minds and the noblest resources of our hearts, coming to the aid of the Lord against the mighty support this happy condition, He will give to us that inward peace which shall leave its bright traces in all the realm of existence. It will make us true men and women; it will make us the torch-bearers of the light of God and will enable us to transmit a radiance by which the peace and pleasure and happiness of the whole world of existence will be adorned. And there is nothing more glorious for man than to realize this bright destiny. God is with us! We can not fail if we are firm in His covenant and steadfast in His commands. This gloomy age will pass away and the radiance of the divine love will penetrate the whole earth, for as 'Abdu'l-Bahá the Great Teacher says, "There is a mysterious power at work in the hearts which moves the rocks, which rends the mountains, which creates new spiritual worlds, which administers all complicated and difficult affairs." This power will not fail, for it is the vibration that emanates from the Kingdom of God.

12

A Slave for Life:
A Story of the Long Ago

Coralie Franklin Cook

This story of a runaway slave's search for freedom was originally published in volume 7 of *Opportunity* magazine, June 1929.

Night had settled down upon the big plantation. All was darkness and stillness. No horse was neighing in the stables, no dog barking in the kennels. Our lone light shone, as was the custom, in the lower hall of the great house. Elsewhere the darkness was so dense that the man had to grope his way along the path to the bay. When nearly there, he turned aside and, still groping his way, crept into a thick shrubbery. Suddenly kneeling, he brushed away some leaves and moss, evidently familiar to his touch, and arose holding a bundle. It was enveloped in a piece of sacking and it contained all his earthly possessions. Attaching it to a stout stick, previously provided, he turned back to the path and with quickening steps reached the water's edge.

Once there, he stopped and, peering about in the black darkness, bent his head, first in one direction then in another, as if listening intently. Apparently satisfied, he waded out into the stream and loosened from its moorings a row boat into which he sprang as lightly as if he had been working in broad daylight.

Ephraim had been wise in his selection of time and tide. Had there been a patrol near, his figure would scarcely have been discernible, so deep was the gloom, and he had no need yet to dip his oars, for the tide was taking the boat out in the very direction he wanted it to go.

When he had drifted far enough away from shore to be satisfied that his departure had not been noted, he rose from his crouching attitude, fitted the oars into their locks and began making strong, swift strokes that sent his bark steadily forward.

The night afforded no friendly North Star to guide this solitary boatman, and he was too intelligent not to be conscious of his danger. Even in the darkness some belated vessel might run him down, overhaul and capture him; yet there was in his heart more fear of what lay behind than of what might await him ahead.

From childhood Ephraim had been familiar with the waters of "old" Chesapeake, and in the ship yards of Baltimore, working for six long years at his trade of caulking, he had learned so much of their art from sailors that he was far from being a novice in the role of seaman.

His plan was to go ahead as rapidly as possible, all the time keeping near enough to shore to be able to make a quick landing in case of need. By daybreak he must be at least twenty miles from the place of starting. He must land where he could hide during the day and resume his journey at night fall.

His capable mind worked clearly and rapidly and, as the blackness changed to gray on sky and water, his muscular arms bent to their task with unflagging energy. Several times he stood up and, balancing himself in the small craft, sought to get his bearings. His whole being pulsed with joy at the certainty that he had made a good time. He felt his muscles strong as tempered steel. "All my life," he murmured, "they've been working for others, now they're working for me." How he loathed the thought of that slavery to which he was still bound!

Listening to the swish of the waters, they seemed to him to follow the stroke of the oars with words like these, on the one side, "A slave!" and on the other, "for life!" The repetition kept up—"A slave!"—"for life!",

"A slave!"—"for life!" What a horrible nightmare it was! He must shake it off and push ahead.

Already it was time to think of landing, for day was breaking—a new day indeed for the man in the boat! His keen eyes watched the dim outline of shore.

There were numerous landing-places, and selecting one which seemed best suited to his purpose, the boatman beached his craft and, with bundle and stick, set forth upon land.

Who can fathom the depth of the conflicting emotions in this free-born soul seeking liberty for its fettered body? Fearful but determined and shunning danger, Ephraim pushed cautiously on. He was well aware that, had he stayed on the water, with the coming of day, he was almost certain to be captured, if not by those directly in pursuit of him, then by others of that scarcely human element who made their living by lying in wait for runaway slaves and securing the prize money awarded when the poor creatures were returned to their masters.

After walking some little distance, the wanderer knew himself to be about twenty-five miles from home. Not wholly unfamiliar with the neighborhood, he felt sure of finding some shelter where he might hide until, under cover of darkness, he could again resume his flight.

Stealthily he set out to find the highway. Before reaching it, however, he came up against a rail fence and there, as if especially provided, beheld with joy, a great straw stack, fresh and sweet and clean. Some distance away and separated by another fence cattle were grazing. It was reasonable to conclude that he was near some habitation. Daylight was dangerously near and he knew the habits of overseers too well to take any risk. He must quickly worm his way into that straw stack so providentially at hand.

Look at him, poor fugitive, before he conceals himself! His physical match would be hard to find. More than six feet tall, his body and limbs are so well proportioned that he does not seem of undue height. A head, noble in outline, is covered with a mass of dark, curly hair. His skin is of that peculiar, golden tint—the legacy of one born of a black mother and white father. His eyes, big, dark, and usually keen, are now full of apprehension and sadness. Running from the accursed soil of slavery he senses all the meaning of liberty and, once on the way, his mind is made up never to be taken alive.

Making several irregular openings near the bottom of the stack and strewing a few handfuls of straw about the ground to simulate the appearance due to the depredations of passing cattle, Ephraim was not long in selecting a place of entrance and, after taking one long, searching survey of his surroundings, bowed his head, and, working his way with shoulders, hands and feet, burrowed far into the stack of straw.

His last thought was to reach out one hand and pull a heavy rail across the very place where he had entered. Half sitting, half lying down and in a decidedly cramped position, the poor fellow settled himself for the long hours of waiting.

After all, the place was not so stifling as he had expected for the straw had been stacked as so to let rain, sunlight and air filter through, and even in his great extremity Ephraim breathed a prayer of thankfulness for the good fortune that had so far attended him.

Lying there, he began to think over his great adventure. How long he had been planning to get away! He could hardly remember a time when the thing had been out of his mind. All his past came before him. Once more he was a little boy tumbling about his "gran' mammy's" door in company with other slave children. Thoughts of her brought memories of the ash cake she used to make, and all at once her runaway grandson became ravenously hungry. Drawing some bread and meat from his pocket he began to eat in considerable discomfort, which was in no sense alleviated by a great thirst that made his throat ache and burn. Reviling the stupidity which had let him forget to provide himself a flask of water, he once more fell into a train of thought.

This time it was his mother who came into his mind. He had seen her so seldom and knew so little about her. She had been a field hand and had visited him mostly at night; but how tender she was, and what happiness it had been to climb into her lap and forget cold and hunger, loneliness, and every childish grief, as she crooned over him and told him those funny stories about "brer" fox and "brer" rabbit. In a childhood so destitute of those things dear to all children, that mother love made the one green spot in the desert of bondage. Tenderly, reverently, he thought of that mother who now lay in a lonely grave on the old plantation.

Ephraim recalled at what an early age he had discovered his social status, and with what deep mortification and sense of injustice he had found himself to be a slave, and not only a slave, but, *a slave for life!* with no way out.

Once more he was going up to the great house to be outfitted for work. He was a big boy now. Hitherto his garb had been of the simplest sort—a tow linen shirt falling just below the knees. He had long been ashamed to be seen in it and had kept out of folks' way as much as possible. Now he came into possession of two pairs of coarse cotton pants, the same number of "hickory" shirts and one pair of heavy shoes. Such continued to be the annual supply of his wardrobe until he had succeeded in hiring his time and had bought clothes of his own choosing. Thus memories of the past surged through his active mind.

He felt glad he had learned to read and write; he laughed even, as there rose before him sidewalks which had stood for him in lieu of blackboards, and the sign boards, bits of newspaper, and barrel heads that had been his teachers.

Again returned the weary days in cotton and corn field, the welcome change from country to city life when he had worked in the great shipping yards, the savage unrest that had made him long for liberty, and, at last, the determination to escape.

One by one, faces of the old slaves he had known, came before him. "Broke-back Mimy," who bore the appellation because she went about terribly bent over, and whose back actually had been broken by a fence rail in the hands of an angry overseer; "Unc' Lem," who had but one eye, having lost the other in a fight with his young master. Ephraim shuddered and tried to banish thoughts of his unfortunate old fellow-servant. It had been because of "young mahstah's" unwelcome attentions to the slave's comely wife that the fight had been so bitter and the punishment so terrible, for poor Lem had come out worsted.

These and similar episodes had made deep and lasting impressions upon Ephraim and had caused him to swear, while yet a stripling, that he would never marry unless he became free, never be the father of a child.

Now, saddest of all the sad thoughts that filled his mind was the memory of Nan, whom he had left behind. He loved Nan. He had not even told her goodbye, trusting her intuition to tell her why. Would she, perhaps, bear a child to some other man, husband or no? True, she was a free woman, but how many free women escaped the slime of the slavery cursed country? Afflicted by all these torturing thoughts, apprehensive concerning the outcome of his attempt to escape, the fugitive's weary body crumpled up and he gave himself to utter misery.

At last he fell asleep and for hours slept as only the healthy, yet worn and weary, can sleep.

Aroused at last by the sound of loud and angry voices, he instantly became alert. Heavy footsteps were close to his hiding-place. Sticks were being thrust into the stack. Merciful God! Was he to be captured like a rat in a hole? Great tremors ran through his body. He broke into a heavy sweat, his very flesh seemed crawling. What was it they were saying? "No use looking for the d—— nigger in here. He's either on the road or on the water." Ephraim knew that voice only too well. It belonged to his master's overseer, a man given to oaths, to whiskey, to the cowhide, and shotgun. He held his breath. Evidently the words had been heeded, for after some further cursing and kicking, footsteps and voices ceased to be heard. Ephraim, forever, was thoroughly alarmed. He must think, *think* what was best to do. The going off might be only a trick to lure him out; in that case he would be perfectly still and give them a game of waiting. So for a long time he remained in his cramped position, not daring to move and breathing softly.

Finally he concluded that the searching party had gone, but for some reason he could not shake off the impression that they would return— and soon. This foreboding became unbearable. It was impossible to stay there longer. He must get away.

Brushing aside the straw, he peered cautiously out; not a creature was to be seen. Looking skyward he was amazed to read by the sun's slanting rays that it was late afternoon. Crawling out from the stack he lay for a short time prone on the ground. He thought of his boat but was too shrewd to go in search of it.

At right angles to the road by which he had approached the stack of straw lay a dense wood. Poplars, maples, oak, and the thick shade of the horse chestnut all were there. Less than a quarter of a mile from where he lay he could safely hide on of those trees. His pursuers would hardly think to look for him there, at any rate it seemed the only present means of escape and he would try it.

Taking from his pocket a small tin box, he scraped from it a quantity of tar with which he smeared liberally the soles of his feet, and after making sure that there was no one in sight, he crept away, at first on hands and knees until some yards from the stack, then rising, he fled in great leaps and bounds to the shelter of the woods.

Selecting a big tree whose branches were covered with broad and thick leaves, Ephraim lost no time in disposing of himself as he had been wont to do when a boy at play and when, as he now remembered hopefully, none of his mates had ever been able to "smoke" him out. Nor was he settled a minute too soon. Whether some Divine prescience or the "root" given him by "conjurah" Sam had guided him, he was not at all certain, but the baying of hounds fell upon his ear and, as cold chills ran up and down his spinal column, sounds of threats and curses mingled with the yelping of the bloodthirsty beasts that had been brought to trail him. To add to his horror, a great blaze of light warned him that the slave hunters had set fire to his late hiding place. The stack had been a big one and, even in the shelter of the tree, Ephraim began to fear that the brilliant light might reveal his presence should the searchers come into the woods. With anxious heart he waited but they never turned in his direction.

What was it that had prompted him to bring the tar? By means of it the hounds had lost scent and his pursuers had been baffled. Was it God? He believed so, and as the sound of horses feet were lost in the distance, and the noise of beasts and men ceased to beat upon his listening ears he was overcome by a strange ecstasy. Instead of feeling scared and despondent as he had in the straw stack, he now rejoiced in the belief that he was destined to escape. Had not the waters of the Red Sea divided for the children of Israel? Were not the three Hebrew children protected from the flames of the fiery furnace? Was not he, Ephraim, in the care of the same Jehovah who had guarded them? With thoughts like these, the lone wayfarer kept his place in the crotch of the oak until darkness had fallen, and stiff and sore he let himself down from his place of sanctuary.

His throat was parched and dry. He could no longer do without water, and in the falling darkness with a woodman's instinct he hunted for a spring. He failed to find one, but a brook was coursing through the woods, and stretched at full length he drank and drank and felt so refreshed that he began, in his sanguine way, to wonder whether these might not be healing waters given him by the "God of Moses."

Not long, however, did Ephraim indulge in fancy. Very cautiously, for there was still a bit of lingering daylight, he made his way to the open road. Every fence rail must be watched; every tree trunk. The slightest sound, even the fall of a dead leaf, stayed his eager footsteps. Were the shadows peopled? To his tense imagination they sometimes were.

With the settling down of night the wayfarer kept steadily on. Presently he came to a crossroad which he recognized with glad surprise, for it meant that he was miles from home and not far from the town of H—— where, if he could reach it before day, he was sure of finding shelter among friends.

At the thought of friends, his heart kindled, for the burning straw stack, the sickening bay of the bloodhounds and the vigil in the tree top had taken toll of his strong nerves, and he felt a choking in his throat and held back unbidden tears.

It was about four o'clock in the morning when, foot-sore and weary, Ephraim entered the little town of H——, at the mouth of the Susquehannah River. Folks were not up yet, and he made his way toward the familiar out of the way spot where his friends lived.

No sound of man or beast broke the quiet. The choking pain that had, for a while, affected him was gone, and breathing far more freely he hurried on. A turn of a corner and poor Ephraim found himself facing a gun! "Halt, nigger!" came the challenge. He obeyed instantly. "Wha's you' pass?" With apparent coolness Ephraim produced one which he himself had written. Swinging his lantern close to the paper the patrol took a long time to look it over. He belonged to the class known as "crackers" and his knowledge of letters was probably less than Ephraim's own. Finally he grunted out, "Papah seems ter be all right, but what yer doin' heah?" "I've been 'lowed time off t' visit some friends," with a show of confidence. "Wal, yer kin go on." The stricture in Ephraim's throat began to relax. He had barely taken two steps forward, however, when the watchman was one more close behind him. "I dunno as I orter let yer go on; yer don't look ner talk like a' eastern sho' darkey; but nevah min', go erlong, I kin soon ketch yer if yer up ter any tricks." "Oh, I'm all right, sir," was the shrewd rejoinder, and Ephraim trudged on.

Silas Jones was a slave who hired his own time. His wife was a free woman and in a tiny house in a back street they lived and toiled.

Ephraim was made heartily welcome. He was permitted to take a warm bath, to eat a substantial meal and to sleep while Silas and Nancy kept watch. At midnight Silas awakened him and he set forth upon the last lap of his journey.

To the watchman at the bridge he presented an entirely different pass, with a different name from the one given the patrol that he had met in the early morning, and was permitted to proceed without question.

Having crossed the bridge, and feeling much better as the result of the kindly ministrations of his humble friends, Ephraim set out almost light heartedly. Silas, who was a teamster, and familiar with all the roads, had given him careful directions and he knew he was not far from the Pennsylvania line—and Freedom! That thought which had haunted him for so long, that he was a slave for life, had fallen into a mental background and in its stead dreams of liberty were shaping themselves—reunion with Nan, a home and—What was that? A footstep in the dark? A falling twig? Which? "It's late for me to be getting scared now," he thought, as he started to cross a field in order to skirt a village where lights were still burning. Once more he stopped, assured now that he was being followed. Turning around abruptly he encountered, not a patrol as he had feared, but a Negro who advanced toward him and in a friendly voice said, "Howdy, man, what's yo' hurry?" The voice and words were reassuring, and with the utmost relief Ephraim answered in an easy way, "Well, it's late, ain't it, to be on the road? Time all honest folks was in bed, eh?" "Oh, I dunno," laughed the newcomer, "I'm heah an' I peahs t' be hones', doesn't I? I jes come this way fo' a sho't cut. I lives on th' aidge o' town an' this brings me out right neah muh stoppin place. Is y' goin fuh, may I ax?"

Thrown completely off guard by the friendly bearing of the follow, poor Ephraim forgot to be cautious and admitted, "Yes, I've got a good bit further to go."

The two chatted amenably, and, leaving the field, after a time, struck back again into the road.

When they had trudged along for about a mile the man halted. "Well, stranjah," he said, "heah we pahts company, I reck'n, lessen you'll cept o' sheltah wive me fo' th' night." Ephraim was not ungrateful for the offer, but too eager to push on to be tempted by it, so reaching out a hand, he was bout to say a cheery goodbye when his new acquaintance uttered so loud a guffaw that it caused him to hesitate. That was no genuine laugh. It seemed like a signal.

Accustomed to the tricks to which slaves often resorted to secure secrecy or give warning, he braced himself for he knew not what.

It flashed through his mind how that officer at the bridge had let him cross without a word. Why had he not thought of it sooner? Anyway, he had been betrayed. Before he had time to realize what was happening a horseman had come upon them, and flashing a lantern in their faces, demanded to know what they were doing here at that time of night. Ephraim recognized in the horseman, who had now dismounted, a white man of low grade, probably a "nigger trader," and as he bent to scrutinize the face of his late friendly companion, he was at once convinced that he had been fooled and betrayed by that lowest and meanest of human beings—a Negro kidnapper of runaway slaves, working in collusion with a poor white.

Righteous indignation gave strength to the poor, hunted creature. He knew himself too near his goal to give up until he had exhausted his every means of self-preservation. Moreover, he did not doubt his ability to match both the other men in a fair fight.

No sooner was he aware that the white man was leveling a pistol at him than he sprang forward with the agility of a panther, knocked the weapon from the threatening hand and, before his would-be captor could recover from his surprise, pinioned both his arms and bore him to the ground, where he beat him almost into insensibility.

What, in the meantime, had become of the Negro, coward that he was? Afraid to openly desert his confederate, though he offered no assistance, he was now cowering before the angry giant who had exhibited such rare courage in assailing one of the master class. Weakly, but mistakenly, he essayed to keep up the role of friend, for Ephraim, enraged by the fellow's treachery and smarting under the humiliation of having permitted himself to be so easily trapped, turned on the black kidnapper with terrible wrath. "You scoundrel!" he cried, heedless of the possibility of being heard, "I've a mind to break every bone in your cursed little body. Don't open your mouth or I'll kill you. Take the rope from that horse's saddle," he commanded, as, at the same time he got possession of the fallen pistol. Compelling the black traitor to cross his hands behind him, he fastened them securely, did the same for his feet, and then gagged him in the most approved fashion.

As the first victim of his physical prowess began to give signs of returning sense, Ephraim lost no time in attending to his needs, omitting the gagging.

"I'll leave you two to keep one another company, and if it wasn't that I have fear of Almighty God, I'd have sent you both to the hell where you belong."

Afterward when he remembered his fury and his profanity, Ephraim was at a loss to account for the latter. Never before had he been half so profane! Accustomed as he was to hear cursing and blasphemy, he had always scorned their use, but on this occasion he seemed not to be able to speak enough of strong and bitter words.

Free now to continue his journey, he felt a sickening sensation come over him, and found himself trembling in every limb.

Great God! Was he to give up now, now so near to freedom? Summoning all his strength, he stumbled along. But it was a stumble, no longer the stead tramp, tramp that was taking him to a "Promised Land." Still he kept on. Once he went straight through a village, making no attempt not to be seen. In a measure dazed, he was conscious of but one thought— On! on! he must keep on! All at once he began to run, slowly at first, then faster and faster. Was it a race? It seemed so to him and that he, Ephraim, was ordained to be the winner. Faster! faster! Harder! harder! Were his lungs bursting? Was he going blind? There was no longer any time, any world, anything, only the race, until finally he tottered and fell.

There he lay, poor, hunted fugitive, pitiful yet noble slave, who had willed to barter life itself in quest of liberty!

When he came to himself, day had broken. A figure was bending over him. A tall, slightly built man of middle age, wearing a drab suit and broad rimmed hat of the same color was shaking him gently and demanding to know if he were ill.

Where was he? What had happened? For a minute or two everything was blank, then it all came back to him—the Negro who had betrayed him, the fight and flight.

He bethought him of the sorry picture he must make, and rose to his feet while the Quaker who had stopped to befriend him took account of his towering height, his breadth of shoulder and his great dark eyes, full of sadness and mystery. "I have lost my way," he faltered, "and I must have fallen asleep." "Thee must be very tired. Get into my wagon and I will give thee a lift."

At these words Ephraim saw for the first time a small spring wagon in the road, from which the stranger had evidently alighted. Slowly he fixed his gaze upon this good Samaritan. The answering look, honest, serene, friendly, sent great waves of confidence and cheer through all his stricken spirit. He asked no questions, felt no fear, but with the faith of a little child seated himself beside this angel of his deliverance.

Was it chance or was it God? The man in drab was one of the most vigilant and untiring "conductors" on the "Under Ground Railroad."

By nine o'clock that August morning, the two were well across the Pennsylvania state line.

In Ephraim's heart a great joy was upspringing and in place of the dirge, "A slave!—for life!" a new song was singing itself through all his being—the Song of Freedom!

13

The Negro as a World Citizen
John B. Shaw

This essay is from notes of an address given at the Bahá'í summer
school in Geyserville, California. It was originally published in
The People's Advocate January 5, 1944.

We will start this discussion with the definition of the word Negro.

The word is derived form the Latin, meaning black, dark, dusk; applied
to the night, the sky, a storm; to pitch, to ivy, to the complexion; and,
more specifically, to the African natives of Sudan, Senegambia, and the
region southward to the vicinity of the equator and the Great Lakes, and
to their descendants in America and elsewhere.

As many Americans may not be well acquainted with the nationals of
other races, or perhaps may have come in contact only with those who
were not a credit to their race, let me discuss the Negro background,
third in point of the world's population, as our special subject this morning.

How many of you ever realized that 10,000 Negro soldiers helped the
American ancestors to win the War for Independence in 1776?

As a matter of fact, Negro blood has provided thousands of soldiers to
defend the Flag in every war in which the United States has been engaged.

But because of this, please do not think that the Negro favors only a
soldier's life.

On the contrary, the Negro race has produced distinguished citizens in every walk of life.

It is especially noteworthy that the Negro is the only non-Caucasian race which has so far furnished rivals to the white man in science, the arts, literature, and mathematics.

There are famous Negro painters, musicians, novelists, botanists, legists, philologists, philosophers, mathematicians, engineers, and general officers whose work is done in the white world and in emulation with the first talent of Europe and of America.

And in the lesser professions and trades the Negro is a valued helper because of his skill and dependability. The Department of Labor some years ago issued a news paragraph reporting a decrease in the accident rate as Negro soldiers and helpers supplanted other labor in the foundries of Indianapolis.

Negroes came to America with the early explorers and took some part in exploration. A Negro of the Fray Mareos Expedition—Stephen Dorantes—was the discoverer of the Southwestern part of North America. There were many Negroes with Balboa, Pizarro, D'Ayllon, and Cortez; and a Negro has now been to the North Pole.

Such brilliant achievements have been, unfortunately, over-shadowed in the public mind by the sad epoch connected with the slave trade that was forced on the Colonies by England in the early days of our history.

As the Dutch and English slave trade of the seventeenth century poured in larger numbers of Negroes, the matter of their control and organization became serious, as they were worked in gangs by severe taskmasters. Their cruel treatment led to repeated revolts throughout the islands and on the Continent, but only two of those uprisings were successful—that of the Maroons in Jamaica in the seventeenth century, and of Toussaint L'Ouverture in Haiti in the eighteenth century.

The Colonists of this country had thought that the slave trade would of itself gradually fade out, and the slaves eventually become citizens or migrate to other places. But, as we know, it required a war to effect their emancipation.

The freedmen then began to demand the ballot and to organize churches and other association in various states, for the purpose of improving their political status and insure their newly acquired rights.

After the Civil War the Negroes started as free laborers without land or capital.

But in less than five years the Negro was in Congress, in the Republican National Convention taking a lead in the National Campaigns, and sharing heavily in the spoils of the Republican Party. In Congress, from 1870 to 1901, he exercised his opportunity quite generally as a leader of his people to promote legislation for Civil Rights for Federal aid for education, a National Election Law, in addition to numerous measures for improvements in rivers, harbors, erection of public buildings, and other projects. Two of the colored legislators were Senators, while the others were members of the House of Representatives. Very soon they counted among their ranks all trades and professions.

By the beginning of the century they had accumulated an estimated wealth of $300,000,000 and their total owned farm land alone amounted to approximately 15,000,000 acres, or an area nearly as large as Holland and Belgium; and by the close of the next decade they had increased their racial wealth by another $300,000,000. Thus, year by year they continued to advance, through education and diligent work, and to occupy many positions of trust in the public service.

Under President Harding a Negro was appointed as Assistant District Attorney to have charge of all Railroad suits brought against the Government in the United States Court of Claims.

President Coolidge assigned a Negro as Comptroller of the Customs at New Orleans; another as a member of the Board of Mediation and Conciliation; one as Assistant to the Director of the Veterans' Bureau; one as Assistant to the Alaskan Railway Engineering Commission; another as Assistant Chief Clerk-at-large to the Railway Mail Service, which was the first highest position ever filled by a Negro in the Post Office Department.

And many others have been appointed to important posts.

In the depression of ten years ago it was natural that the Negroes should be hard hit, perhaps even more so than white Americans when conditions in the South were considered. Lack of steady employment among the white people of the South caused many of them to resort to work which had been traditionally done only by Negroes, thereby increasing the competition for jobs, and lowering the living standards of both white and Negro laborers in the South, the result being that many Negro skilled and educated productive workers emigrated to other sections of the United States in search of a more abundant life. All of this tended to create a problem not solely related to the Negro.

The South having furnished the basis for the population increase of the nation, coupled with the South's large potential market for the nation's goods, the Southern workers leaving for other parts of the country in quest of wider opportunities, have created a problem, according to many reports prepared for the President, that is now a national one of great concern.

But, of course, we are also interested in our individual problems and affairs as well.

Jamaica is my native land. However, I have long been a citizen of the United States.

On first coming to America I lived a while in New York before deciding to try my luck further West.

After reaching San Francisco I presented a letter of introduction to the Manager of the Corporation for which I have since worked many years—to be exact.

He informed me that they had never had one of my race in their employ, but taking into consideration the contents of my letter he felt inclined to make a place for me. This he did with the admonition that it was up to me "to make good" and not to let him "down." I agreed, and have kept my promise working faithfully, to the best of my ability, never shirking my duty.

As a final word, I bring to your thoughtful attention the fact that the Negro undoubtedly has a very important part to play in the future of this country, and in the coming years will probably permeate the life of other continents as well.

In America the Negroes occupy a significant part of the economic strength of the nation.

As I have pointed out, they have furnished persons of ability in politics, literature and art. Just to mention a few well known names like: Banneker, the mathematician and almanac-maker; Phillis Wheatley, the poet; Lemuel Haynes, the theologian; Ida Aldridge, the actor; Frederick Douglass, the orator; Tanner, the artist; Booker T. Washington, educator; Granville Woods, inventor; Kelly Miller, the writer; Rosamond Johnson and Will Cook, musical composers; Dunbar the poet; Chestnut the novelist.

Racial prejudice should have no place in our lives, particularly from a Bahá'í standpoint.

The Bahá'í vision beckons us to make every effort to dispel every cloud of race, prejudice that has darkened our national life.

No solution of the race question is possible which is not based upon an effort to develop every race to its highest capacity, and we Bahá'ís look to the new humanity of this New Day to achieve no greater triumphs than in the field of interracial justice.

This will come about more rapidly and effectively when we all make the world our home and work together for greater international understanding, to the end that all peoples shall be as one family.

14

Votes for Mothers

Coralie Franklin Cook

This editorial was originally published in the August 1915 edition
of the NAACP journal *The Crisis.*

I wonder if anybody in all this great world ever thought to consider *man's* rights as an individual, by his status as a father? Yet you ask me to say something about "Votes for Mothers," as if mothers were a separate and peculiar people. After all, I think you are not so far wrong. Mothers *are* different, or ought to be different, from other folk. The woman who smilingly goes out, willing to meet the Death Angel, that a child may be born, comes back from that journey, not only the mother of her own adored babe, but a near-mother to all other children. As she serves that little one, there grows within her a passion to serve humanity; not race, not class, not sex, but God's creatures as he has sent them to earth.

It is not strange that enlightened womanhood has so far broken its chains as to be able to know that to perform such service, woman should help both to make and to administer the laws under which she lives, should feel responsible for the conduct of educational systems, charitable and correctional institutions, public sanitation and municipal ordinances in general. Who should be more competent to control the presence of bar rooms and "red-light districts" than mothers whose sons they are meant to lure to degradation and death? Who knows better than the girl's mother at what age the girl may legally barter her own body? Surely not the men who have put upon our statute books, 16, 14, 12, aye, be it to their eternal shame, even 10 and 8 years, as "the age of consent!"

If men could choose their own mothers, would they choose free women or bond-women? Disfranchisement because of sex is curiously like disfranchisement because of color. It cripples the individual, it handicaps progress, it sets a limitation upon mental and spiritual development. I grow in breadth, in vision, in the power to do, just in proportion as I use the capacities with which Nature, the All-Mother, has endowed me. I transmit to the child who is bone of my bone, flesh of my flesh and *thought of my thought;* somewhat of my own power or weakness. Is not the voice which is crying out for "Votes for Mothers" the Spirit of the Age crying out for the Rights of Children?

———

1 5

———

Letter to 'Abdu'l-Bahá 'Abbás

Coralie Franklin Cook

This previously unpublished letter was sent by Coralie Franklin Cook to 'Abdu'l-Bahá in March 1914.

Honored and dearly beloved Teacher:

Only a short time ago, after many months of waiting, I dared to send you a brief letter expressing my love for the Cause and telling you in what way your visit to this Institution had planted seed, which, already begins to grow and bear fruit.

Writing a letter to you is like no other writing. No sooner do I take up the pen with that intention than I seem somehow, to be ushered into your very Presence. The pen is indeed only a medium and you yourself seem very near.

Perhaps the subject I shall try to write upon is one of such import as to invoke your Presence. However that may be, you will know that I shall write no thoughtless word and shall try to be just and honest in every statement.

It has seemed wise to my good friends Mr. and Mrs. Hannen and Mrs. Haney that I should write you concerning some aspects of the Race Problem in its relation to the Bahá'í Cause here in America. We do not make the mistake of supposing that 'Abdu'l-Bahá does not understand far more about this matter than any believer can possibly show him, but we do feel it fitting to put on record and into your hands certain facts as expressing the attitude of the colored people themselves concerning race prejudice. Since we are the ones whose progress it impedes and whose footsteps it hounds surely we must be better prepared to speak than those who view the situation ON THE OUTSIDE.

Race relationship, in the Southern States especially, but more or less thru out the country is in a deplorable condition. In many instances where friendship, mutual sympathy, and good will ought to exist, hostility and venom are manifested by the whites and are met by distrust and dislike on the part of the colored people. To cite the contributing causes which have led up to this direful situation—culminating recently in acts of certain public officials, leading toward segregation and discrimination among the employees of the federal government itself—would be to write a book. Chief among them however it is safe to say is the popular delusion called "social equality." By some strange phenomenon certain white people think or affect to think, that if a colored person shares in the ordinary privileges which pertain to comfort and convenience, or political or civic right that it means "social equality"—that is to say, if permitted to vote, to take part in civic festivities or parades, to ride in the same car, to attend the same public school or place of worship or to be buried in the same grave yard means "social equality." To any but a morbid mind or diseased mind this seems like unbelievable absurdity, which. practically carried out, is making the position of the colored people almost unbearable and robbing the American white people of any rightful claims to an exalted position among the nations of men, because they are either active participants in, or silent witnesses of the gross injustice. And yet, as in the days of slavery, when certain heroics rose up against the iniquities of that awful system and said, "These things must not and shall not be," so now the maligned and persecuted black man is not without friends. New Abolitionists, who SEE the nations peril as well as the black man's extremity, have banded together to readjust the situation in ways becoming a Christian nation and a Democratic Government. The Southern Sociological Congress which held its Second Annual Meeting in Atlanta, Ga., last year considered "Six Great Questions," one of which was the

Race Problem. It reported that for three days 300 white and 100 black men and women in a spirit of perfect harmony and helpfulness, discussed race relationship and reached a basis of agreement upon co-operative investigation and action which is bound to result in material benefit to both races. Efforts on the part of the hot-headed demagogues to annul the amendments to the National Constitution which conferred citizenship and the franchise upon the black man, have been met by uncompromising opposition from some few members of both houses of Congress who have not yet forgotten the Declaration of Independence nor that message handed down through the ages: "He hath made of one blood all nations of men."

No phase of the color question excites so much rancor and misrepresentation as the one of mixed marriage. It is constantly made use of by all classes of whites from the Statesmen to the boot-black and now includes some so-called Bahá'ís to arouse passion and strife and to flatter Saxon vanity. If the whole truth were told, it must be said that many colored people are as strongly opposed to inter-racial marriage as the whites who rant and tear continuously, the difference being that colored people entertain no fear of whole-sale absorption as some whites apparently do. I use the word absorption meaning that in the ratio of 4 to 1 must in time result in the racial identity of the smaller group being lost in that of the larger. Former President Roosevelt has explained in a recent number of *The Outlook* that this is the accepted mode of race adjustment in Brazil, South America, and is provocative of no race friction whatever, but on the contrary establishes harmony and good will.

So far as the matter of amalgamation goes here in the United States, it is settled past undoing. 250 years of domestic slavery with the female slave at the command of her master has bequeathed to the country hundreds, yes thousands, of mixed bloods ranging in type from a dark rich brown skin with curly hair to the perfect blond with golden hair and blue eyes all classed as negroes and all—if known to have a drop of negro blood—subject to the same restrictions, insults, and persecutions. What is even more significant is just as you find the white skin, the fair hair bespeaking white blood among the colored people you find the open nostril the full lips the large and melancholy eye distributed among those who suppose themselves to be pure white. Surely "the Judgments of the Lord are true and righteous altogether." This mixing of the two Races we are told is biologically unfit, will degrade posterity and vitiate the noble Saxon blood. But even from such unholy alliance came the great Fredrick Douglass, and our Gifted Du Bois is plainly of mixed blood, this same admixture gave to France her Dumas, to Russia her Pushkin, while some go so far as to claim the African strain courses through the blood of the Great Robert Browning and the early American Patriot Alexander Hamilton. Surely such examples in no wise incite the alarming theory of race deterioration. Numerous examples might be given where colored boys and girls in competition with whites outstrip the latter amazingly. For example a fourteen year old colored girl has recently taken a prize for proficiency in German over 107 white competitors, EIGHTEEN OF WHOM WERE OF GERMAN DESCENT. Nor do these instances in any way reflect upon the capacity of the full blooded negro. The Flower of the French Army was defeated by the military genius of Haiti's black General, the most popular note in American music today is given by a Negro Composer and no writer of verse of the present generation has displayed finer poetic fire than Paul Laurence Dunbar. Intelligent colored people have no craving for intermarriage, nor do they inveigh against it, they take the position that it is a question for the two parties concerned to settle for themselves, with which no one has a right to interfere and most of all do they deem it an outrage that in a free Republic laws should be enacted prohibiting such legal union while concubinage between white men and black women goes unpunished. Writers who oppose mixed marriages almost always assure the reader that there is a "natural antipathy between the races," but is more than likely to follow up this statement by saying that social equality must not be tolerated, because it inevitably leads to mixed marriage. To a normal mind the query naturally suggests itself: "Why make laws to prevent a thing which an 'inherent God-given instinct' has already provided against?"

Knowledge of the progress of the colored people during their fifty years of freedom has astounded the world and incited the envy and hatred of those who prophesied their extinction and argued their inability to work for themselves. In the midst of unfriendly surroundings they have accumulated $7,000,000,000 worth of property raising a million and a half of dollars in the past year alone for educational work, coming out of slavery with 95 percent of their whole number unable to read or write to say that number is reduced to only 30 percent an advance surpassing that of the whites during the same period. Instead of this marvelous achievement appealing to all that is best and noblest in the whites it has seemed to have a contrary effect. Laws are being passed in many sections compelling colored people to live in segregated districts, where they have had handsome houses among white residences these houses have been attacked, lives endangered, valuable property ruthlessly destroyed, anonymous orders to vacate, if ignored, have even resulted in the use of dynamite and total destruction of a house and its contents, the Law Courts offer no redress for the word of a black man is not taken against that of a white man where Judge and Jury are all of the dominant class. Back, back and evermore back! "Be ye hewers of wood and drawers of water" only! Come thus far and no further! is the slogan dinned into his ears until the average person of color is almost a state of desperation. Most naturally the afflicted one would turn and look to the followers of Christ for protection and championship, but one by one they have given into the mandates of the Race Problem or Prejudice that is enclosing the white race almost as much as the black, one by one various religious bodies have departed from their original teachings. For a colored person to enter almost any white Church in the City of Washington and attempt to share in its worship would be to virtually break up the meeting. The Seventh Day Adventists who at one time were in perfect harmony and fellowship disgraced the Cause of God and outraged the souls of men by finally dividing on racial lines, the same thing is true of the Salvation Army. Where then is the black man to turn. The Bahá'í Cause is his last hope. If he be asked to face a line of cleavage in it, his faith will be broken and not only HIS faith but the faith of all those white persons who believe in a Divine teachings, worse than all to discriminate would be to furnish the enemies of the Negro with new weapons both of offence and defiance for would they not say, "See, we are right! Even the Bahá'ís could not hold out." Because the Race situation is so acute, because the colored people and their brave friends feel this is the most crucial period in all the Nations History, I pray God that no one who has ever embraced the Faith will step aside to so contribute to the Nations' shame and so abandon the Cause. Let them say like Luther, "Here I stand, God helping me I can do no other," like Garrison will not retreat a single inch and will be heard. "I will not hesitate, I will not equivocate."

It is an awful moment! Our children and our children's children will reap as we sow. Let us sow in righteousness that our cause may be exalted and that we may shield generations yet unborn from the calamities that follow evil doing.

In the light of all these things and many more but time will not here allow is it not evident that the Bahá'í teaching, reiterating the Gospel of the Fatherhood of God and the Brotherhood of man is not only the last hope of the colored people, but must appeal strongly to all persons regardless of race or color who have come to say I am my brother's keeper. To any one of the Bahá'í faith to whom the tempter says "temporize" or let the matter work itself out, I say beware! When was ever a mighty Principle championed by temporizing or delay? I know some must suffer both white and black, but who better able to wear the mantle of suffering than the real Bahá'í? The blessed Báb, Bahá'u'lláh, and the Center of the Covenant, have blazed the path for our feet to tread. Dare we turn back? If any one has come to realize his duty to the community in which he lives, to the country to which that community is a part, to the world to which that country must contribute its share in the making of the world Progress and to His God, must he not embrace the Teachings of Bahá'u'lláh as the Greatest instrument put in the hands of man for bringing all the nations of earth under conscious harmony with the Will of God? To open closed doors, to enable mothers to look into the faces of their beloved children and know that they may aspire to serve their day and generation in whatever way their capacity will allow, to remove hate and malice and evil doing, to be no respecter of persons, but to let worth and goodness fix man's status would indeed be the coming of His Kingdom, the doing of His Will, on earth as it is in heaven. Weary and heart sore, discouraged with the Churches that close their doors to them, the silent pulpits that should thunder forth in trumpet tones against the iniquities in the pews, it were strange indeed if the Bahá'í Teachings wakened no response of great hope in the hearts of colored people. If the true believers only stand by the teachings though it requires superhuman courage, and live the life it is only a question of time when every seeker after truth will be swept into Bahá'í embrace! To falter, to let go one divinely approved Principle would be disastrous! No one could then have faith for Truth is unalterable and cannot change. There are ministers filling hundreds of pulpits today who dare not preach the Truths beating in their breasts for utterance! There are hundreds of hungering souls who never enter the churches because of the hollow mockery they find there. "They ask for bread and are given a stone."

Every noble principle, every lofty ideal, every rule of conduct in the Bahá'í Faith can be defended by passages of our own Bible, the Faith is seeking followers at a time when it would seem as if the Universe itself were challenged to choose between Peace and War, brotherhood and disunion, right and wrong. It is not plain to all that the TEST is crucial and that the times are so momentous that what may seem for the present to put back the Cause of Bahá'í may be in reality the one thing that will put world progress forward immeasurably.

My greetings and my prayer for your blessings,
Coralie F. Cook

16

The Spiritual Heritage
of African-Americans

Bonnie Fitzpatrick-Moore

This letter to Wilma Ellis appears in
Bonnie Fitzpatrick-Moore's book, *My African Heart.*

As we enter this new phase in South African history, several things come
to mind that should be spoken of and attended to. I wonder how many
Black Americans have any idea about what it is they can contribute to
the world. We were uniquely placed so that we could receive that which
would set us apart from the rest of the Black people of the earth. Despite
the hardships, and maybe to a real measure because of them, we were
placed into a system where we could be educated, could achieve, and
develop to our full potential. That has not been true for any other group
of Black people. I do not think for a minute that the evils of slavery,
segregation, and repression came to be our lot by an accident of birth. I
do rather think that it was ordained by God in His mercy, so that we
would be placed in a country where we could be educated and develop to
our full potential, within a governmental system that would allow us to
develop. I certainly am not making light of how hard the task has been
and how many tears have been shed in our collective efforts to achieve, or

how many have given their lives, most often not willingly, to achieve this freedom of development and choice. "All things are of God."

What I am saying is that, now that we have a recorded past that starts with degradation and goes on to record outstanding achievements in all fields of life, do we not owe our Creator a tremendous debt for the bounties that He has bestowed upon us? As I look around the world, I am struck by the fact that Negroes are a unique race of people. They are perceived by so many of the Black races of the world as a people who have overcome the hardship and succeeded against all odds. They are an inspiration to the Black peoples of the world. "All things are of God."

But they are about to lose their glorious heritage, their abundance of gifts bestowed upon them by a Loving and Kind Father, because they for the most part have chosen to sink into the mire of self-pity, anger and materialism. Sometimes, we carry all of these negative feelings with us to the Cause, and often unconsciously view the teachings of Bahá'u'lláh from behind a "black wall." We, like most people, do not take the words of the Guardian about the "most challenging issue" personally.[1] In our vanity we think "he couldn't possibly be talking to me." To accept his words we would have to give up all our preconceived ideas about who and what we are and where we as a people are going. The Báb says, "O peoples of the World! Whatsoever ye have offered up in the way of the One True God, you shall indeed find preserved by God, the Preserver, intact at God's Holy Gate."[2]

I wonder how many know that the first pioneer to go out under the Guardian's African campaign was a Negro? Our history is before us. What historians write about the Negroes in future Bahá'í history books is up to us now, today. So many of us are still trying to outrun the "jungle bunny" labels. I am sure that you are familiar with the saying "call me anything, just don't call me late for dinner." Well, a new one might be "call me anything, but just don't call me a Bahá'í who didn't arise to serve while there was still time."

The Negroes, though they themselves may not realize it, have a contribution to make to the World Order of Bahá'u'lláh. His Teachings and the society He has come to establish are for every race and every nation, and each one of them has his own part to play and the gift of his own qualities and talents to give to the whole world.[3]

I appeal particularly to its dearly beloved members belonging to the Negro race to participate in the contemplated project marking a significant milestone in the world unfoldment of the Faith.[4]

The Negro believers must be just as active as their white brothers and sisters in spreading the Faith, both among their own race and members of other races. It has been a great step forward in the Cause's development in America to have Negro pioneers go forth, and their work has been of the greatest help and very productive of results.[5]

The Bahá'ís in villages, the simple people, are so touched by the fact that Black people have come to be with them. The color barrier is not there. Certainly in this part of the world, it is of great advantage to have a black skin and be allowed to travel to the villages to be with and to teach and be taught by the "salt of the earth." But, we must hurry before the salt loses its taste.

Along this line, I think that Black American women would be ideal role models for African women. Black American women have a strength, a radiance and resilience needed to awaken and help develop African women. They represent the ability not only to overcome, but to develop continually in what can only be realistically described as a hostile environment. The circumstances endured by the American Black woman in her efforts to raise a family and personally develop, the progress she has thus far achieved can and must be used to inspire and awaken in her African sisters the knowledge of the true and high destiny to which all women have been called by the Revelation of Bahá'u'lláh.

To read and study the compilation on women is to grasp the reality of our true inheritance, an inheritance which must be learned of and accepted by the world community of women, so that we may join hands in our "spiritual sisterhood" each connected by the knowledge that the attributes given and the bounties bestowed upon them by an All-Embracing Father will enable them to arise and contribute significantly to their families, their work places, their communities, and the world. The future of the world's development hangs in the balance. "As your faith is, so shall your powers and blessings be. This is the balance."

> And let it be known once more that until woman and man recognize and realize equality, social and political progress here or anywhere will not be possible.[6]

> As long as women are prevented from attaining their highest possibilities, so long will men be unable to achieve the greatness which might be theirs.[7]

I guess what I am saying is, is there not a way that we could work together to wake up the African-Americans?

I'll tell you a secret that I've discovered. In Africa I found that my ancestors are lost in the mist of time, found only through prayers. I am not an African and never will be. No matter how hard I try to be, wearing the clothes, speaking the language will not make me an African. But if I were to make a true search for my roots, they would be in the heart and soul of Africa. The true roots of man are spiritual and not material nor physical. In this land there is a kindness, a gentleness of heart, a quality so precious that I cannot name it. It is fragile beyond belief, and each day that we keep the Revelation to ourselves, each time that we think or say, "I'm not going over there to that awful place," this precious, nameless quality lessens, and one day it might disappear due to our neglect, only to be revived by another race of man.

> The handmaidens of God and the bondsmaids in His divine Court should reveal such attributes and attitudes amongst the women of the world as would cause them to stand out and achieve renown in the circles of women. That is, they should associate with them with supreme chastity and steadfast decency, with unshakable faith, articulate speech, and eloquent tongue, irrefutable testimony and

high resolve. Beseech God that thou mayst attain unto all these bounties.[8]

One of the most important lessons that I've learned in my life is that if we are not very careful, we will become whatever it is that we abhor. "All things are of God."

By now, I'm sure that you can see how strongly I feel that Black America has a profound role to play in the world arena of women. I often think of the lives of Louis Gregory, Mag Carney, Amoz Gibson and of their sacrifices. Of those who were not Bahá'ís, I think often of Dr. Martin Luther King and Rosa Parks. In fact all people who have had the thought, made the decision, taken the action, and lived the life.

Several years ago, the Universal House of Justice wrote to [the Bahá'ís of] South Africa and said "the winds of change that are sweeping throughout the world have not by-passed South Africa." They went on to say the words that never fail to strike terror in my soul . . . "while there is yet time." The only time that lasts forever is God's own time and not ours.

Can we not enter into consultation on what can be done to awaken our People to their obligation to the peoples of the world? At the risk of sounding melodramatic, I fear that we will become people without a future.

17

Heroines of the Faith
Zylpha Mapp Robinson

This presentation was originally given at the 6th Annual Association for Bahá'í Studies Regional Conference, Green Acre Bahá'í School, Eliot, Maine, on September 4, 1988.

Beloved Friends,

Alláh-u-Abhá

It is with deepest love that I stand before you today. Please understand that it is my great privilege to have been asked to come and share with you some memories of my dear mother, Zylpha Odysell Mapp (Gray).

Early Childhood

Zylpha Johnson was born in Boston, Massachusetts, on October 7, 1890. She spent her early years in Plymouth, Massachusetts, where she was exposed to the great outdoors. Often she would join her father William Johnson, then somewhat delicate in health, at his easel by the seaside painting seascapes in oil on canvas. She would sit quietly by reading until he was ready to gather up his things and return home. It was during these walks that she would ask all kinds of questions.

Whilst quite young, Zylpha's parents sent her to four different Sunday Schools. They all met at different times, and each one claimed it was the only one that was right and all the others were wrong. This attitude puzzled her a lot and often she would lie down in the meadow, listen to the birds, look up into the blue sky and ponder about God and the universe.

Being a precocious child, one day she asked her father: "Father, why did God make so many people if He's going to send them all to Hell? The Catholic priest says that unless you're a Catholic, you will go to Hell. The Baptist minister says that unless you're a Baptist, you won't get to Heaven. I want to know, what about all those people in Africa, India, China, and other places in the world who have never even heard of Jesus Christ? Father, is God going to send them all to Hell? Why would a Just God do that?

Her father answered: "Child, don't ask such questions, that's sacrilegious." For this dear man really didn't know how to answer her question.

And so it was from that tender age, she became aware that something was amiss as far as her religious understanding was concerned.

Youth and Marriage

After graduating from Plymouth High School in 1908 (her father had been the first Black person to have graduated from PHS in the mid-1880s, and she was the first female) she returned to Boston to further her education. But in those years it was not possible to pursue professional training in nursing until she had become 21. Meanwhile, she had met my father. However, as he was a foreigner from Barbados, West Indies, there was some reluctance on the part of her mother (Josephine Houston Johnson) to allow the union to take place. But Zylpha had a strong sense of justice and an inborn belief in the oneness of mankind, so she consulted with her family doctor, an Englishman, Dr. Partridge. He told her: "Marry the man, for in mixed marriages bright progenies are born." Dr. Partridge then proceeded to smooth the way with her mother and the marriage took place in 1910. The couple moved to Cambridge, Massachusetts. Alexander Mapp studied and became an architect, contractor, and builder.

In 1916, when Zylpha was in her mid-twenties, she was undergoing dental treatment after the birth of her fourth child. Her dentist, Dr. Tomlinson, was a West Indian practicing in Cambridge, Massachusetts. She told us later that during these visits she used to ask him questions of a religious nature. Then one day he said to her: "Madam, I think you are ready to hear a Message, would you like to come to a meeting tonight?" On handing her the address, she said she was interested but would have to speak to my father about it.

Bahá'í Faith

That evening they went to the home of Mr. Harlan and Grace (Robarts) Ober. The speaker explained that the religion of God was like a great tree, and His prophets were like the branches of the tree, sent to give shade to all the people of the earth. One branch here shaded the Africans, one here for the Europeans, one over here for the Asians, and so on until all the peoples of the world are under the shade of the same tree. Now the coming of Bahá'u'lláh as the latest prophet of God is to bring unity to all the peoples of the earth, and all are sheltered under the shade of the one tree of life (God). Zylpha listened with great intensity, for to her, at last the question which she had asked her father so many years before had finally been answered. And she became afire with His Love.

As Zylpha was an avid reader, she began to study the Faith and was matured along by such dear souls as Grace (Robarts) Ober, Ella Robarts, Marion Jack, and others, and from that time onward dedicated herself to the service of Bahá'u'lláh.

In those early years the whole family would go to the Bahá'í Feasts and gatherings on Commonwealth Avenue in Boston. I remember once the children were all seated on the floor during a talk, when Auntie Victoria Bedikian (a very dear and dramatic soul) pointed to the Mapp children and said: "Look, we have such beautiful Black pansies among us, how sweet they are." Mother was careful to explain later that Auntie Victoria was pure-hearted and her reference to color was in praise of God's kingdom on earth. Such an action on mother's part was most commendable. My mother and Auntie Victoria became close friends and used to correspond with one another. Here is a brief note:

> Our home in Cambridge became an international gathering place. I remember the visits of scholars from all over the world such as, the Persian Janabi Fadil, who greeted my elder sister, Janice, in French. And she responded excitedly saying: "Oh, mother, he has called us beautiful flowers of the rose garden." (At that time Janice was about 9 and had never studied French, her understanding was through the power of love.) A Mr. Trott, Black South African scholar, who sat at our table often, brought back a diamond ring, and presented it to me at age 5, as a token of his appreciation of the warmth and love and friendship he had experienced in our home. Mother used to encourage the foreign students to study the Faith so as to help enlighten their people back home when they'd return.

Power of Prayer

My younger sister Josephine was born on October 5, 1921. Mother's Dr. Partridge had been alerted and the midwife had left her room to answer the doorbell on the first floor. My elder sister and I had crept down the stairs from the 3rd floor when we heard my mother crying out: "Yá Bahá'u'l-Abhá, Yá Bahá'u'l-Abhá, Yá Bahá'u'l-Abhá!"[1] But we stopped in our tracks when we saw Dr. Partridge and the midwife running upstairs to reach my mother's room. We heard a distant baby's cry and learned the next morning that when the doctor entered my mother's room, our baby sister had already been born through the power of prayer.

Zylpha was known to be somewhat "deep and mystic" and was prone to have "visions and feelings." One day the telephone rang in our den. She remarked that the telephone is ringing with a foreboding tone. Upon answering she was informed of the passing of 'Abdu'l-Bahá (November 1921). She said the signal she had received had prepared her for the shock of His passing.

Life in Avon

In August 1922, my parents, with some degree of foresight, moved to a country home in Avon, Massachusetts, seventeen miles out of Boston, toward the Cape. It was a small town of 2,000 White people—we integrated the town—although not without some hardships. When we went to school, mother instilled in us that "Bahá'í children should study hard and surpass the other children." She expected us to do our homework and would help us to understand things, if it was necessary. She even encouraged us to go beyond the assignments. Avon was the family home for twenty-three years.

One day during the 1920s my Mother took my younger sister, Josephine, with her on an errand to Brockton, Massachusetts. Whilst they were gone, our home caught on fire. My elder brother, Bennie, then about 12 years old, heard the fire engines pass our school, and going to the window saw the flames at the top of the hill coming from our house. He ran home, up the front stairs and tried to salvage things. There on mother's dressing table he saw *The Hidden Words* opened to the page which read: "O Son of Being, busy not thyself with this world, for with fire We test the gold, and with gold We test Our servants."[2]

Needless to say, this was a difficult experience, but the tragedy opened the hearts of some townspeople and three families offered and provided shelter for us. My parents returned to the house in less than a week and gradually rebuilt it, leaving us children with neighbors for awhile.

Zylpha explained: "The message from the Hidden Words tells us that the fire was God's way of bringing about a better understanding amongst the races in Avon."

Green Acre

During the latter part of the 1920s, Mother took us to Green Acre for long weekends in August. There we would stay with Ella Robarts in her cottage and walk down the lane to the Sarah Farmer Inn for activities and a visit to the 'Abdu'l-Bahá room on the third floor. She took us to the river bank to see the sunset, and there she later wrote a poem.

Green Acre
I stood on the bank of a river
The sunset to behold
And lo from each side of the river
Appeared a bridge of gold.
They told me the story of red men,
Awed by this vision one night
Named the river Piscataqua
In Our word "River of Light"
And now high on the hilltop
Overlooking this river of light
Stands a village where people gather
To learn of a new found knight
Who has brought to the world a new vision
Of love and new hope for all
He found it deep down in a prison
Away from all ports of call.
Now thousands have caught this vision
Ignited like a burning flame
Caught from that spark in prison
Bearing the Greatest Name.

Mother meanwhile began to correspond with Shoghi Effendi in Haifa. In one of his letters he asked her "to devote her life to the unity and harmony of the black and white races in America." She immediately was obedient and began to communicate with Mr. Louis Gregory about race amity affairs. By the time of the third annual Amity Conference at Green Acre in August 1929, she had become very actively engaged in presenting the Faith to various groups in Cambridge, Boston, and Brookline. At Green Acre she would serve with Mr. Gregory in discussion groups. It was in these early years that I sat on Mr. Gregory's knee. He seemed to be such a kind, gentle man from the eyes of a child.

Secretary to LSA-Boston

From Riḍván 1928 through 1934, mother served as the secretary of the Boston Spiritual Assembly. She would commute by train to the meetings. I remember one winter the snowdrifts had piled up so high that she got caught up to her hips as she tried to walk three-quarters of a mile from the train station, arriving home in a state of exhaustion with frozen hands and knees. She told us that she had reached home only by calling aloud the Greatest Name[3] as she took each step in the unplowed, drifting snow.

It was about 1931, when a group of Bahá'ís in the Boston area met at the home of Mrs. Nancy Bowditch and signed a piece of paper which was then sent off to Shoghi Effendi in Haifa registering us officially as Bahá'ís. All members of my family were present except my elder brother Bennie, whose name went in also.

Camp Azjaowé

Zylpha was influenced by the Teachings of Bahá'u'lláh in many different ways. For example, His words: "He who educates his son, or any other's children, it is as though he hath educated one of My children,"[4] inspired her to establish a camp for underprivileged children from the Boston area (sponsored by the Boston Urban League). The building of Camp Azjaowé, a permanent structure on our property in Avon, was a unifying family venture, designed and built by my Dad with the help of professionals and family members. Once the campers had arrived each of us had a specific role to play. Whilst the camping experience for the youngsters helped them to learn new skills, under mother's guidance they developed a sense of sharing and caring for each other. Love motivated the camping program, and our days began and ended with prayers. Studies, drama, gardening, walks, games, arts and crafts—everyone could find his niche. To many who had never been to a country town before, the fresh air, good food, and the pine grove with a running brook and ample playing space improved their sense of well-being.

As one camper wrote some years later: "Mother Mapp always made me feel that I was someone 'special' and that had never happened to me before."

Another one said: "Mother Mapp spent many hours guiding and inspiring us, she was busy giving of herself from morning till night."

One wrote from overseas: "I'll always remember how you treated us all with such fairness, everyone was welcomed in your home, it's important to me now to think on those days."

Randavonian Orchestra

Zylpha continually focused on the need to provide concrete evidence of the oneness of mankind. She encouraged my brothers, Bennie and Dickie, along with their musical friends to set-up the Randavonian Orchestra. Its members comprised of diverse nationalities—Italian, Swedish, Irish, Anglo Saxon, and so on. Mother played the piano, Bennie the drums, and Dickie the trumpet. Dickie was also a vocalist (as well as myself), and the other friends played string and wind instruments. The Randavonian Orchestra performed for charitable organizations, hospitals, churches, and other functions. Among the highlights of their years together was driving to Boston to give concerts for the Bahá'ís.

During the long rehearsals at the house, Zylpha would say, our music is to stir the hearts and souls of men as we give thanks and praise to God. She looked upon the orchestra as a means of giving thanks to the townspeople of Avon.

Portia Law School

In addition to being our spiritual mother, Zylpha was aware of the need to continue her own advancement. Thus whilst we children were still in school, she enrolled at Portia Law School "to keep up with my family," she said. She commuted to Boston and completed two and a half years, but the death of our grandfather (William Johnson) and the Great Depression interfered with her completing her studies.

I remember the story she told of how God is ever-present in one's life. One evening she went to her class in torts at Portia Law and found an examination in progress. She had been absent from the previous class owing to my grandfather's illness, so the exam came as a surprise to her. Zylpha took the exam paper, closed her eyes and bent her head to say, "Is there any Remover of difficulties, save God? Say: Praised be God! He is God! All are His servants, and all abide by His bidding!"[5] nine times. She opened her eyes read the paper and answered all the questions receiving in the end a mark of ninety percent. "Put your faith in Him, for He is always there, no matter how small or how large your difficulty may be," she would say. How many times thereafter did we use that key?

Bahá'í Youth

Our parents facilitated our movements as Bahá'í youth to attend activities in Boston, Cambridge, or Brookline communities. In the summer months, when our garden would be replete with corn, string beans, tomatoes, lettuce, and fruits from the trees, mother would foster picnics for the young people to come to our pine grove in Avon. I remember Sylvia Paine Parmelee, Betty Shook, Wilfred Barton, and Beth Murray would be present. Sometimes Lorna Tasker, Rachel Small, and Nancy Bowditch would be present, too. Our school friends and the Randavonian Orchestra would join to make a happy diverse group.

With the growth of the Faith, Shoghi Effendi in his letters to America instructed us to develop Assemblies according to the city jurisdictions. Thus, we in Avon became isolated believers.[6] This plunged mother into even greater activity. We lived in the first house on the street at the top of a hill. Whenever anyone came to the house, mother would find a way to give them "the Message." She told us that God had sent them to her, and it was her duty to teach the Faith, regardless of what their mission might have been . . . traveling salesman, hobo, rag-picker, it didn't matter. Once a Rosicrucian came and tried to convince her of his teachings, but in the end he left with some typewritten pages on the Bahá'í Faith. (In those days we had few teaching tools.)

Father died in 1944 whilst I was living overseas (Jamaica). Two years later Mother left Avon for good and moved to New York to be nearer to my two sisters. She became affiliated with the Riverdale Children's Orphan Association and served as housemother in its home for girls on a 200-acre plot of ground on the Hudson River in New York. When for financial reasons this home was closed, she was asked to remain to live in the director's home and provide a home for eight orphan boys. This she did for three years, providing them with love and care to help them improve in their studies and gain self-esteem.

Some of her happiest moments came when in later years she would receive a letter or phone call from one of her many "adopted children" telling her of the positive changes in their life as a result of her attention to them earlier.

In 1950, whilst I was living in England, mother returned to Plymouth, Massachusetts, where she married a childhood friend, Mr. George Gray. Even though she again became an isolated believer, she prayed for the progress of the Faith. Each week she would go to the seaside and the hillside and shout "Yá Bahá'u'l-Abhá" to the four corners of the earth. Zylpha was active in community affairs there and volunteered to play the organ in her husband's church. He died in 1959. Some years later she learned that Plymouth had a thriving Bahá'í community.

Life in Springfield

Josephine and her husband, Howie, encouraged Mother to relocate to their house in Springfield, Massachusetts, in 1960, which proved to be an excellent decision. Soon she learned that there was another Bahá'í in Springfield, Beulah Timmerman, and the two of them began to hold Feasts together, say prayers and open her home to the Faith.

Meanwhile, as Zylpha was always community-minded, she took an active part in the Springfield Federation of Women's Clubs and served as their first Black president for four consecutive years. Under her supervision many worthwhile projects were undertaken including the establishment of a "Tot Lot" (children's playground) in the north end of the city.

She turned one of her hobbies, sewing, into a service. And for five years (1961–5) she designed, cut out, and sewed from 50 to 60 dresses a year which she sent to the Indian children on the reservation at the White Earth Mission in the west. This project she undertook while attending the women's group at Christ Church Cathedral in Springfield as the Bahá'í representative in its thrust for ecumenism.

Zylpha also found another avenue for serving mankind when she joined the Golden Agers at Winchester Square branch in Springfield and became an assistant treasurer. They met every week, and it was not long before she caught their attention by reading a quotation from the writings of Bahá'u'lláh or 'Abdu'l-Bahá. Many times thereafter she was called upon to speak on her favorite subject, "The Oneness of Humanity," through the contacts she had made with the Golden Agers.

By responding to the appeal from the colleges in the area, Zylpha happily offered hospitality to foreign students during the holiday seasons. Again her home took on an international flavor as she encouraged the young people to share their culture with others. Sometimes they'd prepare special dishes together—recipes from Africa, the West Indies, Asia, or South America. She was more than a mother to them, often helping the student to improve his English through the playing of the game Scrabble. One student later said, "After playing Scrabble with 'Nana Mapp' I would go home and study the dictionary, so as to learn new words; this helped me a lot with the language. She was really challenging us to learn."

By 1964, the Springfield Bahá'í Group gained three more members as I returned to the States (after an absence of 20 years), Jane Grover and her family moved to Springfield, and my brother Bennie (whose work had its headquarters in Boston) began to commute from Springfield to Boston, enabling him to participate in the Springfield community. We established regular Firesides at Zylpha's home, which served thereafter as the Bahá'í center for five years.

Just prior to this, Zylpha had had the bounty of visiting the Holy Land. It had come about as a total surprise. While she had served at Riverdale, she had befriended a young doctoral student and, over the years, Dr. Olivia Hooker had kept in touch. One day Dr. Hooker invited mother to go to the Holy Land, in appreciation of her previous kindnesses and as an answer to mother's dream. It was an exhilarating experience early in the morning when she went to the Shrines and was greeted by Mr. Amoz Gibson, who permitted her to say prayers on Mt. Carmel. There, in the Shrine of the Báb, she knelt to pray with tears streaming down her cheeks; she emerged "feeling like utter nothingness." The visit to the Shrine of 'Abdu'l-Bahá gave her a sense of exaltation, and she knew that she was living in a joyous era. Thus, she rededicated herself to the service of Bahá'u'lláh.

Comments

"Her Firesides were something special," said a young Caucasian seeker of high school age, "I had never been in the home of a non-White before and was completely enraptured by her warmth, wisdom and knowledge of the Faith."

It was always a delight for Mother to turn to any Bahá'í book and find an answer to a seeker's question directly from the words of the Manifestation of God.

Dick Grover was still a seeker when he moved to Springfield. I'm sure he would like to give us some thoughts on how he perceived Zylpha before he became a Bahá'í. It was through Dick's declaration that we finally reached nine and could form an Assembly in Springfield.

"Everyone loved Nana, for she took time to listen and pay attention to you," said her grand-daughter Juanita. "She instilled confidence in me, telling me to reach for the stars. Nana was unique, she would design clothes for me that would be different and give me a sense of individuality. She also believed that by interacting with young people, keeping busy and involved with promoting harmony and unity, she would stay alert."

In July 1967, the *Springfield Daily News* honored her as a "friend to children" and presented her with orchids as a symbol of someone special. In that same year, she visited Wilmette to take part in the intercontinental conference. The next year she went travel teaching to Barbados, West Indies (the home of her husband, Alexander Mapp), and there made several presentations on the Faith. (She was accompanied by my elder sister, Janice.) She was warmly welcomed by the indigenous friends for having journeyed to my father's birthplace at her age, 77, to enlighten them with the Message of Bahá'u'lláh.

"As you know, mothers-in-law and sons-in-law usually don't hit it off well," said Howie Edmonds, "but in Nana's case, she loved me and I loved her. She was the most lovable, energetic, knowledgeable, and admired soul with a great sense of justice for all. And her name lives on, for as part of the American Bicentennial celebration (1976) a publication entitled *Women of Springfield's Past* cited her for her work among the children."

"Mother had been active in the Faith up to her last breath and passed her last days peacefully," remarked my sister Jo. "We knew her life was ebbing. One day she asked: 'When will Joel be back here?'" (Joel, my sister's son and Nana's grandson, was living and teaching in New York College but wasn't expected before the Christmas holidays.) "However, he came to Springfield that same evening quite unexpectedly as if he had caught Nana's thought wave. The next day (early December 1970) she passed on quietly to the Abhá Kingdom, at the age of 80."

In summary, you might ask, what sort of lady was this handmaiden of Bahá'u'lláh, this "wonderful soul," as some have referred to her?

Zylpha always thanked God for everything. I have heard her say: "Thank God for a bed to sleep in." She would always praise the Source for whatever bounty came her way.

She had friends in all walks of life; she was warm-hearted, fearless, compassionate, trustworthy, honest and just. Wherever she went people looked up to her. "An elegant lady who set the standards for the community in which she lived," said a colleague of mine, "she made a tremendous impact on us all."

Thank you all for listening.

---

1 8

Sadie Rebecca Johnson Ellis

Adrienne Reeves

This biography of Sadie Ellis is previously unpublished.

"I was born July 20, 1863, in Rolla, Missouri. I was the child of very poor slave parents. Both Father (James, born 1839) and Mother (Matilda Ballinger, born 1840) was of the independent spirit. Hence when the Civil War of [the] '60s began, Father left the man who owned him and enlisted in the Union Army, stating he would rather die than remain in slavery."

Thus begins a sketch of the life of Helen Josephine Ballinger Walker, written in 1937 in her own hand when she was seventy-four years old. Helen's sister, Mary, younger by three years, was the mother of Sadie Rebecca Johnson Ellis. Details from Helen Walker's chronicle give some insight into the remarkable ancestry of Sadie Ellis.

Matilda (Sadie's grandmother), less than five feet tall, disguised herself as a fat young man because she was over six months pregnant and took her baby, Will, whom she called her brother, and set out from Virginia to join her husband, James. James had sent her a message from the Union Army encampment in Rolla, Missouri, that he was nearly blind due to measles.

Matilda "at once began to pray, requesting of God to help her make her escape from the man who owned her and go to the army to be near father in his lonely time of blindness and distress."

The master's son and another slave hunter sat on a log just above where Matilda and her baby were hiding in a dugout, covered by leaves and twigs. The baby had been given something to make him sleep quietly. The man decided that "Tillie" couldn't have made it that far and turned back. Some friendly people helped Matilda get to James at Rolla, where, a few months later, Helen was born. Upon his discharge, James and his family set out for Iowa in a covered wagon, but he found work as a skilled harness maker in Alton, in the free state of Illinois. Through industriousness and good business sense James and Matilda were able to purchase first one forty-acre plot and later another one on which they built a hilltop two-story white house, which is still standing and occupied. Little Sadie Johnson often visited her maternal grandparents at this house in Wood Station, known as the Ballinger Homestead, a few miles outside of Alton. Sadie's mother, Mary, was the first of the nine Ballinger children to be born in freedom, and she (Matilda) grew up in this house.

Sadie was born on February 7, 1892, in Wood Station, to Mary Ballinger Johnson and William Madden Johnson on a farm first purchased by James Henry and Eleanor Johnson in 1854. It has been continuously occupied and farmed by four generations of Johnsons.

A few miles from the Johnson farm is Salem Baptist Church, first organized in 1854. This small church had a deep effect upon both the spiritual and social life of the Black community. Sadie was raised as a Christian by her devout parents in that church where the Johnsons served the clerkship for seventy-six years.

Sadie had eight brothers and three sisters. During childhood she became seriously ill, very thin, and nearly died. Friends named Dorsey who lived in St. Louis prevailed upon the Johnsons to let Sadie live with them to be near the doctors and the hospital. Her health gradually improved as she lived with the Dorseys in St. Louis, and she graduated from Sumner High School there. Her sisters were also sent to high school in St. Louis or nearby because of the racial prejudice in the Alton schools.

Sadie was an excellent student and earned the distinction of being selected salutatorian of her graduating class. The valedictorian was a young man named Charles Everett Ellis from the small town of Altamont, Illinois, some seventy miles northwest of Alton. He had been sent to high school in St. Louis by his father, Levi G. Ellis, who, with his brother Albert, operated the oldest barbershop on record in that town.

After graduation Charles returned to Altamont, to the barbershop which became his after his father and uncle retired. Charles and Sadie were married on September 4, 1943. She was twenty-one; he was twenty-six.

The Ellis family had always been the only black family in Altamont. The two brothers, Levi and William, had married two sisters, Lina Eudora and Jennie Sellers. William's family of eight children migrated to Chicago, as did a number of Levi's six children. One wonders, therefore, what it was like for Sadie, reared in a large family in the midst of an expanding black community, to come to Altamont. She was a bride coming from cousins, friends, family whom she saw often, and a black church which provided both spiritual and social sustenance into a totally white community used to the phenomenon of this single black family and certainly not free from racial prejudice.

Charles Ellis kept a diary which spanned some forty-three years. It began on January 1, 1927, and ended December 5, 1970, four months before he died. When the diary begins, Charles and Sadie have been married thirteen years. Five children have been born: Charles, Marguerite, Howard, Adrienne, and William. William died in infancy of pneumonia. Caswell was born in April of the year the diary begins. Wilma was born in Altamont two years later, and the youngest child, Marilyn, arrived after the family moved to Alton.

The pattern of life that Charles recorded in his diaries at this time includes long hours for him at the barber shop, the family attending church twice on Sundays, the planting and harvesting of vegetables, entertaining family from Chicago and Alton, and Sadie occasionally in bed with pleurisy. The children took part in church plays; the pastor and his wife visited.

Charles and Sadie played rook in the evenings, with Sadie as the most frequent winner. They saw each picture show as it changed at the local movie house. They frequently walked, especially on moonlit nights, and sometimes stopped in to visit someone. Some friend with a car took them on a ride. Sadie belonged to the Ladies Aid Association at the church and participated in their quilting bees. She went to Alton, and Charles went to Chicago to see family.

As the Great Depression spread and deepened, unemployment was felt even in a town as small as Altamont. In his diary Charles notes that business was very slow, as the farmers had no money for haircuts and shaves. He and Sadie made plans to move the family to Sadie's home while he stayed in Altamont, living in the back of the shop. On June 5, 1930, Sadie and the children went to Wood Station to share the family farmhouse with her brother, Cyrus Johnson, and his family. Charles visited regularly by train and bus. Once they met in Chicago. In 1933 a fire destroyed the farmhouse, and Sadie moved into Alton. The farmhouse was rebuilt, but Sadie's family remained in Alton. In June of that year Charles finally was forced to close the shop and went to Chicago to try to find work. He sold eggs in Chicago as long as he could, then tried working in Detroit, but without success. He left Detroit on October 12, 1933, and hitchhiked west, arriving in Prescott, Arizona, eight days later. He stayed briefly with a friend, working at whatever small job he could find. On October 28 he records, "Lambert Taylor quitting the job. I take it with much gratitude. A start at last."

The older children remembered the hard days following the fire as a time when they had to live in their grandmother's small basement, as the rest of the house was full, and being laughed at by some of the school children because of the clothes they wore. One basket of laundry was snatched from the upstairs landing of the house before the flames engulfed the upper story. Very little else was saved. Eventually Sadie found a house to move into, and for the next three years she and the children struggled to make ends meet. Charles, Junior, and Howard eventually followed their father west. In Phoenix, Arizona, Charles met and married Rena Alexander.

It was to their house in Phoenix that Charles, Sr., now firmly established as a barber in a resort hotel in Prescott, Arizona, made arrangements for his family to come to in December 1936. Sadie and the children left Alton on a Greyhound bus around December 16; the children were in a state of excitement about the trip and going to far away to live. Sadie once said of this trip, "Knew we would finally be together again as a family, and I was thankful about that, but I had no idea about how much our lives would change because of this decision."

They arrived at the house on North 9th Street on December 21, 1936. In Alton they had left a heavy snowfall. In the well-kept yard around the house, the roses that Charles had planted were in bloom. The weather was sunny and warm. It seemed like paradise.

The serpent in this paradise was racial discrimination. Blacks could not eat at lunch counters except for a small Chinese place called Sing High's. They were not welcome in the better stores, as Sadie discovered when she went into Goldwater's Department Store downtown and was refused service. There were black schools, churches, parks. Seating in movie theaters was segregated and blacks did not live in white neighborhoods.

Sadie joined the First Baptist Church on 5th and Jefferson, and Charles, the Tanner AME Church when he was able to leave Prescott in January 1938 to begin barbering in Phoenix. The professional and skilled worker positions for blacks in Phoenix were very limited; most work was as domestics or in the service areas such as waiters and porters.

Charles Jr. and his wife, Lina, found employment as a couple in a domestic service job that had live-in accommodations. They turned the house over to Sadie and the children.

The Phyllis Weatley Community Center was the site of black activities. It was there, for instance, that her daughters gave Sadie a "dancing party" on her birthday in 1939. Charles and Sadie played whist and Chinese checkers with friends; visits and dinners were exchanged. They went to the Little Theatre occasionally and to the movies frequently. Charles was active in the Masonic Lodge, and for a while Sadie went to the auxiliary body for women.

Adrienne began attending Phoenix Junior College in 1937. Late in 1938 she was invited to join a small singing group with a classmate, Betty Hogan. Betty's mother was known for her rich alto and rehearsed the group in singing spirituals. The group was invited to sing at a meeting held in the home of some people named Schoeny who lived on Portland Street. Most of the people at the meeting were white, as were the Schoenys. There was a friendliness and warmth, and when the group left, they were invited to come again. In speaking of the meeting later to her mother, Adrienne spoke about how welcomed she felt and showed her mother a small blue pamphlet about the Bahá'í Faith and its ten principles, which Mrs. Schoeny had given her.

Adrienne went again, and each time she was invited to return, which she did. Meanwhile a Mrs. Lucy Lucas had taken a room in the large house on Washington Street to which the family had moved in June 1938. She was affiliated with the Bahá'ís. On October 8, 1938, Sadie and Adrienne accompanied Mrs. Lucas to a Bahá'í picnic. On November 6 Charles attended his first Bahá'í function, going with the group to Coolidge, Arizona, for a meeting.

By 1939 Adrienne was attending Bahá'í meetings regularly. One day Mrs. Zahrah Schoeny said, "Don't you want to join us and be a Bahá'í?" Adrienne said, "Yes," instantly, unequivocally. Paul and Zahrah Schoeny explained that she would need to read certain books and then meet with the Spiritual Assembly so they could ascertain if she had the basic understanding of the Central Figures and tenets of the Faith. She began studying a book by J. E. Esslemont called *Bahá'u'lláh and the New Era,* which gave the origin of the Faith, a brief history, its teachings, and application to the present and future.

Sadie began working as a housekeeper-companion, taking jobs which sometimes called for her to be away, returning home for overnight visits. One day she said to Adrienne, "You're spending a lot of time with the Bahá'ís. Are you serious about the Faith?" Adrienne said she was. "I'm studying now to learn what I have to know in order to be a Bahá'í." "If you're that serious about it," Sadie said, "then I'll have to look into it seriously."

Sadie and Adrienne had both been steadfast members and workers in the Baptist Church of which Rev. Favors was pastor. Adrienne went to school with his daughters. At that time one could be a Bahá'í without formally ending one's ties with a church. However, Adrienne had gradually replaced church activities with Bahá'í activities, and when she had studied the Will and Testament of 'Abdu'l-Bahá and successfully met with the Phoenix Spiritual Assembly to become a Bahá'í in June, 1939, she withdrew from the church.

Sadie told her son Caswell later that when Adrienne had told her that Bahá'u'lláh claimed to be the return of Christ, she remembered that her father had told her that one day she might hear this claim made by "a man among men," and that if and when she did she should investigate it because this is how the Return would occur, not by a person descending on a cloud. Sadie was three months old when Bahá'u'lláh ascended in May 1892. She was forty-six when she finally learned about Bahá'u'lláh and His Revelation. She began classes preparatory to enrollment on June 20, 1939, and became a member of the Bahá'í Faith on June 24, 1939.

Sadie had been raised as a Christian by devout parents, William and Mary Johnson, who were leaders in the church. Inspired by and supported by her love for God, the source of her spirituality was the teaching to Jesus Christ, the church and the constant example of her parents whom she loved and respected. But when one considers how hard she worked, how loving and caring she was, how trusting in God she was, it is not surprising that once she learned of Bahá'u'lláh, her heart recognized Him, and she became a declared believer four months and seventeen days after her forty-seventh birthday.

The Bahá'í community of Phoenix, of which she became a member, established its first Spiritual Assembly in April 1930. Lily Wiggins was the first Black Bahá'í in the community. Among other black believers were Bea Durando, Marie Payne, and Lucy Lucas. Matthew and Noble A. White were also affiliated but were not declared Bahá'ís. Also in the community were Clinton and Miriam Beaglee, Nancy Phillips, and Paul and Zahara Schoeny. Sadie wrote a letter to the pastor of the church she had been attending, explaining why she would no longer be a member. Rev. Favors came to visit her and she told him about the Faith. He could not understand nor accept the fact that Christ had thus returned, but he said he had to respect Sadie's wishes and that he was very sorry to lose her from the church.

There was a lot of activity in the Phoenix community which Sadie and her family immediately participated in. The three younger children, Caswell, Wilma, and Marilyn went to the children's classes. Feasts were attended. Bahá'ís on their way to and from other places stayed in the Ellis home; a youth conference was held there. In August all of Phoenix went out to the country to help raise a house for Walter and Emma Jones and their children. A picnic was held there the following month. In November Clarence Iverson left to pioneer, and the Ellis family went to the farewell. The American Bahá'í community was trying to achieve the goals of the First Seven Year Teaching Plan at the time. It was given to the community by Shoghi Effendi, Guardian of the Bahá'í Faith, in 1937 and was to end in 1944. The chief goals were to establish a Spiritual Assembly in each state and province of North America and in Alaska, to establish a center in each republic of Latin America and the Caribbean, and to complete the exterior of the House of Worship in Wilmette. Clarence Iverson and Johnny Eichenauer went from Phoenix to the Central American country of El Salvador as pioneers.

From the beginning Sadie was a diligent and persevering student of the Bahá'í writings. She eagerly bought and studied each new pamphlet, as there were few books available in 1939. Through the years as books were published they became part of her Bahá'í library. She began teaching her children, including the older ones, Charles, Marguerite, and Howard, who were already out of the home, and eventually all of them became confirmed believers. She was also anxious to tell her brothers and sisters and her mother about this wonderful News. The first time she was able to do this was when she returned to Alton during her mother's final illness. She later told Adrienne, "At least Mama died knowing about Bahá'u'lláh."

"How did Grandmother respond?" Adrienne asked.

"I think she understood that the Lord had returned."

By the early forties her three older children, Charles, Marguerite, and Adrienne were now living in Los Angeles, and Howard was in the army. Regular travels between Phoenix and Los Angeles became commonplace. Sadie was in Los Angeles when Marguerite and her husband, Roscoe Johnson, had their first child, Gloria. The younger children joined her there for the summer. In February 1942 the family moved to 9 North 12th Street in Phoenix. Directly across the street lived a teacher, Miss Manila Smith, who had come from Los Angeles to teach in the black elementary school and who became like a member of the family. She was exposed to the Faith and embraced it later. She returned to Los Angeles eventually and served for many years on the Spiritual Assembly.

Although she herself could not physically go pioneering, Sadie and her husband, Charles, gave their wholehearted consent to Adrienne to interrupt college and pioneer in North Carolina with Eva Lee Flack in the fall of 1942 where the first Spiritual Assembly was to be established in Greensboro. The Local Spiritual Assembly was formed, with Adrienne and Eva as two of its members on April 21, 1943. While at their pioneer post Eva married a Bahá'í named Charles McAllister, and Adrienne married William A. Reeves, who became a Bahá'í later in Los Angeles. Joyce Dahl writes that she got to know Sadie Ellis at Geyersville. "Sadie Ellis first won my heart when she offered to take my baby, Keith, while I went to the afternoon gathering in the grove."

In the summer of 1942 Sadie took the children and went by bus to the Bahá'í School in Geyersville, California. A receipt shows that she paid thirty dollars to Irene L. Chittenden for the upstairs apartment from July 4 to July 25. This was the beginning of a summer ritual which helped to deepen Sadie's knowledge of and commitment to the Faith and formed the Bahá'í ideal in the hearts of Caswell, Wilma, and Marilyn during their formative years, for this Bahá'í School on property given to the Faith by John and Louise Bosch in the 1920s was a living laboratory. Here believers from all over the U.S. and often from other countries could come with their families and friends to live and study the Faith in unity in beautiful surroundings of the hills and redwoods of northern California.

A family move to Los Angeles had begun when Charles and Marguerite established themselves there. Sadie and children arrived in March 1944, and the move was completed when Charles and Sadie moved into a house at 793 East 47th Street in 1945, which they had purchased earlier. The family became a part of the Bahá'í community in Los Angeles, which was large and had many activities growing out of its center at 331 South New Hampshire Avenue. All Nineteen-Day Feasts and Holy Days were observed; adult and children's classes held, a large library maintained. Many noted Bahá'í visitors visited the city and spoke at the center during the regular teaching programs, usually on Sunday.

Sadie and the children attended everything regularly, and in May 1944, Sadie went with Adrienne to her first National Bahá'í Convention in Wilmette, Illinois.

Living in Los Angeles with its many Bahá'í activities, people coming in and out of the city, and connections made by Geyersville Bahá'í School all provided Sadie with occasions to extend the gracious hospitality which was a natural part of her being. Firuz Kazemzadeh recounts the following:

Amin Banani, Shidan Fathe A'zam, and I were invited by Caswell to stay at the Ellis home in Los Angeles, where we visited in the fall of 1945. Mrs. Ellis—and, by the way, we never called her Sadie—was the most charming and kind hostess.

She made no fuss over us but managed to make us feel at home. We knew somehow that we belonged, that our presence was not a burden, that she was our friend.

On that occasion, and on later ones, most of my interaction with Mrs. Ellis was in her kitchen, which was in effect the parlor, the living room where the "living" was done. The kitchen was always full of people who floated in and out, and there was always plenty of delicious food on the table.

Mrs. Ellis inspired respect not only because she was an older person and the mother of my friend Caswell. Her demeanor and her appearance were such that one felt in the presence of someone important. Mrs. Ellis was dignified and aristocratic without being artificial or still.

Watching Mrs. Ellis interact with members of her family and others who happened to be in her home, one could not help noticing the influence she exerted over them. Behind the soft exterior there was enormous strength. It must have been that strength that led her first to become a Bahá'í and then to assume a position of leadership in the Bahá'í community in Los Angeles. It was the strength of devotion to God and His trust, the strength of love for people, the strength that comes from an inborn desire to serve.

One afternoon Sadie received a call from a young man who was visiting in Los Angeles from Palo Alto, California. He said his mother, who was a Bahá'í, had instructed him to be sure to look up the Bahá'ís. Sadie invited him to her fireside that evening. When he came, he had with him a young woman and explained they would not stay long, as they were going out, but he wanted to carry out his mother's wishes. Sadie welcomed them, and when they left a little later, she invited the young lady to come again as she was living and working in Los Angeles. The young lady, Valerie Wilson, came back the very next week, said she was greatly attracted to the Faith and wanted to study it seriously. The young man never became a Bahá'í, but Valerie was a physical therapist, in town for a special course. She became a member of the Ellis extended family and soon a declared believer. When she returned home, she immediately contacted Joyce and Arthur Dahl and plunged wholeheartedly into the Bahá'í work. Her mother, Octavia Jones, became a Bahá'í and was a pillar in the Palo Alto community for some forty years. Valerie's profession took her various places, but when Shoghi Effendi called for a teaching campaign in Africa during the Second Seven Year Plan 1946–53, and asked America especially to send its "dearly beloved members belonging to the Negro race"[1] to pioneer, Valerie left her profession and her home and went to Liberia, where she made a significant contribution to the establishment of the Faith in that country.

One of the earliest black believers in Los Angeles was Robert Franklin Willis. Born in Atlanta, Georgia, in 1886, he became a Bahá'í in Boston, Massachusetts, where he had a rooming house for shipyard workers. Some friends took him to a home, where he was introduced to the Faith. He often mentioned Mrs. Alice Higginbotham among his friends he met there. He also knew Juliet Thompson and Lua Getsinger. He told how the Bahá'ís took part in a parade in which he played the coronet. The Boston Bahá'ís met in downtown hotels. In 1924 he moved his family to Los Angeles and became a part of that community. He served on an early Regional Teaching Committee for Nevada, California and Arizona. His niece, Norah Newman, moved from Ohio to California in 1948. Her Uncle Robert took her to many Bahá'í activities, and in 1956 she became a believer. She served on the Los Angeles Assembly from 1957 to 1966. In 1969, at age seventy-six, her mother also embraced the Faith. (These notes courtesy of Norah Newman, now living in Mira Loma, California.)

19

Arrival in Haifa, March 11, 1927
Sadie Oglesby

These notes of Sadie Oglesby's pilgrimage are previously unpublished.

During our first visit with Shoghi Effendi, which was a few hours after our arrival in Haifa, Shoghi Effendi having greeted us (the American pilgrims, five in the party) and having asked of the American believers as to health, unity, etc., he turned to me and said he was very pleased that I had come to visit Haifa, that I was the first colored believer to visit there during his time, etc. Then proceeded to ask how many colored believers there are in America.

I told him we were very few. He then asked about the number of colored believers in Boston, New York, and other centers. He said the Master[1] loved the colored people very much and that the Cause needs the colored people and cannot be established without them.

He said, "The believers should practice great kindness and show great love so that the colored people may be attracted to the Cause. Until the doors are opened and the colored people are attracted into the Cause the white people who are not believers will not have confidence in the sincerity of the friends and will not enter the Cause. The friends should practice all the teachings and not only a part, and this will draw the colored people to the Cause."

At another time he said, "He is not pleased that so few colored people are in the Cause," and that special effort must be made to attract them. He asked if I had been urgent in this matter, if I had been forceful in explaining this feature of the teachings to the understanding of the believers.

I told him I had thought that if we should meet together, read the teachings, and practice great love, doing all possible at the same time to draw others into the Cause all other matters would adjust themselves and perfect amity among the believers would ultimately be attained.

He said I should be insistent and urgent upon this matter. That I should be persistent and not quiet so that the believers may learn of this great need. He told me I had been negligent, indifferent, and had not done my duty upon this subject.

I told him Mr. Oglesby had often been persistent in speaking to the friends upon this subject but that I had just as often tried to keep him quiet. He said, "Mr. Oglesby's way is the better way."

I told him I had tried all I could to be in harmony and amity with friends, that I had understood the Master to say we must give up even the right and accept the wrong for the sake of harmony and unity. He then said, "Yes, the Master said that and the Master wrote that, but that was then. This is another time. It is important that we have a center in America composed of colored and white believers, where all differences are removed. A center established upon the teachings of the Master. This is most important."

Continuing, he said, "Racial unity and harmony, cooperation and freedom from racial prejudice is the first principle. If we will not keep the first principle, how can we hope to keep the following principles? We must find unity and harmony upon the principles. If we find unity and harmony other than upon the principles, we will establish that which is not the Cause."

I told Shoghi Effendi that I thought the friends of America loved him very much, and I believed if they know how anxious he was upon this matter that they would do all they could to satisfy his desire.

He said when I returned to America, I should seek no rest but be constant and urgent. That the importance of this matter should be understood by the friends. That I should be fearless and compelling. I expressed my great sorrow to him and told him I was quite unprepared, unqualified for the work he wished me to do. I said to him, "I have no strength or importance in America. I am so sorry."

To this, Shoghi Effendi said, "When you return to America, do as I have told you. Be fearless and know that the invisible concourse will assist you and I will supplicate at the Holy Shrine in your behalf."

Another day when Shoghi Effendi had talked upon this subject, I said to him, "Shoghi Effendi, it presents itself to me thuswise: since the infancy of the human family, races and nations one after another have arisen and fallen in their long march around the cycles and to maturity and at this time, the oldest race represented upon the earth is the colored race, while the youngest or last to have attained a high civilization is the white race, and in order to close this cycle and save the civilization of this day, the oldest and youngest or first and last, that is the white and colored, or outer ends of the cycle must link together, then the inner, or intermediate races will automatically take their places in the circle. Thus the family of Bahá'u'lláh will be established."

Shoghi Effendi said, "That is true, but if we fail to do this, we will be dispersed."

Again, Shoghi Effendi said, "The believers must establish in America a center composed of white and colored people who are living in perfect harmony and unity, having settled all their differences through the revelation of Bahá'u'lláh. When the people have suffered and are tired and weary, ready to seek hope and comfort, the attention of the ruling heads of the nations may be called to this center in America and establish the world of Bahá'u'lláh, but if we fail to establish such a center, the people will find no hope anywhere."

One day at dinner with the pilgrims, both Eastern and Western, Shoghi Effendi, as he discoursed upon the matter of unity between the white and colored people, was interrupted several times and to each of those who sought information upon other matters he said, "That is not important," but urged the need of a center in America composed of the two races saying, "India has her problem, Germany has her problem, Persia has her problem, the other nations each has its problem, but

America's problem is the establishment of unity and harmony between the white and colored people." He said, "Racial prejudice and differences on the part of non-believers is a problem, but there should be no racial problem on the part of the believers."

He said the believers should astonish the world by their fellowship and cooperation with the colored people. This, he said, is an open door of service in which the Bahá'is will not be molested.

March 23

During the dinner period, Shoghi Effendi said a colored believer should be elected upon each committee even if it required that the same one be elected upon each committee. I then asked him this question. "If after having gone into the meeting for election, we prayed for spiritual guidance, proceeded to vote and no colored believer was elected, what should we do in such a case?" He said, "To pray for spiritual guidance is not sufficient, we should also study the needs of the Cause, discuss the needs of the Cause at the Nineteen Day Feasts, speak of the needs and the qualifications the committees require (not at the time of election), discuss it during the year so that the friends may be informed. At present, the colored are overwhelmed by the white."

Shoghi Effendi asked, "Have the friends read the Master's teachings upon racial amity? Have they enough teaching upon this feature of the Cause? Do they understand its great importance? Do they know of the Master's fearless example in His attitude toward Mr. Gregory in Washington and elsewhere?"

I told Shoghi Effendi I had often heard the friends read the Master's teachings upon this subject in the meetings. Then he said, "I have never written upon it; I will write."

March 27

As I sat with Shoghi Effendi in the Master's parlor, he said to me, "My charge to you is that when you go back to America, tell the friends to look within themselves and find there the reason of so few colored people being in The Cause. Until this is removed, the Cause cannot grow. If we wish The Cause to grow in America, that which is the Cause of so few colored believers must be removed. This is vital."

I told Shoghi Effendi I had believed that since the colored people were not responsible for this breach or chasm, never having desired a separation from the whites, that the white believers would be the ones to work this feature of The Cause. Shoghi Effendi said, "Yes, but we must help them."

I asked Shoghi Effendi if it would not be well for us to have prayer meetings. Answer: "Yes it would be very effective if the believers should gather and engage in prayers from different friends even as many as would take part. It would no doubt be of much benefit in bringing out amity and harmony, but this should not be forced upon any one."

One day I asked Shoghi Effendi if a Bahá'í should have a last will and testament [and] a desire to be cremated, [but] it [was] within the power of the friends reasonably to deny this request and inter according to the teachings, should this be done. Answer: "Undoubtedly, to inter according to the teachings is most important and will be a favor to the departed."

Shoghi Effendi said that when I felt I had done all I could upon the feature of racial amity among the believers, to take trips south and teach there. The South is in great need of the teachings.

During my last interview with Shoghi Effendi he said, "You must be earnest and constant in your effort to press to the understanding of the believers the vital need of a perfect unity between the white and colored people. Be eager, earnest and forceful in this matter, and be assured that the invisible concourse will assist you in your work and we will support you, I will pray for you, I will pray for you at the Holy Shrine. I will pray for you. Be confident."

Having spent twenty days in Haifa and having had many private interviews with Shoghi Effendi and listened to his daily dinner talks during each of which he emphasized and urged upon racial amity, yet the one impression that stands out most paramount is that Shoghi Effendi wishes nothing done in regards to the Cause that is not according to the will of the National Spiritual Assembly and sanctioned by that body.

20

Mary Brown Martin: 1877–1939

Lydia Jane Martin

This previously unpublished recollection was written in July 1973.

"To love all the world, to love humanity and to try to serve it, to work for universal peace and universal brotherhood," these were the religious precepts which motivated the life of Mary Brown Martin, who was born to the Winfield Scott Browns in Raleigh, North Carolina, on May 31, 1877. The only girl in a family which was to number six boys meant that Mary was quite a prize. Everyone loved her at once because of some special sunshine in her soul, whose rays warmed and brightened the lives of all she touched. There was a gaiety and buoyancy about Mary which she kept all the days of her life.

Swinging on her front gate as a small child on a day that happened to be her birthday, a neighbor said to her: "Born on the last day of May, you almost did not get here, little girl!" "Oh no," piped up Mary, "I'd 'uv come tomorrow!" It was this kind of reasoning which rescued Mary many times from the vicissitudes of life which were to follow. Brothers feel that they were put in this world to tease their sisters, even when there is a great deal of love for each other. Mary, being the only sister, came in for more than her share of this show of love. However, in the long run, the teasing in early life only strengthened her spirit and understanding of men, so that she grew to have the ability to outthink and parry the thrust of many associates in her professional life. Without losing any of her womanly loveliness, Mary became a tower of strength.

This sweet and beautiful daughter was nine years old when the Brown family moved from Raleigh to Cleveland, Ohio, where Mary entered school. Shortly thereafter Mary began to show signs of being possessed of a very alert mind. She loved learning and teaching. As a child she began to teach younger children around her. As soon as she would acquire some bit of new knowledge at school, she would hasten home and try to teach it to her younger brothers. She would correct their errors of speech while striving hard herself to emulate her teachers. She was thoughtful and had a very inquiring mind and spirit. She loved all humanity and accepted all children, regardless of race, or class, or evident signs of external differences, as her bosom friends and playmates. Mary seemed early in life to have caught the Message of the Day, of love, mercy, and justice. One day as a mother, she told the following story to her own children.

In Raleigh, North Carolina, in the nineteenth century, the garbage collection was made by little waifs and orphans who, for a small fee, would carry it away to a burying place. The little girl who collected in the neighborhood of the Browns was herself less than ten—about the age of Mary. Mary loved her so much that when her chores were finished, Mary would embrace her and invite her over to play. The result was that by evening, unless Mary's mother had intervened, Mary's clothes were as soiled and smelly as those of her playmate. This kind of appreciation of the human soul enabled Mary Brown to associate with all, high and low alike, treating them all as they crossed her path, with the same love and understanding.

When Mary learned that there was but one God and all are His creatures, she began to wonder why all the people of the world could not belong to one and the same church. She had realized that she and her family attended one church, but that some of her friends and playmates went to another. In her reasoning, this seemed rather strange. Why couldn't they all be together? Mary Brown was to find her answer one glorious day in 1913.

In Cleveland Mary Brown studied voice and piano while a public school student. When she graduated from Central High School, she was elected class vocalist. This meant she sang a solo at the class night exercises which preceded the commencement. She used this talent as a member of the choir of Mt. Zion Congregational Church, singing high soprano, where one Sunday morning she noticed a tall, dark young man as he entered the church and seated himself. Her little heart must have done a flip-flop, for the next Sunday and the next, she gave this youthful lawyer a warm smile, which he always remembered.

After a year of study at the College for Women (Flora Stone Mather College) of Western Reserve University, and one additional year at the old Normal School, Miss Brown received an appointment to teach at an academy for Negroes in Cotton Plant, Arkansas. She taught at the academy for two years and then returned to Cleveland to marry attorney Alexander H. Martin. As success came to her brilliant husband, Mrs. Martin turned her attention to building a happy family life and rearing their four children.

While teaching in the South, her students were young Negroes, eager to learn but greatly deprived and needy. Miss Brown had made lasting friendships in her loving association with these young people. Not only through the subject matter she taught them, but also by precept and example, she was able to give them much hope and inspiration. While remaining at home in Cleveland to give guidance and care to her own young children, she utilized many evening hours by tutoring young immigrants, men and women who needed help and training in learning the English language after their arrival from foreign shores. At the end of World War I, Mrs. Martin's children were old enough for her to venture out into public life and take a role in the Suffragists' Movement. She was one of the leaders in Cleveland in the movement to obtain the vote for women, and she was known as an influential suffragette.

Mrs. Martin also worked steadfastly with the Parent-Teachers Organization in Cleveland, and for a few years in the early 1920s she went back into the classroom as a teacher. It was early in 1929 that a group of friends from all walks of life, public-minded citizens, urged her to consider becoming a candidate for the Cleveland Board of Education, because she had distinguished herself as a public servant, devoted mother, and educator. She was to become the second woman to serve on the Cleveland Board of Education and the first Negro to be so honored.

In 1933 Mrs. Martin was elected to a second four-year term on the School Board. At the end of that four years, her family, sensing that perhaps the work was a bit too strenuous for her at that time, urged her not to accept the invitation to run for the office a third time. As she was busily preparing for a daughter's wedding, Mrs. Martin acquiesced to the desires of her loved ones. However, the pleas of the friends were too strong in 1939, and, running again (always on a non-partisan ballot), Mrs. Martin received 101,000 votes and was elected to her third term. What a victory for a woman whose parents had been slaves!

The telegrams and messages of congratulations were still arriving when two weeks later this saintly and productive life came quickly to a close after a very short illness and a cerebral hemorrhage. Friends who came in tears to her home expressed stark dismay that their "mother, teacher, the one who had helped so many to attain a job or some coveted goal" had left them forever. The suddenness of her passing on November 19, 1939, was a great shock to the city. On the day of her funeral the flags were flown at half-mast on schools and other public buildings; the city schools were closed and the streets along the route to and from the church were lined with throngs of people, many of whom had lost their best friend.

However, Mrs. Martin still lives in the activities and service of those whom she helped and inspired along life's pathway. Many outstanding business and professional men and women of Cleveland are proud today of having been her pupils. She enjoyed the respect, confidence, and intimate friendship of all classes and all races of people. This great woman had served her city with distinction, for uppermost in her mind always were the precepts of love and justice for all. The work of her own four children, who have university educations, very remarkably reflects the wonderful force and personality of Mrs. Martin as they endeavor to perpetuate her quality of service to humanity.

Her older daughter, Lydia Martin, a professional librarian, held a position for many years at the Case Western Reserve University Library in the Catalog Department. The second daughter, Dr. Sarah Martin

Pereira, is professor of Romance Languages and head of the Department at the District of Columbia Teachers College in Washington, DC. Both daughters have worked diligently in the Bahá'í community. Dr. Pereira had served thirteen years as one of the nine members of the National Spiritual Assembly of the Bahá'ís of the United States, when she was appointed as one of the four members of the Continental Board of Counselors for North America. Attorney Alexander H. Martin, Jr., is a practicing lawyer in Cleveland, and Stuart Martin, the younger of the two sons, teaches English in the high school of St. Thomas, Virgin Islands. Her grandson, Dr. Carlos Martin Pereira, is an assistant professor of physics at the University of Maryland, and Paul Martin, another grandson, is at present a high school student.

In 1965 the Cleveland Board of Education named a new elementary school the Mary B. Martin Elementary School in honor of Mrs. Martin. Her four children, two daughters-in-law, the two grandsons, and a host of friends were present to witness the dedication of the building and the presentation to the principal of a portrait of Mrs. Martin to be hung in the hallway.

In 1972, on October 6, a letter came to Sarah, Mrs. Martin's second daughter, from a dear friend in Cleveland. It read:

> Dear Sarah,
> This is a hastily-written letter, but I had to let you know that I have cause to think of you *daily!* Why? Because I am the principal of MARY B. MARTIN SCHOOL! I am proud to be associated with a building named after your mother—a wonderful woman, who was instrumental in helping me to get my first playground-instructor job.
> With love,
> Helen West

Mary B. Martin was possessed of great poise, charm and a rare spiritual sensitivity. When the Light of the Bahá'í Revelation came to her in 1913, shortly after the visit of 'Abdu'l-Bahá to Cleveland in 1912, she became illumined, strengthened, and inspired. Her activities as a teacher of the

Revealed Word grew and expanded. The Bahá'í Faith became the ruling force in her life, as Christianity had been previously. As a lover of all humanity she heard with appreciation the fact that Bahá'u'lláh enjoined all believers to "consort with all the people with love and fragrance. Fellowship is the cause of unity, and unity is the source of order in the world."[1] "The best beloved of all things in My sight is Justice; turn not away therefrom if thou desirest me."[2]

Inasmuch as Mrs. Martin was always an active teacher and promoter of the Faith in Cleveland, the Martin home on Fortieth Street came to be known as a rallying point and spiritual center for the Bahá'í activities in the early days of the Faith in that city. In very truth, her life was a power, drifting steadily forward to hasten the day of the fulfillment of the promise of Bahá'u'lláh—

That all nations shall become one in faith and all men as brothers; that the bonds of affection and unity between the sons of men be strengthened; that diversity of religion shall cease, and difference of race be annulled. . . . These fruitless strifes, these ruinous wars shall pass away, and the "Most Great Peace" shall come.[3]

Notes

Preface

1. Milton C. Sernett, *Afro-American Religious History*, pp. 413–20.
2. E. Franklin Frazier, "The Negro Church and Assimilation," quoted in Sernett, p. 375.
3. C. Eric Lincoln, *Race, Religion, and the Continuing American Dilemma*, pp. 140–69.
4. Ibid., pp. 148–51.
5. 'Abdu'l-Bahá, quoted in Shoghi Effendi, *The Advent of Divine Justice*, p. 37.
6. C. Eric Lincoln, *Race, Religion, and the Continuing American Dilemma*, p. 139.
7. For accounts of the American Bahá'í community's contribution to the promotion of better race relations see: Bonnie J. Taylor, *The Power of Unity*, Gayle Morrison, *To Move the World*, and Richard W. Thomas, *Racial Unity*.
8. Robert Stockman, *The Bahá'í Faith in America*, vol. 1, p. xiii.
9. Ibid., p. 139.
10. Ibid., p. 126–7.

Chapter 1

1. "Statistics," *The Bahá'í World 2003–2004*, p. 241.
2. William S. Hatcher and J. Douglas Martin, *The Bahá'í Faith*, p. xiii.
3. 'Abdu'l-Bahá, *Selections*, p. 34.
4. William S. Hatcher and J. Douglas Martin, *The Bahá'í Faith*, p. 82.
5. Shoghi Effendi, *God Passes By*, p. 100.
6. Ibid.
7. Ibid.
8. Ibid.
9. Ibid.
10. Bahá'u'lláh, *Gleanings*, p. 288.

11. Bahá'u'lláh, Ishráqát, *Tablets,* p. 130.

12. Bahá'u'lláh, Hidden Words, Arabic, no. 68.

13. 'Abdu'l-Bahá, *Selections,* no. 225.24.

14. William S. Hatcher and J. Douglas Martin, *The Bahá'í Faith,* p. 6.

15. Ibid., p. 26.

16. Peter Smith, *The Bahá'í Religion,* p. 2.

17. For a view of the history of the Bábí religion from an eyewitness of many of the events, see Shoghi Effendi, *The Dawn-Breakers.* The study by Denis MacEoin, "Early Reactions to the Bab and His Claims," in Moojan Momen, *Studies in Bábí and Bahá'í History,* pp. 1–47, also shed light on the early history of the Bábí religion, explains its theological connection to nineteenth-century Persian (Iranian) Shia Islam and how it emerged as "a Messianic reform movement within Islam."

18. Shoghi Effendi, *God Passes By,* pp. 89–150.

19. Smith, *The Bahá'í Religion,* pp. 4–5.

20. Ibid., p. 6.

21. Ibid.

22. Ibid.

23. William S. Hatcher and J. Douglas Martin, *The Bahá'í Faith,* pp. 46–7.

24. Ibid., p. 47.

25. Ibid.

26. H.M. Balyuzi, *'Abdu'l-Bahá,* p. 50.

27. William S. Hatcher and J. Douglas Martin, *The Bahá'í Faith,* p. 50. For a more comprehensive study of the Covenant of Bahá'u'lláh, see Adib Taherzadeh, *The Covenant of Bahá'u'lláh.*

28. Smith, *The Bahá'í Religion,* p. 7; Taherzadeh, *The Covenant of Bahá'u'lláh,* pp. 164–291; Shoghi Effendi, *God Passes By,* pp. 244–308.

29. William S. Hatcher and J. Douglas Martin, *The Bahá'í Faith,* p. 59.

30. Ibid.

31. Shoghi Effendi, *God Passes By,* p. 295.

32. Ibid., p. 279.

33. English translations of these letters are published as *Tablets of the Divine Plan.*

34. William S. Hatcher and J. Douglas Martin, *The Bahá'í Faith,* p. 60.

35. Ibid.

36. See June M. Thomas, *Planning Progress.*

37. Ibid, p. 59–60.

38. William S. Hatcher and J. Douglas Martin, *The Bahá'í Faith,* p. 63. For an analysis of "institutionalization in the formative age" of the Bahá'í Faith see, Peter Smith, *The Bábí and Bahá'í Religion,* pp. 115–35; Rúḥíyyih Khánum Rabbani, the widow of Shoghi Effendi, describes his lifetime work in her book, *The Priceless Pearl.*

39. Shoghi Effendi, *God Passes By,* p. 324.

40. These letters are collected in Shoghi Effendi, *Bahá'í Administration.*

41. William S. Hatcher and J. Douglas Martin, *The Bahá'í Faith,* p. 68.

42. Peter Smith, *The Bábí and Bahá'í Religions,* p. 158; Shoghi Effendi, *This Decisive Hour,* p. 11; June M. Thomas, *Planning Progress,* pp. 45–7.

43. "Appointment of the Hands of The Cause of God," *The Bahá'í World,* vol. 12, pp. 38–40; Paul E. Haney, "The Institution of The Hands of the Cause of God," *The Bahá'í World,* vol. 13, pp. 333–94; Paul E. Haney, "The Institution of The Hands of the Cause of God," *The Bahá'í World,* vol. 14, pp. 459–74.

44. William S. Hatcher and J. Douglas Martin, *The Bahá'í Faith,* p. 70; "The Completion of the Bahá'í World Crusade, 1953–1963: Summary of Achievements under the ten year international Bahá'í teaching and consolidation plan," *The Bahá'í World,* vol. 13, pp. 459.

45. Rúhíyyih Khánum, "The Passing of Shoghi Effendi," *The Bahá'í World,* vol. 13, pp. 207–28.

46. William S. Hatcher and J. Douglas Martin, *The Bahá'í Faith,* p. 60.

47. Charlotte M. Linfoot, "First International Convention," *The Bahá'í World,* vol. 14, pp. 427–30.

Chapter 2

1. Peter Smith, *The Bahá'í Religion,* p. 4; John Hope Franklin and Alfred A. Moss, Jr., *From Slavery to Freedom,* p. 208.

2. William S. Hatcher and J. Douglas Martin, *The Bahá'í Faith,* p. 49; Franklin and Moss, Jr., *From Slavery to Freedom,* pp. 259–63.

3. Thomas O'Toole, "The Historical Context,"; Donald L. Gordon, "African Politics," in April A. Gordon & Donald L. Gordon, ed., *Understanding Contemporary Africa,* pp. 45, 53.

4. George M. Fredrickson, *White Supremacy,* passim; Thomas F. Gossett, *Race,* pp. 86, 261–4; 280–1, 343; George L. Mosse, *Toward the Final Solution,* pp. 68, 71, 112.

5. Shoghi Effendi, *The Advent of Divine Justice,* p. 31.

6. Dr. Mary Khaden Czerniejewski & Dr. Richard Czerniejewski, "The Pupil of the Eye," quoted in Bonnie J. Taylor, compiler, *The Pupil of the Eye,* p.vii.

7. 'Abdu'l-Bahá, *Selections,* no. 78.1.

8. Ibid.

9. Ibid.

10. Rúhíyyíh Khánum, "Rúhíyyíh Khánum Shares Teaching Observations," *Bahá'í News* (U.S. Supplement) no. 40 (June 1961), pp. 1–2.

11. Ibid., p. 2.

12. Ibid.

13. Bahá'u'lláh, Hidden Words, Arabic, no. 68.

14. Robert H. Stockman, *The Bahá'í Faith in America,* vol. 1, p. 139.

15. May Maxwell, *An Early Pilgrimage,* pp. 20–1; Louis G. Gregory, "Robert Turner" in *World Order,* vol. 12 (April 1946), p. 28.

16. Louis G. Gregory, "Robert Turner," p. 28.

17. Ibid., p. 29.

18. Ibid.; Robert H. Stockman, *The Bahá'í Faith in America,* p. 156.

19. See chapters 3 and 4 for more information about these women and those described in subsequent paragraphs.

20. Gregory, p. 10.

21. "Will Read of Dorothy Champ One Hundred Years From Today," *The Evening Bulletin,* Providence, Rhode Island, November 29, 1979—the "talk" referred to in the quote is a presentation entitled "The Promised Day Is Come," which she gave in Syracuse, New York. "Eulogy," "Literary Notes," Dorothy Champ Papers, box 1, folder 50, National Bahá'í Archives, Wilmette, IL.

22. "Will Read of Dorothy Champ One Hundred years From Today," p. 1.

23. Gayle Morrison, *To Move the World,* p. 3.

24. Ibid., p. 5.

25. Quoted in ibid, p. 7.

26. Quoted in ibid.

27. Ibid.

28. Ibid, p. 7.

29. Ibid, p. 8.

30. Ibid, p. 5.

31. Ibid.

32. Louis G. Gregory, *A Heavenly Vista,* p. 10; Louis G. Gregory Papers, National Bahá'í Archives, Wilmette, IL.

33. Louis G. Gregory Papers.

34. Ibid.

35. Ibid.

36. Ibid.

37. Gayle Morrison, *To Move the World,* p. 64.

38. Louis G. Gregory, *A Heavenly Vista,* p. 15.

39. 'Abdu'l-Bahá, *Promulgation of Universal Peace,* p. 113.

40. Gayle Morrison, *To Move the World,* Gregory, pp. 66–7.

41. Ibid, p. 70.

42. C. Eric Lincoln, *Race, Religion and the Continuing American Dilemma,* pp. 23–59; Diana L. Hayes and Cyprian Davis, O.S.B., eds., *Taking Down Our Harps;* Joel L. Alvis, Jr., *Religion and Race;* Forrest G. Wood, *The Arrogance of Faith.*

43. George Washington Carver, letter to Roy C. Wilhelm, July 3, 1932, in Roy Wilhelm Papers, National Bahá'í Archives, Wilmette, IL.

44. Gayle Morrison, *To Move the World,* p. 32.

45. Louis G. Gregory, "Racial Amity In America: An Historical Review," in *The Bahá'í World,* vol. 7, p. 654. The full text can be read on pp. 175–201.

46. Allen L. Ward, *239 Days*, p. 40.

47. 'Abdu'l-Bahá, *Promulgation of Universal Peace*, p. 44.

48. Louis G. Gregory, "Racial Amity In America: An Historical Review," in *The Bahá'í World*, vol. 7, p. 654.

49. Gayle Morrison, *To Move the World*, p. 132.

50. 'Abdu'l-Bahá, quoted in ibid., p. 141.

51. Louis G. Gregory, "Racial Amity In America: An Historical Review," in *The Bahá'í World*, vol. 7, p. 657.

52. Louis G. Gregory, "Light on Basic Unity," in *The Bahá'í World*, vol. 4, p. 496; "Inter-racial Amity Activities," in *Bahá'í News* (April, 1933) p. 6.

53. Gayle Morrison, *To Move the World*, p. 32.

54. Ibid.

55. Gayle Morrison, *To Move the World*, pp. 83–4; Louis G. Gregory, "Booker T. Washington and Tuskegee," in *Star of the West*, vol. 15 (August, 1924), p. 136; Obituary, "Ellsworth-Blackwell, 1902–1978," in *The Bahá'í World*, vol. 16, pp. 452–3; Obituary, "Matthew W. Bullock, 1881–1972," in *The Bahá'í World*, vol. 15, pp. 535–9.

56. Gayle Morrison, *To Move the World*, p. 161.

57. Ibid., pp. 159–60.

58. Mark Lloyd Perry, "The Chicago Bahá'í Community, 1921–39," unpublished dissertation, University of Chicago, 1986, pp. 299–300.

59. Ibid, p. 301.

60. Gayle Morrison, *To Move the World*, p. 296.

61. Written on behalf of Shoghi Effendi, letter to an individual Bahá'í, December 18, 1943, quoted in Bonnie Taylor, ed., *The Power of Unity*, p. 107.

62. "Elsie Austin Biographical Sketch," National Bahá'í Archives, Wilmette, IL; Elsie Austin, "The Bahá'í Faith and Problems of Color, Class, and Creed," *The Bahá'í World*, vol. 3, pp. 829–33; Elsie Austin, "Social Basis of World Unity," *The Bahá'í World*, vol. 10, pp. 694–8; Elsie Austin, "World Unity as a Way of Life," *The Bahá'í World*, vol. 11, pp. 694–8.

63. "Sarah Martin Pereira Biographical Sketch," Bahá'í National Archives, National Bahá'í Center, Evanston, IL; "Amoz Gibson Biographical Sketch," Bahá'í National Archives, National Bahá'í Center, Wilmette, IL.

64. "Sarah Martin Pereira Biographical Sketch," Bahá'í National Archives, Wilmette, IL; "Amoz Gibson Biographical Sketch," Bahá'í National Archives, Wilmette, IL.

65. "Dr. Wilma Ellis Biographical Sketch," Bahá'í National Archives, Wilmette, IL.

66. "National Spiritual Assembly Members and Their Length of Service," Bahá'í National Archives, "93rd Bahá'í National Convention," *The American Bahá'í*, June 5, 2002.

67. Stephen Grant Meyer, *As Long as They Don't Move Next Door*, pp. 7–9; Douglas S. Massey and Nancy A. Denton, *American Apartheid*, pp. 54–5; Daniel Kryder, *Divided Arsenal*, pp. 30–1, 37–8, 153–8, 163; Jules Tygiel, *Baseball's Great Experiment*, pp. 10–46.

68. Written on behalf of Shoghi Effendi, letter to two Bahá'ís, September 27, 1941, quoted in Helen Hornby, ed., *Lights of Guidance,* p. 533.

69. Written on behalf of Shoghi Effendi, letter to two Bahá'ís, December 10, 1942, quoted in ibid., p. 526.

70. Written on behalf of Shoghi Effendi, letter to an individual Bahá'í, March 17, 1943, quoted in Bonnie Taylor, ed., *The Power of Unity,* p. 5.

71. An example of racial identity among Black Bahá'ís throughout the diaspora can be seen in a book of short biographies of Black Bahá'ís collected by an Afro-Brazilian Bahá'í: Gabriel Marques, *Of Acendedores de Velas: Contribucoes de Afroo-descendtes Bahá'ís á construcao da Nova Ordem Mundial* (Sao Paulo, Brazil: Editora Planeta, 2000). For an example of African and African-American Bahá'ís racial identity based upon the Bahá'í teachings of the "pupil of the eye," see Lally Warren, "An open letter to all Black Americans from Mrs. L. Warren, Member of the Continental Board of Counsellors of the Bahá'í Faith in Africa," in Bonnie Fitzpatrick-Moore, *My African Heart,* pp. 180–1.

72. Ibid.

73. Hermione C. Pickens, "Vanguard of the Dawning Conference: Through the Pupil of the Eye." Typewritten account of the conference in author's possession.

74. James A. Williams and Ted Jefferson, *The Black Men's Bahá'í Gatherings,* p. 22.

75. Ibid, pp. 23 and 28.

76. Ibid.

77. Ibid., p. 3.

78. Ibid., p. 1.

79. Ibid., p. 21.

80. Ibid., pp. 22–3.

81. Ibid., pp. 27–8.

82. Bonnie Fitzpatrick-Moore, *My African Heart,* p. 176.

83. Lally Warren, "An open letter to all Black Americans," in Bonnie Fitzpatrick-Moore, *My African Heart,* pp. 180–3.

84. Ibid.

85. Ernest D. Mason. "Alain Locke's Social Philosophy," *World Order,* vol. 7, no. 13 (Winter 1978–79), p. 25–26. Locke wrote several articles which were published in *The Bahá'í World,* see "Unity Through Diversity: A Bahá'í Principle," *The Bahá'í World,* vol. 4, pp. 372–4; "The Orientation of Hope," *The Bahá'í World,* vol. 5, pp. 527–8; "Lessons in World Crisis," *The Bahá'í World,* vol. 9, pp. 745–7.

86. "Margaret Danner Biographical Sketch"; "Robert Hayden Biographical Sketch," Bahá'í National Archives, Wilmette, IL; John Hatcher, *From The Auroral Darkness,* p. 17.

87. "John Birks 'Dizzy' Gillespie Biographical Sketch," Bahá'í National Archives, Wilmette, IL; Dizzy Gillespie with Al Fraser, *To Be or Not To Bop,* pp.

473–5. For a brief but interesting "outsider's" perspective on Dizzy Gillespie's life as a Bahá'í, see Alyn Shipton, *Groovin' High* (New York: Oxford University Press, 1999), pp. 325, 331–4, 336, 349, 354.

Chapter 3

1. See Robert Stockman, *The Bahá'í Faith in America.*
2. Darlene Clark Hine, "Lifting the Veil, Shattering the Silence: Black Women's History in Slavery and Freedom," in *The State of Afro-American History,* p. 228.
3. "Say: Beware, O people of Bahá, least ye walk in the ways of them whose words differ from their deeds. . . . It is through your deeds that ye can distinguish yourselves from others." Bahá'u'lláh, *Gleanings,* no. 139.8.
4. Bahá'u'lláh himself instituted this, in passages such as the following: "He hath, moreover, ordained that His Cause be taught through the power of men's utterance, and not through resort to violence. . . . Beware least ye contend with any one, nay, strive to make him aware of the truth with kindly manner and most convincing exhortation. If your hearer respond, he will have responded to his own behoof, and if not, turn away from him, and set your faces towards God's sacred Court, the seat of resplendent holiness." *Gleanings,* no. 128.10.
5. Roger Dahl, archivist, National Bahá'í Archives, in a letter to the author dated October 19, 1989; Robert Stockman, *The Bahá'í Faith in America,* pp. 126–7.
6. Robert Stockman, *The Bahá'í Faith in America,* p. 227, n16.
7. Bahá'í Historical Card, National Bahá'í Archives, Wilmette, IL. The historical record card was a survey instrument used to collect information for the first "Bahá'í census" that began the summer of 1935. The cards were distributed to local spiritual assemblies, groups and individuals. "The record cards, which were collected over the next few years, finally reached a total of 1,813 . . . this figure represented about 60 percent of the Bahá'í population in the United States and Canada. Thirty-seven men and sixty-two women—identified themselves in some way as being Black." In Gayle Morrison, *To Move the World,* pp. 203–4.
8. Bahá'í Historical Record Card.
9. In Morrison, *To Move the World,* pp. 203–4.
10. "Biographical Sketches of Noteworthy Bahá'ís of African-American Background," National Bahá'í Archives, Wilmette, IL.
11. An informal meeting open to the public for the purpose of providing individuals with information about the Bahá'í Faith. See William S. Hatcher and J. Douglas Martin, *The Bahá'í Faith,* p. 179.
12. Dr. Sarah Martin Pereira, interview with the author, August 16, 1986.
13. Bahá'í Historical Record Card, National Bahá'í Archives, Wilmette, IL.

14. See Zylpha Mapp Robinson, "Heroines of the Faith," on pp. 251–63.

15. Elected governing bodies within the Bahá'í community at the local and national level.

16. Zylpha O. Mapp, letter to Victoria Bedikian, 22 May 1930, Bedikian Papers, National Bahá'í Archives, Wilmette, IL.

17. "Biographical Sketches of Noteworthy Bahá'ís of African-American Background," National Bahá'í Archives, Wilmette, IL.

18. Dr. Zylpha Mapp Robinson, interview with the author, June 16, 1988.

19. Ibid.

20. Vivian Dunlap Wesson, interview with the author, March 26, 1989.

21. Ibid.

22. 'Abdu'l-Bahá dedicated the site of the second Bahá'í House of Worship in the world during his visit to the US in 1912. The temple was completed in 1953. See J.E. Esslemont, *Bahá'u'lláh and the New Era,* p. 187.

23. Erma Hayden, interview with the author, June 26, 1988.

24. Eulalia Bobo Taylor, interview with the author, July 13, 1986.

25. Teachings of the Bahá'í Faith warn against developing simple rites into "a system of uniform and rigid rituals by introducing into them man-made forms and practices." See Helen Hornby, *Lights of Guidance,* p. 138.

26. Hilda Strauss Papers (unprocessed), National Bahá'í Archives, Wilmette, IL.

27. Ibid.

28. Ibid.

29. Reference to the Bahá'í House of Worship, Wilmette, IL, that was in the preliminary stages of its construction at this time.

30. Strauss papers. The full text of the poem reads
    Perfect Union
    We are living, sweetly living in the Blessed Light of Love,
    We are living in the Radiance of God's Glory from above.
     Naught on earth that light can hide
    While we in His Love abide.
    It's clear shining leads us to the Heavenly Dove.
    We are loving, truly loving as He tells us we should do;
    In His daily Life He shows us in the way we men shall woo
    To the Blessed Cause of God,
    In the Path His Prophets lived;
    Perfect Love shall keep us firm and true.
    We are praying, we are praying as we never prayed before,
    And this brings us countless blessing, for the key unlocks the Door.
    May each breath become a prayer,
    That we all, in God, may share
    The sweet comfort which the prayers of love bestow.
    We are working daily, hourly, every moment for God's Word,
    In loving, prayerful service in the Great Day of our Lord.

His pure Knowledge brings us peace,
While His Joy our cares release,
All because His Voice our ears have gladly heard.
In love, and prayer, and service may we all united be,
That the Coming of our Beloved to these shores we soon may see;
To prove our perfect union, raise the Temple while we may.
'Abdu'l-Bahá calls to union; let us hasten to obey!

31. *Star of the West,* vol. 2, September 8, 1911, p. 9.
32. Bahá'í Historical Record Card, Washington, DC, Bahá'í Archives.
33. Jessie Carney Smith, *Notable Black American Women,* book 2, p. 312.
34. Bahá'í Historical Record Card; Linda M. Perkins, "The Education of Black Women in the Nineteenth Century," in John Mack and Florence Howe, eds., *Women and Higher Education in American History,* p. 70; Washington Conservatory of Music Records, Collection Guide, pp. 5–6, Moorland-Spingarn Research Center, Howard University.
35. Correspondence, Oberlin College, 25 November 1960, Washington Conservatory of Music Records, box 1, folder 1, Moorland-Spingarn Research Center, Howard University; *Washington Tribune,* 1 March 1941; Washington, DC, *Evening Star,* 26 February 1941.
36. The Washington Conservatory of Music Records, Collection Guide, pp. 3–5.
37. Ibid., p. 5.
38. Hannen-Knobloch Family Papers (unprocessed), National Bahá'í Archives, Wilmette, IL.
39. Washington Conservatory of Music Records, box 1, folder 24.
40. Washington, DC, Bahá'í Archives; Washington Conservatory of Music Records, Collection Guide pps. 5–6.
41. *Washington Tribune,* 1 March 1941.
42. Zylpha Mapp Robinson, "Heroines of the Faith," see pp. 251–63.
43. Ibid.
44. Roberta Grahame and Catherine Blakeslee, et. al., *Women of Springfield's Past,* p. 34.
45. Mrs. Mapp sent a copy of her poem "Our First Lady" to Eleanor Roosevelt in 1939 and received a warm thank you note written on behalf of the First Lady.
46. A reference to 'Abdu'l-Bahá. "The Master," was a title given to him by his father, Bahá'u'lláh.
47. All poems in this section are from the Zylpha Gray Mapp Papers, Zylpha Mapp Robinson Personal Collection.
48. Abraham Lincoln Monument.
49. Bahá'u'lláh, *Gleanings,* no. 4.1.
50. Zylpha Mapp Robinson, "Heroines of the Faith."
51. Dorothy Champ Papers, box 1, folder 50, National Bahá'í Archives, Wilmette, IL.

52. *The Evening Bulletin of the Amsterdam News,* Thursday, Nov. 29, 1979, p. B-2.

53. Dorothy Champ Papers, box 2, folder 36, National Bahá'í Archives, Wilmette, IL.

54. Champ Papers, box 1, folder 50, National Bahá'í Archives, Wilmette, IL.

55. The Seven Year Plan (1937–44) was the first teaching plan designed by Shoghi Effendi for the purpose of systematically expanding the Bahá'í Faith throughout the world. For more information, see pp. 16, 97.

56. Champ Papers, box 1, folder 40, National Bahá'í Archives, Wilmette, IL.

57. Ibid., box 1, folder 51.

58. Ibid., box 1, folder 40.

59. Ibid., box 1, folder 50.

60. See pp. 283–88 for Lydia Martin's biographical essay, "Mary Brown Martin, 1837–1939."

61. Paula J. Giddings, *When and Where I Enter,* p. 126.

62. Ibid., p. 170.

63. Lydia Martin Papers, National Bahá'í Archives, Wilmette, IL; Dr. Sarah Martin Pereira, interview with the author, August 18, 1986.

64. Lydia Martin, "Mary Brown Martin, 1837–1939."

65. Dr. Sarah Martin Pereira, interview with the author, July 19, 1987; Lydia Martin Papers, National Bahá'í Archives, Wilmette, IL.

66. Bahá'í Historical Record Cards, National Bahá'í Archives, Wilmette, IL.

67. Esperanto is a constructed/synthetic language invented by Russian physician Ludwig Zamenhof. It appeared in print for the first time in 1887. See Dwight Bolinger, *Aspects of Language,* 2nd ed. (NY: Harcourt Brace Jovanovich, Inc., 1975) p. 580. Incidentally, Dr. Zamenhof's daughter Lydia became a Bahá'í.

68. "The day is approaching when all the peoples of the world will have adopted one universal language and one common script. . . . These things are obligatory and absolutely essential." Bahá'u'lláh, *Gleanings,* no. 117.1.

69. San Francisco Bahá'í Archives (unprocessed).

70. The text of this lecture can be found on pp. 229–33.

71. The exact date of Ms. Queen's enrollment has not been determined. She was listed as a member of the Washington, DC, Bahá'í community as early as 1913.

72. Joseph J. Boris, *Who's Who in Colored America,* p. 164; Howardiana Biographical File, Moorland-Spingarn Research Center, Howard University.

73. A letter to 'Abdu'l-Bahá from an individual Bahá'í dated August 3, 1913, briefly mentions that he encouraged Hallie to extend her stay at the school in Puerto Rico in order to teach the Bahá'í Faith to local people there. Hannen-Knoblock Papers, box 1, folder 1, National Bahá'í Archives, Wilmette, IL.

74. Hannen-Knobloch Papers, box 1, folder 1, National Bahá'í Archives, Wilmette, IL.

75. A title of Ṭáhiríh, an early Bábí heroine and the first woman to enroll in the Bábí religion. She was killed because of her religious beliefs and subsequently became a role model for all Bahá'í women. See J. E. Esslemont, *Bahá'u'lláh and the New Era*, p. 148.

76. Hannen-Knobloch Papers, box 1, folder 1, National Bahá'í Archives, Wilmette, IL.

77. *The Crisis*, vol. 8, (October 1914), p. 268.

78. *The University Journal*, 14.21 (30 March 1917): 1–2, Moorland-Spingarn Research Center, Howard University.

79. Ibid.

Chapter 4

1. Darlene Clark Hine, ed., *Black Women in America*, p. xix.

2. Shoghi Effendi, *The Advent of Divine Justice*, p. 33–4.

3. Gerda Lerner, *The Majority Finds Its Past*, p. 63.

4. Ibid., p. 63.

5. Joseph J. Boris, *Who's Who in Colored America*, p. 46.

6. Press Release, Department of Public Information, Howard University, August 21,1931; George Cook Papers, Moorland-Spingarn Research Center, Howard University.

7. Joseph J. Boris, *Who's Who in Colored America*, p. 46.

8. Ibid.

9. Roger Dahl, Correspondence, National Bahá'í Archives, Wilmette, IL.

10. Ibid.

11. Hannen-Knobloch Papers, box 3, folder 12. National Bahá'í Archives, Wilmette, IL.

12. Ibid., box 8, folder 33.

13. Ibid., box 11, folder 59.

14. See pp. 237–43 for the full text of the letter.

15. 'Abdu'l-Bahá, quoted in Gayle Morrison, *To Move the World*, p. 64.

16. Hannen-Knobloch Papers, box 3, folder 13, National Bahá'í Archives, Wilmette, IL.

17. Washington, DC, Bahá'í Archives (unprocessed).

18. Ibid.

19. Gayle Morrison, *To Move the World*, p. 206.

20. Roberts Papers, box 10, folder 4, National Bahá'í Archives, Wilmette, IL.

21. Ober Papers, box 3, National Bahá'í Archives, Wilmette, IL.

22. A July riot in Washington, DC, began with a familiar pattern: inflamed white mobs, in this case consisting mainly of white servicemen, attacked Blacks. The riot turned to race warfare when white gangs attempted to burn the Black district and its residents arose to defend themselves and their property. Later that month in Chicago, Bahá'ís were caught up in

the worst race riot the nation had ever experienced. One Bahá'í home was bombed, and two members of a Bahá'í family were jailed briefly before the charges against them were dropped. Dr. Zia M. Bagdadí, a Persian physician in Chicago, was, as a fellow Bahá'í recalled, the one white man who went into the Black sections during the riot and brought food to the hungry. See Gayle Morrison, *To Move the World*, p. 130.

23. Ober Papers, box 1, folder 0, National Bahá'í Archives, Wilmette, IL.

24. Gayle Morrison, *To Move the World*, p. 130.

25. Sadie Oglesby's "Arrival in Haifa." The full text of the report of her pilgrimage can be found on pp. 277–81.

26. Ibid.

27. Shoghi Effendi, *The Advent of Divine Justice*, p. 33.

28. Sadie Oglesby, "Arrival in Haifa." The "Holy Shrine" referred to by Shoghi Effendi is the burial place of Bahá'u'lláh.

29. Ibid.

30. "As to racial prejudice, the corrosion of which, for well-nigh a century, has bitten into the fiber, and attacked the whole social structure of American society, it should be regarded as constituting the most vital and challenging issue confronting the Bahá'í community at the present stage of its evolution." Shoghi Effendi, *The Advent of Divine Justice*, pp. 33–4.

31. Sadie Oglesby, "Arrival in Haifa."

32. Robarts Papers, box 4, folder 75, National Bahá'í Archives, Wilmette, IL.

33. Lunt Papers, box 3, folder 82, National Bahá'í Archives, Wilmette, IL.

34. Mary Maxwell was the maiden name of Rúḥíyyih Rabbani, also known as 'Amatu'l-Bahá Rúḥíyyih Khánum, wife of Shoghi Effendi and a Hand of the Cause of God.

35. Lucy Marshall, "Reminiscences," January 1937, Lucy Marshall Papers, San Francisco Bahá'í Archives.

36. Obituary, *Detroit Free Press*, May 26, 1988, p. 4C.

37. Naomi Oden, interview with the author, August 7, 1987.

38. Ibid.

39. Ibid.

40. Paula J. Giddings, *When and Where I Enter*, p. 309.

41. Naomi Oden, interview with the author, August 7, 1987.

42. Ibid.

43. Obituary, *Detroit Free Press*, May 26, 1988, p. 4C.

44. Erma Hayden, interview with the author, June 26, 1988.

45. Paula J. Giddings, *When and Where I Enter*, p. 285.

46. Erma Hayden, interview with the author, June 26, 1988.

47. Ibid.

48. Ibid.

49. Dorothy Champ Papers, box 1, folder 50, National Bahá'i Archives, Wilmette, IL.

50. Biographical Sketches, National Bahá'í Archives, Wilmette, IL.

51. Ibid.
52. Paula J. Giddings, *When and Where I Enter*, p. 7.
53. Bahá'u'lláh, quoted in *Women*, p. 3.
54. Paula J. Giddings, *When and Where I Enter*, p. 170.
55. Ibid.
56. For an example of one of her essays, see "Votes for Mothers" on pp. 235–6.
57. Earlita Flemming, interview with the author, January 9, 1989.
58. Ibid.
59. Zylpha Mapp Robinson, interview with the author, June 16, 1988.
60. Ibid.
61. Roberta Grahame and Catherine Blakeslee, *Women of Springfield's Past*, p. 34.
62. Elsie Austin, interview with the author.
63. Ibid.
64. Zenobia Perry became a Bahá'i in 1982 according to her interview in 1987.
65. Zenobia Perry, interview with the author, 1987.
66. Lecile Webster, interview with the author, 1988.
67. Elsie Austin, interview with the author.

Chapter 5

1. Amin Banani, foreword to the 1977 edition, 'Abdu'l Bahá, *Tablets of the Divine Plan*, p. xix.
2. Ibid, pp. 5–107.
3. Ibid, p. 40.
4. "Tablets Revealed by 'Abdu'l-Bahá to the Bahá'ís throughout the United States and Canada," *Star of the West*, vol. 7, no 10. (September 8, 1916), pp. 87–91; Banani, foreword to the 1977 edition, 'Abdu'l Bahá, *Tablets of the Divine Plan*, p. xix.
5. Joseph H. Hannen, "The Convention of 'Abdu'l-Bahá," *Star of the West*, vol. 10, no. 4 (May 17, 1919), pp. 54–6.
6. Ibid., p. 54.
7. Louis G. Gregory, "Opening of the Convention and Congress—The Feast of El-Rizwan," ibid. pp. 56–62.
8. Shoghi Effendi praised both Martha Root and Marion Jack for their great accomplishments in spreading the Bahá'í teachings among various peoples and countries around the world. "A new episode began when, in quick response to those same Tablets [Tablets of the Divine Plan] and their summons, that star-servant of Bahá'u'lláh, the indomitable and immortal Martha Root . . . embarked on the first of her historic journeys which were to extend over a period of twenty years, and to carry her several times around the globe, and which ended only with her death far from

home and in the active service of the Cause which she loved so greatly." See, Shoghi Effendi, *God Passes By*, p. 308; For a full length discussion of Root's life as Bahá'í teacher around the globe, see, M.R. Garis, *Martha Root: Lioness at the Threshold* (Wilmette, IL: Bahá'í Publishing Trust, 1983); Shoghi Effendi also praised another great women teacher and pioneer praised Marion Jack: "It was a Canadian woman (Marion Jack), one of the noblest in the ranks of the Bahá'í pioneers, who alone and single-handed, forsook her home, settled among an alien people, braved with the leonine spirit the risks and dangers of the world conflict that raged around her, and who now at an advanced age is still holding the Fort and is setting an example worthy of emulation by all her fellow pioneers of the East and West." Quoted in *Quickeners of Mankind*, p. 85.

9. Shoghi Effendi, *Citadel of Faith*, pp. 4–6.
10. Melanie Smith and Paul Lample outline the objectives and outcomes of each plan during the first and second epochs of the Divine Plan, see "Systematic Unfoldment of the Divine Plan," in Melanie Smith and Paul Lample, *The Spiritual Conquest of the Planet*, pp. 16–17, 19; In *Planning Progress*, June Manning Thomas discusses the planning principles and methods used by Shoghi Effendi in developing and implementing the plans
11. "Announcement by the Hands of the Cause of God of the Historic Election of the First Universal House of Justice," *The Bahá'í World*, vol 14, p. 425.
12. The Báb, *Selections*, p. 56.
13. Bahá'u'lláh, *Gleanings*, no. 96.3.
14. 'Abdu'l-Bahá, *Tablets of the Divine Plan*, nos. 8.11, 4.4.
15. Shoghi Effendi, *Bahá'í Administration*, p. 69.
16. Ibid.
17. Shoghi Effendi, *Directives from the Guardian*, p. 75.
18. Ibid.
19. Bahá'u'lláh, quoted in Shoghi Effendi, *The Advent of Divine Justice*, p. 68.
20. Shoghi Effendi, letter dated March 13, 1944, in *This Decisive Hour*, p. 92–3.
21. Ibid. The "Heroic Age" is explained by Shoghi Effendi in *God Passes By* as the first century of the Bahá'í era, pp. xiii, 46, 50, 55, 157, 158, 223, 256, 309.
22. See chapter 1, n17.
23. Gayle Morrison, *To Move the World*, p. 247.
24. Ibid., pp. 246–52.
25. Ibid., pp. 252–5.
26. Shoghi Effendi, letter to Lydia Martin, 20 May, 1939, quoted in Gayle Morrison, *To Move the World*, p. 255.
27. Ibid.
28. Ibid., pp. 255–6.
29. Ibid.
30. Lydia Martin Biographical Sketch, Bahá'í National Archives, Wilmette, IL.

31. "Ellsworth Blackwell," In Memoriam, *The Bahá'í World,* vol. 17, p. 453.
32. Ibid.
33. Ibid., p. 452
34. Ibid., p. 453.
35. Shoghi Effendi, *Citadel of Faith,* pp. 87–88.
36. "The Guardian's Letter to Mr. William Foster," quoted in the Bahá'í News, September, 1951, p. 1.
37. "Ethel Stephens," *They Answered the First Call,* p. 1.
38. Written on behalf of Shoghi Effendi, letter to the African Teaching Committee of the National Spiritual Assembly of the United States, January 24, 1952.
39. *Bahá'í News,* February 17, 1952, p. 1.
40. "Ethel Stephens," *They Answered the First Call,* p. 1.
41. Ibid.
42."Valerie Wilson," Ibid, p. 2.
43. "International Survey of Current Bahá'í Activities," *The Bahá'í World,* vol. 13, p. 245.
44. Elsie Austin, "Matthew W. Bullock (1881–1972) Knight of Bahá'u'lláh," In Memoriam, *The Bahá'í World,* vol. 15, p. 538.
45. Ibid.
46. Ibid.
47. Ibid.
48. Ibid., p. 539
49. "George and Bessie Washington," *The American Bahá'í,* October 16, 1997.
50. Ibid.
51. Ibid.
52. Ibid.
53. Ibid.
54. Ibid. In 1971 during their travels in Liberia, 'Amatu'l-Baha Rúḥíyyih Khánum and Violette Nakhjavání visited the graves of the Washingtons. Later, Nakhjavání would write: " Next to the their home, on a hilltop, he (George) buried Bessy, and on the same day dug a grave for himself next to her. He planted a frangipani tree, which by the time we visited the graves was a beautiful mighty tree with fragrant white flowers." See Violette Nakhjavání, *The Great African Safari,* p.146.
55. David M. Earl, "Joy Hill-Earl (1912–1972)," In Memoriam, *The Bahá'í World,* vol. 15, p. 532.
56. Ibid.
57. Ibid.
58. Ibid.
59. Ibid., p. 533.
60. Ibid.
61. Ibid.
62. Ibid.

63. Ibid.

64. Ibid.

65. Ibid.

66. Dempsey and Adrienne Morgan, "Pioneer Notes: 1958–1980" p. 1; For the call for pioneers at the Bahá'í conference in Chicago in 1958, see: "The International Conference in Wilmette, IL, May 2–4, 1958," in *The Bahá'í World,* vol. 13, pp. 324–25.

67. Dempsey and Adrienne Morgan, "Pioneer Notes: 1958–1980," p. 1.

68. Ibid.

69. Ibid.

70. Ibid., p. 2.

71. Ibid.

72. Ibid., p. 4.

73. Ibid., p. 5.

74. Ibid.

75. Ibid., pp. 6–7.

76. Ibid., p. 7.

77. "The Historic Election of the First Universal House of Justice," *The Bahá'í World,* vol. 14, p. 425; Beatrice Ashton, "The Most Great Jubilee: Report on the Bahá'í World Congress held in London, April 28–May 2, 1963," *The Bahá'í World,* vol. 14, pp. 57–80. In early 1970 while traveling in Chad, 'Amatu'l-Bahá Rúḥíyyih Khánum and Violette Nakhjavání had contact with the Morgans. Nakhjavání recalled this meeting. "In Fort-Lamy, the capital of Chad, we found Dempsey and Adrienne Morgan, two faithful and devoted pioneers, waiting for us in the lobby of our prearranged hotel . . . there was no room in any of the hotels and they very kindly invited us to stay with them. . . . Mr. and Mrs. Dempsey Morgan and Bill Davis were valiant pioneers who gave of their time and knowledge to spread the Cause of God." Violette Nakhjavání, *The Great African Safari,* pp. 103–4.

78. Gwili Posey, interview with the author, July 2001; Part of the objectives of the Nine Year Plan were the twin objectives of expansion and universal participation, see Melanie Smith and Paul Lample, *The Spiritual Conquest of the Planet,* p. 19.

79. "Africa's Descendants Return with the Message of Bahá'u'lláh," *The Four Year Plan and the Twelve Month Plan,* p. 40.

80. Ibid.

81. Ibid.

82. Ibid.

83. Ibid.

84. Bonnie Fitzpatrick-Moore, *My African Heart,* pp. 170–1.

85. Ibid., p. 172.

86. Ibid., p. 173.

87. Ibid.

88. Ibid.
89. Ibid., p. 175.

Chapter 6

The epigraph for this chapter is from Bahá'u'lláh, *Gleanings*, no. 161.2.
1. 'Abdu'l-Bahá, *Promulgation of Universal Peace*, p. 134.
2. "Any believer [in the Bahá'í Faith] who arises and leaves his home to journey to another country for the purpose of teaching the Cause is a pioneer." Universal House of Justice, letter to the National Spiritual Assembly of the Bahá'ís of the United States, in Helen Hornby, ed. *Lights of Guidance*, p. 573.
3. Elsie Austin, interview with the author.
4. Bahá'u'lláh, *Gleanings*, no. 43.1.
5. Joseph J. Boris, *Who's Who in Colored America*, p. 164; Howardiana Biographical file.
6. Hannen-Knobloch Papers, box 1, folder 1, National Bahá'í Archives, Wilmette, IL.
7. Ibid. Here, Mrs. Queen enumerates some of her successes in Puerto Rico:

> The hope of Puerto Rico is the younger generation. Thus it was with my own pupils, the graduating class, that I mostly worked. I made small mention of the Cause *as a Cause*, but strove to instill its *teachings*. What little I have been able to do, I lay at ['Abdu'l-Bahá] Feet.
>
> 1st. I formed a welfare society in my class. At Christmastime we found the names of all the needy and deserving women of our city, and took to them baskets of fruit and clothing.
>
> 2nd. At the time of the recent floods in Ohio, we collected forty two dollars, which we sent to the sufferers and for which we were personally thanked by the Acting Governor of Puerto Rico, Mr. M. Drew Carrell.
>
> 3rd. We held weekly discussions on the Beauty of Universal Peace and the horrors of war.
>
> 4th. An essay on the Life of Kurrut-ul-Aine was sent by one of my pupils to the Insular Fair, and received a first prize.
>
> 5th. All pupils were taught to recognize and respect the portraits of 'Abdu'l-Bahá.
>
> 6th. I sent out Bahá'í literature to American Friends.
>
> 7th. I instilled into the minds of my boys that the girls were their equals.
>
> 8th. I myself learned how not to be afraid of life.
>
> 9th. I taught my pupils the vanity of laziness and instilled within them the beauty of honorable work I am just beginning; I have done but little,

and if, in this, there by any good, I offer it as a sacrifice at the Throne of my Savior.
—Hallie E. Queen

8. Ober Papers, National Bahá'í Archives, Wilmette, IL.
9. Will C. van den Hoonaard, *The Origins of the Bahá'í Community of Canada*, p. 229.
10. The text of this talk can be found on pp. 229–33.
11. *Washington Tribune*, Saturday, March 1, 1941.
12. Washington Conservatory of Music Papers, box 1, folder 5, Moorland-Spingarn Research Center, Howard University.
13. Washington Conservatory of Music Papers, box 1, folder 24, Moorland-Spingarn Research Center, Howard University.
14. Vivian Dunlap Wesson, interview with the author, March 26, 1989.
15. Lecile Webster, interview with the author, 1988.
16. Dr. Zylpha Mapp Robinson, interview with the author, June 16, 1988.
17. Written on behalf of Shoghi Effendi, letter to the British Africa Committee, 4 June 1954, in *Unfolding Destiny*, p. 329.
18. Elsie Austin, interview with the author.
19. "Biographical Sketches," National Bahá'í Archives, Wilmette, IL.
20. 'Abdu'l-Bahá, *Tablets of the Divine Plan*, no. 7.8.
21. Written on behalf of Shoghi Effendi, letter to two Bahá'ís, December 10, 1942, in *Lights of Guidance*, no. 1785.
22. Bonnie Fitzpatrick-Moore, *My African Heart*, p. 12.
23. See Bonnie Fitzpatrick-Moore, "The Spiritual Heritage of African-Americans," on pp. 245–9.
24. Lecile Webster, interview with the author, 1988.
25. Dr. Zylpha Mapp Robinson, interview with the author, June 16, 1988.
26. Elsie Austin, interview with the author.
27. The Hands of the Cause in the Holy Land, letter to the Fifth Intercontinental Conference in Singapore, *Bahá'í News*, no. 333, pp. 3–4.
28. Bonnie Fitzpatrick-Moore, *My African Heart*, p. 8.
29. Written on behalf of Shoghi Effendi, letter to the British Africa Committee, 4 June 1954, in *Unfolding Destiny*, p. 330.
30. These sketches were partially selected on the basis of availability of information and not necessarily for their historical importance.
31. For more information about Knights of Bahá'u'lláh, see pp. 107–8.
32. Vivian Dunlap Wesson, interview with the author, March 26, 1989.
33. Ibid.
34. Ibid.
35. Ibid.
36. Ibid.
37. Ibid.
38. Ibid.

39. Ibid.
40. Ibid.
41. "Obituaries," *The Bahá'í World 1993–94,* p. 322.
42. Dr. Zylpha Mapp Robinson, interview with the author, June 16, 1988.
43. Ibid.
44. Obituary, *The American Bahá'í,* August 20, 2001, p. 28.
45. *Biographical Sketches,* National Bahá'í Archives, Wilmette, IL.
46. Elsie Austin, interview with the author.
47. Ibid.
48. Ibid.
49. Ibid.
50. Ibid.
51. Ibid.
52. Ibid.
53. Lecile Webster, interview with the author, 1988.
54. Ibid.
55. Ibid.
56. Ibid.
57. Ibid.
58. Ibid.
59. Ibid.
60. Ibid.
61. Ibid.
62. Ibid.
63. Ibid.
64. Ibid.
65. Written on behalf of Shoghi Effendi, letter to two Bahá'ís, *Lights of Guidance,* no. 1784.
66. Earlita Flemming, interview with the author.
67. *The Call to Arise,* US National Bahá'í Center, Wilmette, IL.
68. Bahá'u'lláh, *Gleanings,* no. 157.1.

Chapter 7

1. Portions of this historical account have been published in Will C. van den Hoonaard, *The Origins of the Bahá'í Community of Canada.* We have also made good use of Lynn Echevarria-Howe, "Life History as Process and Product: The Social Construction of Self through Feminist Methodologies and Canadian Black Experience" master's thesis, Department of Sociology and Anthropology, Carleton University, Ottawa. 1992.
2. James H. Morrisson, "Portrayal of Black History," *The Atlantic Provinces Book Review,* vol. 14 (February–March 1987), p. 1.
3. Leo W. Bertley, *Canada and Its People of African Descent,* p. 23.

4. Don H. Clairmont and Fred Wien, "Blacks and Whites: The Nova Scotia Race Relations Experience," in D.F. Campbell, ed., *Banked Fires*, pp. 141–82.

5. James H. Morrisson, "Portrayal of Black History."

6. Michel Laferrière, "Blacks in Quebec: Minorities Among Minorities" in Cora B. Marrett and Cheryl Leggon, eds., *Research in Race and Ethnic Relations*, p. 24.

7. Don H. Clairmont and Fred Wien, "Blacks and Whites."

8. Keith Henry, *Black Politics in Toronto Since World War I*.

9. Ibid.

10. "Old-line families" is a term used by Daniel Hill and cited by Keith Henry, *Black Politics in Toronto Since World War I*.

11 S. Lightman, "The Negro Community in Toronto," unpublished research paper, Department of Sociology, University of Toronto, 1948.

12. Esther Hayes, letter to Will C. van den Hoonaard, January 6, 1997; Keith Henry, *Black Politics in Toronto Since World War I*.

13. S. Lightman, "The Negro Community in Toronto."

14. Keith Henry, *Black Politics in Toronto Since World War I*.

15. D. Braithwaite, ed., *The Council Drum*, newsletter of the Joint Council of Negro Youth, Toronto, 1944.

16. Sylvia D. Hamilton, "Our Mothers Grand and Great: Black Women in Nova Scotia." *Canadian Women's Studies*, 11.2 (1991) pp. 32–7.

17. Ibid.

18. S. Lightman, "The Negro Community in Toronto."

19. Canadian Citizenship Branch, *Notes on the Canadian Family Tree*.

20. Gwendolyn Etter-Lewis, "African American Women in the Bahá'í Faith, 1897–1919," *World Order*, Winter 1994, p. 44.

21. Reportedly, a Black couple attended the first reception at the Maxwell home held in honor of 'Abdu'l-Bahá, on the evening of August 30, 1912. Mr. And Mrs. Archibald Eddington, who "played such an active part in securing the most outstanding newspaper publicity of 'Abdu'l-Bahá's visit to America" were assumed to have been the first Black believers in Canada (see Amine De Mille *'Abdu'l-Bahá in Canada*, pp. 55–7). However, in a recent interview with one of Canada's earliest believers, Mr. Rowland Estall, by Will C. van den Hoonaard, February 1992, in Toronto, it came to light that the Eddingtons were not Black.

22. Amine De Mille *'Abdu'l-Bahá in Canada*, p. 56.

23. See chapter 4, n34.

24. Interview with Ann Lilly Irwin, Penticton, BC, October 6, 1982, by Carrie Jensen.

25. Linda O'Neil, "A Short History of the Bahá'í Faith in Canada, 1989–1975" (mimeo, 1975), p. 44. There is some question as to what organization May Maxwell belonged to. The Coloured Women's Club, started in 1902, was limited to 15 members and served purely recreational and artistic purposes. Between 1914–18, one also found the Coloured Women's Charitable and Benevolent Association. There were about half a dozen

other organizations in Montréal (Wilfred E. Israel, "The Montreal Negro Community," unpublished master's thesis, McGill University, Department of Sociology, 1928, pp. 199–218). Braithwaite's *The Council Drum* contains a more detailed description of the Coloured Women's Club of Montreal, which would lead one to believe that it is this organization of which May Maxwell was the honorary president.

26. Rella Braithwaite, *The Black Woman in Canada,* p. 59.

27. Gayle Morrison, *To Move the World,* p. 117.

28. Montréal Council of Social Agencies, *Welfare Work in Montréal in 1928,* pp. 178–9.

29. Gayle Morrison, *To Move the World,* p. 178.

30. Bertley, *Canada and Its People of African Descent,* p. 165.

31. Ibid, p. 279.

32. Rowland Estall, "Melodies of the Kingdom: The Memoirs of Rowland Estall" (mimeo, 1977), p. 32. This particular event must have occurred around 1929, for Estall's account started in 1926 and the event was reported to have happened "some years later." This activity may well have been cojoined with the work of the Interracial Amity Committee which had a successful local meeting in Montréal in the Bahá'í year ending in March 1930.

33. Rowland Estall, "Melodies of the Kingdom."

34. Ibid.

35. Though they are not prevented from attending services of other religions, Bahá'ís are expected to withdraw from membership in churches or other religious organizations. See Helen Hornby, compiler, *Lights of Guidance,* nos. 530–8.

36. Rena-Millie Gordon, interview with Will C. van den Hoonaard, July 18, 1990.

37. Ibid.

38. Rowland Estall, "Melodies of the Kingdom," p. 53.

39. *Canadian Bahá'í News,* no. 39 (April 1953), p. 2.

40. Eddie Elliot was not a member of the Montréal Branch of the International Union of Electrical Workers. His obituary appears in *Canadian Bahá'í News,* no. 45 (October 1953), p. 4.

41. Rowland Estall, "Melodies of the Kingdom," p. 53.

42. *Montreal Star,* July 11, 1953.

43. Montréal Council of Social Agencies, *Welfare Work in Montréal in 1928,* p. 178.

44. De Mille, *'Abdu'l-Bahá,* p. 56.

45. Rowland Estall, "Melodies of the Kingdom," p. 53.

46. Raymond Flournoy, letter to Will C. van den Hoonaard, November 13, 1988.

47. Bob Ferguson, *Who's Who in Canadian Sport,* p. 78.

48. By 1930, McGill's Faculty of Medicine had six or seven Black students and became a focal point in the medical education of many West Indian doctors. See Ida Greaves, *The Negro in Canada,* (Montréal: McGill University, Department of Political and Economic Studies, 1930), p. 69.

49. Bahá'í Registration Card, Bahá'í National Centre, Thornhill, ON, February 28, 1989.

50. Suzanne Maloney, e-mail to Will C. van den Hoonaard, December 9, 1997.

51. Gayle Morrison, *To Move the World,* p. 120.

52. *The Bahá'í World,* vol. 9, p. 919.

53. Ted Anderson, letter to Will C. van den Hoonaard, August 24, 1993.

54. Ted Anderson, letter to Will C. van den Hoonaard, October 4, 1987.

55. *U.S. National Bahá'í Review,* September 1971, p. 1. According to Bahá'í Historical Record Cards, Mrs. Bray would have been 102 years old in 1971, not 105. Born on May 30, 1869, in Lexington, Kentucky, she was apparently a dual national (English and Indian). In 1923 she married Mr. Gulliford, but became a widow in 1935, when she settled in Seattle. Mrs. Bray last resided in Pasadena, CA.

56. Jean E. Nixon, letter to Kenosha, WI, Bahá'í Spiritual Assembly, April 7, 1924. Kenosha Records, box 5, folder 52, National Bahá'í Archives, Wilmette, IL.

57. Keith S. Henry, in *Black Politics in Toronto since World War I,* makes mention of a Jamaican clergyman in Nova Scotia, Rev. Cecil A. Stewart, an activist with a "vision and vigor," moving later to Toronto. We must presume that this is the same pastor who had invited the Bahá'ís to speak to his congregation in Saint John.

58. Jean E. Nixon, letter to Kenosha, WI, Bahá'í Spiritual Assembly, April 7, 1924. Kenosha Records, box 5, folder 52, National Bahá'í Archives, Wilmette, IL.

59. Jean E. Nixon, letter to Victoria Bedikian, January 13, 1924. Victoria Bedikian Papers, National Bahá'í Archives, Wilmette, IL.

60. *Canadian Bahá'í News,* March 1941, p. 7.

61. Paul Williams, "Candles of Guidance: The History of Early Halifax Baha'i Community," unpublished, 1985, p. 4.

62. Paul Williams, "Candles of Guidance," p. 4.

63. See also Gwendolyn Etter-Lewis, "African-American Women," p. 50.

64. Paul Williams, "Candles of Guidance," p. 10; Audrey Rayne, telephone conversation with Will C. van den Hoonaard, February 19, 1989.

65. Dorothy Wade, interview with Will C. van den Hoonaard, July 16, 1990.

66. Bahá'í Registration Card, Bahá'í National Centre, Thornhill, ON, February 28, 1989.

67. Ken Bolton, interview with Will C. van den Hoonaard, October 27, 1990.

68. Bahá'í Registration Card, Bahá'í National Centre, Thornhill, ON, February 28, 1989.

69. Lloyd Gardner, interview with by Joan Anderson, November 13, 1988.

70. Reginald G. Barrow, Jr., e-mails to to Will C. van den Hoonaard, May 20, 2000, June 8, 2000, and June 10, 2000. According to Barrow (Jr), his father had done the same in Brooklyn, NY, years earlier and there were 173 church members who wanted to declare their faith in Bahá'u'lláh. None were accepted, however.

71. Bahá'í Registration Card, Bahá'í National Centre, Thornhill, ON, February 28, 1989; Paul Williams, "Candles of Guidance," p. 20, states that he declared in July 1946.

72. Audrey Rayne, telephone conversation with Will C. van den Hoonaard, February 19, 1989.

73. Ibid.

74. Milwyn Adams Davies, "A Brief History of the Edmonton Bahá'í Community," mimeo, July 1949.

75. Don Carty, letter to Lynn Echevarria, February 17, 1992.

76. Ibid.

77. Audrey Robarts, interview with Lynn Echevarria, 1990.

78. John Robarts, letter to Esther Hayes and her family, October 25, 1971.

79. Bahá'ís between the ages of 15 and 70 who are in good health observe a yearly fast where they abstain from food and drink from sunrise to sunset from March 2 through 20.

80. Esther Hayes, interview with Lynn Echevarria, December 1988.

81. Ibid.

82. Bahá'í Registration Card, Bahá'í National Centre, Thornhill, ON, February 28, 1989.

83. Esther Hayes, interview with Lynn Echevarria, December 1988.

84. Doris Richardson, letter to Esther Hayes, September 7, 1966.

85. Elizabeth Rowan "Testimonial to Inez Hayes: A Portrait of Inez Hayes," 1974.

86. Ibid.

87. National Spiritual Assembly of the Bahá'ís of Canada, letter to Esther Hayes, November 1974.

88. The information is derived from telephone interviews with Don Carty by Lynn Echevarria, December 1988 and March 1989.

89. Bahá'í Registration Card, Bahá'í National Centre, Thornhill, ON, February 28, 1989.

90. Don Carty, interview with Lynn Echevarria, February 17, 1990.

91. Ibid.

92. Ibid.

93. Ibid.

94. Bahá'í Registration Card, Bahá'í National Centre, Thornhill, ON, February 28, 1989.

95. Guysboro was the end of the "Underground Railroad."

96. A good account of the Black community in the historical and contemporary context in Nova Scotia is Thompson's work, *Born with a Call: A Biography of Dr. William Pearly Oliver,* (Halifax: Black Cultural Centre for Nova Scotia, 1986).

97. See John Porter, *The Vertical Mosaic.*

Chapter 8

1. Bahá'u'lláh, *Gleanings,* no. 109.2.
2. Ibid., nos. 131.2, 132.3.

Chapter 9

1. A reference to 'Abdu'l-Bahá. See chapter 3, note 46.
2. "'Akká Lights, Teachings Imparted to Mr. and Mrs Jof. H. Hannen Upon the Occasion of a Visit to 'Abdu'l-Baha, Feb. 19–27, 1909," National Bahá'í Archives, Wilmette, IL, p. 11.
3. Translations of 'Abdu'l-Bahá's talks during his travels in America, including those listed here, can be found in *The Promulgation of Universal Peace.*
4. Bahá'u'lláh, Ishráqát, *Tablets of Bahá'u'lláh,* p. 125
5. 'Abdu'l-Bahá, *'Abdu'l-Bahá in London,* p. 19.
6. The Will and Testament of 'Abdu'l-Bahá, which is considered the charter document of the administrative structure of the Bahá'í community. The document also appointed 'Abdu'l-Bahá's grandson, Shoghi Effendi, as Guardian of the Faith.

Chapter 10

1. 'Abdu'l-Bahá, *Promulgation of Universal Peace,* pp. 192–3.

Chapter 11

The epigraph for this chapter is from 'Abdu'l-Bahá, *Paris Talks,* no. 45.12–3.
1. A reference to the Báb, called "The Herald" because he heralded the coming of Bahá'u'lláh.

Chapter 16

1. See chapter 4, n30.
2. The Báb, *Selections,* p. 48.
3. Written on behalf of Shoghi Effendi, letter to two Bahá'ís, December 10, 1942, in *Lights of Guidance,* no. 1785.
4. Shoghi Effendi, letter to the American Bahá'í community, August 5, 1950, in *Citadel of Faith,* p. 87.
5. Written on behalf of Shoghi Effendi, letter to two individual Bahá'ís, March 19, 1944, in *Lights of Guidance,* no. 1784.
6. 'Abdu'l-Bahá, *Promulgation of Universal Peace,* p. 77.

7. 'Abdu'l-Bahá, *Paris Talks*, no. 40.33.
8. 'Abdu'l-Bahá, quoted in *Women*, p. 5.

Chapter 17

1. An Arabic phrase meaning "O Glory of Glories." It is one of the forms of the "Greatest Name," an invocation of God.
2. Bahá'u'lláh, Hidden Words, Arabic, no. 55.
3. Bahá'u'lláh, quoted in J. E. Esslemont, *Bahá'u'lláh and the New Era,* p. 151.
4. The Báb, *Bahá'í Prayers,* p. 226.
5. This is an expression used to indicate when someone is the only Bahá'í in a particular jurisdiction.

Chapter 18

1. Shoghi Effendi, letter of August 5, 1950, published in *Citadel of Faith,* p. 87.

Chapter 19

1. A reference to 'Abdu'l-Bahá.

Chapter 20

1. Bahá'u'lláh, *Bahá'í Scriptures,* p. 157.
2. Bahá'u'lláh, Hidden Words, Arabic, no. 2.
3. Bahá'u'lláh, words recorded by E. G. Browne in *A Traveller's Narrative,* p. xl.

Bibliography

Works of Bahá'u'lláh

Gleanings from the Writings of Bahá'u'lláh. 1st pocket-size ed. Translated by Shoghi Effendi. Wilmette, IL: Bahá'í Publishing, 2005.

The Hidden Words. Translated by Shoghi Effendi. Wilmette, IL: Bahá'í Publishing, 2002.

Tablets of Bahá'u'lláh revealed after the Kitáb-i-Aqdas. Compiled by the Research Department of the Universal House of Justice. Translated by Habib Taherzadeh et al. Wilmette, IL: 1988.

Works of the Báb

Selections from the Writings of the Báb. Compiled by the Research Department of the Universal House of Justice. Translated by Habib Taherzadeh et al. Haifa: Bahá'í World Centre, 1976.

Works of 'Abdu'l-Bahá

'Abdu'l-Bahá in London: Addresses and Notes of Conversations. London: Bahá'í Publishing Trust, 1982.

Paris Talks: Addresses Given By 'Abdu'l-Bahá in Paris in 1911. 12th ed. London: Bahá'í Publishing Trust, 1995.

Promulgation of Universal Peace: Talks Delivered by 'Abdu'l-Bahá during His Visit to the United States and Canada in 1912. Compiled by Howard MacNutt. 2nd ed. Wilmette, IL: Bahá'í Publishing Trust, 1982.

Selections from the Writings of 'Abdu'l-Bahá. Compiled by the Research Department
  of the Universal House of Justice. Translated by a Committee at the Bahá'í
  World Center and Marzieh Gail. 1st pocket-size ed. Wilmette, IL: Bahá'í
  Publishing Trust, 1996.

Tablets of the Divine Plan: Revealed by 'Abdu'l-Bahá to the North America Bahá'ís.
  1st pocket-sized ed. Wilmette, IL: Bahá'í Publishing Trust, 1993.

Will and Testament of 'Abdu'l-Bahá. Wilmette, IL: Bahá'í Publishing Trust, 1944.

Works of Shoghi Effendi

Advent of Divine Justice. 1st pocket-size ed. Wilmette, IL: Bahá'í Publishing
  Trust, 1990.

Bahá'í Administration: Selected Messages, 1922–1932. 7th ed. Wilmette, IL: Bahá'í
  Publishing Trust, 1974.

Citadel of Faith: Messages to America, 1947–1957. Wilmette, IL: Bahá'í Publishing
  Trust, 1965.

God Passes By. New ed. Wilmette, IL: Bahá'í Publishing Trust, 1974.

*This Decisive Hour: Messages of Shoghi Effendi to the North American Bahá'ís,
  1932–1946.* Wilmette, IL: Bahá'í Publishing Trust, 2002.

*The Unfolding Destiny of the British Bahá'í Community: The Messages from the
  Guardian of the Bahá'í Faith to the Bahá'ís of the British Isles.* London:
  Bahá'í Publishing Trust, 1981.

Compilations of Bahá'í Writings

Bahá'u'lláh and 'Abdu'l-Bahá. *Bahá'í Scriptures: Selections from the Utterances of
  Bahá'u'lláh and 'Abdu'l-Bahá.* Edited by Horace Holley. 2nd ed. New York:
  Bahá'í Publishing Committee, 1928.

Helen Hornby, compiler. *Lights of Guidance.* New ed. New Delhi, India: Bahá'í
  Publishing Trust, 1994.

Bonnie J. Taylor, compiler. *The Pupil of the Eye: African Americans in World
  Order of Bahá'u'lláh: Selections from the Writings of Bahá'u'lláh, the Báb,
  'Abdu'l-Bahá, Shoghi Effendi, and the Universal House of Justice.* 2nd ed.
  Rivera Beach, Florida: Palabra Publications, 1998.

Quickeners of Mankind: Pioneering in a World Community. Wilmette, IL: Bahá'í Publishing Trust, 1980.

Women: Extracts from the Writings of Bahá'u'lláh, 'Abdu'l-Bahá, Shoghi Effendi and the Universal House of Justice. Toronto: Bahá'í Canada Publications, 1991.

Other Works

Alvis, Joel L. Jr., *Religion and Race: Southern Presbyterians, 1946–1983.* Tuscaloosa, AL: University of Alabama Press, 1994.

The Bahá'í World: An International Record, vol. 3, 1928–1930. Compiled by the National Spiritual Assembly of the Bahá'ís of the United States and Canada. New York: Bahá'í Publishing Committee, 1930.

The Bahá'í World: A Biennial International Record, vol. 7, 1936–1938. Compiled by the National Spiritual Assembly of the Bahá'ís of the United States and Canada. New York: Bahá'í Publishing Committee, 1939.

The Bahá'í World: A Biennial International Record, vol. 8, 1938–1940. Compiled by the National Spiritual Assembly of the Bahá'ís of the United States and Canada. Wilmette, IL: Bahá'í Publishing Committee, 1942.

The Bahá'í World: A Biennial International Record, vol. 9, 1940–1944. Compiled by the National Spiritual Assembly of the Bahá'ís of the United States and Canada. Wilmette, IL: Bahá'í Publishing Committee, 1945.

The Bahá'í World: A Biennial International Record, vol. 10, 1944–1946. Compiled by the National Spiritual Assembly of the Bahá'ís of the United States and Canada. Wilmette, IL: Bahá'í Publishing Committee, 1948.

The Bahá'í World: An International Record, vol. 11, 1946–1950. Compiled by the National Spiritual Assembly of the Bahá'ís of the United States and Canada. Wilmette, IL: Bahá'í Publishing Committee, 1952.

The Bahá'í World: An International Record, vol. 12, 1950–1954. Compiled by the National Spiritual Assembly of the Bahá'ís of the United States and Canada. Wilmette, IL: Bahá'í Publishing Trust, 1956.

The Bahá'í World: An International Record, vol. 13, 1954–1963. Compiled by the Universal House of Justice. Haifa: Universal House of Justice, 1970.

The Bahá'í World: An International Record, vol. 14, 1963–1968. Compiled by the Universal House of Justice. Haifa: Universal House of Justice, 1974.

The Bahá'í World: An International Record, vol. 15, 1968–1973. Prepared under the supervision of the Universal House of Justice. Haifa: Universal House of Justice, 1975.

The Bahá'í World: An International Record, vol. 16, 1973–1976. Prepared under the supervision of the Universal House of Justice. Haifa: Universal House of Justice, 1978.

The Bahá'í World: An International Record, vol. 17, 1976–1979. Prepared under the supervision of the Universal House of Justice. Haifa: Universal House of Justice, 1981.

The Bahá'í World: An International Record 1993–1994. Haifa: Bahá'í World Centre, 1994.

The Bahá'í World: An International Record 2003–2004. Haifa: Bahá'í World Centre, 2005.

Balyuzi, Hasan M. *'Abdu'l-Bahá: The Center of the Covenant of Bahá'u'lláh.* London: George Ronald, 1971.

Bertley, Leo W. *Canada and Its People of African Descent.* Montréal: Bilongo, 1977.

Boris, Joseph J. *Who's Who in Colored America.* Yonkers, NY: 1927.

Braithwaite, Rella. *The Black Woman in Canada.* Toronto: OISE, 1976.

Browne, E. G., translator. *A Traveler's Narrative Written to Illustrate the Episode of the Báb.* Rev. ed. Wilmette, IL: Bahá'í Publishing Trust, 1980.

Campbell, D. F., editor. *Banked Fires: The Ethnics of Nova Scotia.* Port Credit, ON: Scribbler's Press, 1978.

Canadian Citizenship Branch. *Notes on the Canadian Family Tree.* Ottawa: Department of Citizenship and Immigration, 1960.

De Mille, Amine. *'Abdu'l-Bahá in Canada.* Forest, ON: Forest Free Press, 1962.

Esslemont, J. E. *Bahá'u'lláh and the New Era: An Introduction to the Bahá'í Faith.* 5th rev. ed. Wilmette, IL: Bahá'í Publishing Trust, 1980.

Ferguson, Bob. *Who's Who in Canadian Sport,* Scarborough, ON: Prentice-Hall, 1977.

Fitzpatrick-Moore, Bonnie. *My African Heart*. Johannesburg: Bahá'í Publishing Trust, 1999.

The Four Year Plan and the Twelve Month Plan, 1996–2001: Summary of Achievements. Haifa, Israel: Bahá'í World Centre, 2002.

Franklin, John Hope and Alfred A. Moss, Jr., *From Slavery to Freedom: A History of African Americans*. 7th ed. New York: McGraw-Hill, Inc., 1998.

Frazier, E. Franklin. *The Negro Church in America*. New York: Schocken Books, 1974.

Fredrickson, George M. *White Supremacy: A Comparative Study in American and South African History*. Oxford: Oxford University Press, 1981.

Giddings, Paula J. *When and Where I Enter*. New York: Bantam Books, 1985.

Gillespie, Dizzy with Al Fraser. *To Be or Not To Bop: Memoirs of Dizzy Gillespie*. New York: Doubleday, 1979.

Gordon, April A. and Donald L. Gordon, editors. *Understanding Contemporary Africa*. 2nd ed. Boulder: Lynne Rienner Publishers, 1996.

Gossett, Thomas F. *Race: The History of an Idea in America*. New York: Schocken Books, 1965.

Grahame, Roberta and Catherine Blakeslee, et. al. *Women of Springfield's Past*. Springfield, MA: USA Bicentennial Committee of Springfield, Inc., 1976.

Gregory, Louis G. *A Heavenly Vista: The Pilgrimage of Louis G. Gregory*. Washington, DC: NPND.

Hatcher, John. *From The Auroral Darkness: The Life and Poetry of Robert Hayden*. Oxford: George Ronald, 1984.

Hatcher, William S. and J. Douglas Martin, *The Bahá'í Faith: The Emerging Global Religion*. Wilmette, IL: Bahá'í Publishing, 2002.

Hayes, Diana L. and Cyprian Davis, O.S.B. eds., *Taking Down Our Harps: Black Catholics in the United States*. Mary Knoll, NY: Orbis Books, 1998.

Henry, Keith. *Black Politics in Toronto Since World War I*. Toronto: The Multicultural History Society of Ontario, 1981.

Hine, Darlene Clark. Editor. *Black Women in America: An Historical Encyclopedia.* New York: Carlson Publishing Inc., 1993.

Hine, Darlene Clark. Editor. *The State of Afro-American History.* Baton Rouge: Louisiana State University Press, 1986.

Kryder, Daniel. *Divided Arsenal: Race and the American State During World War II.* Cambridge: Cambridge University Press, 2000.

Lerner, Gerda. *The Majority Finds Its Past: Placing Women in History.* New York: Oxford University Press, 1979.

Lincoln, C. Eric. *Race, Religion and the Continuing American Dilemma.* Rev. ed. New York: Hill and Wang, 1999.

Mack, John and Florence Howe, editors. *Women and Higher Education in American History: Essays from the Mount Holyoke College Sesquicentennial Symposia.* New York: W. W. Norton and Company, 1988.

Marques, Gabriel. *Of Acendedores de Velas: Contribucoes de Afroo-descendtes Bahá'ís á construcao da Nova Ordem Mundial.* Sao Paulo, Brazil: Editora Planeta, 2000.

Marrett, Cora B. and Cheryl Leggon, editors. *Research in Race and Ethnic Relations: A Research Annual,* vol. 3. Greenwich, CT: Jai Press, 1982.

Massey, Douglas S. and Nancy A. Denton, *American Apartheid: Segregation and the Making of the Underclass.* Cambridge, Massachusetts: Harvard University Press, 1993.

Maxwell, May. *An Early Pilgrimage.* Rev. ed. Oxford: George Ronald, 1969.

Meyer, Stephen Grant. *As Long as They Don't Move Next Door: Segregation and Racial Conflict in American Neighborhoods.* Lanham, MD: Rowman & Littlefield Publishers, Inc., 2000.

Momen, Moojan. *Studies in Bábí and Bahá'í History,* vol. 1. Los Angeles: Kalimat Press, 1982.

Montréal Council of Social Agencies. *Welfare Work in Montréal in 1928.* Montréal: 1928.

Morrison, Gayle. *To Move The World: Louis G. Gregory and the Advancement of Racial Unity in America.* Wilmette, IL: Bahá'í Publishing Trust, 1982.

Mosse, George L. *Toward the Final Solution: A History of European Racism*. New York: Harper and Row, 1980.

Nábil-i-A'zam. [Muḥammad-i-Zarandí] *The Dawn-Breakers: Nabíl's Narrative of the Early Days of the Bahá'í Revelation*. Translated and edited by Shoghi Effendi. Wilmette, IL: Bahá'í Publishing Trust, 1962.

Nakhjavání, Violette. *The Great African Safari: The Travels of 'Amatu'l-Bahá Rúḥíyyih Khánum in Africa, 1969–73*. Oxford: George Ronald, 2002.

Pinn, Anthony B. *Varieties of African-American Religious Experience*. Minneapolis: Augsburg Fortress, 1998.

Porter, John. *The Vertical Mosaic,* Toronto: University of Toronto Press, 1965.

Rabbani, Rúḥíyyih. *The Priceless Pearl*. London: Bahá'í Publishing Trust, 1969.

Raboteau. Albert J. *Canaan Land: A Religious History of African-Americans*. New York: Oxford University Press, 2001.

Sernett, Milton C., editor. *Afro-American Religious History: A Documentary Witness*. Durham, NC: Duke University Press, 1985.

Smith, Jessie Carney. *Notable Black American Women, Book 2*. New York: Gale Research, 1996.

Smith, Melanie and Paul Lample. *The Spiritual Conquest of the Planet: Our Response to Plans*. Riviera Beach, FL: Palabra Publications, 1993.

Smith, Peter. *The Bábí and Bahá'í Religions: From Messianic Shi'ism to a World Religion*. Cambridge: Cambridge University Press, 1987.

Smith, Peter. *The Bahá'í Religion: A Short Introduction to Its History and Teachings*. Oxford: George Ronald, 1998.

Stockman, Robert H. *The Bahá'í Faith in America: Origins, 1892–1900*, vol 1. Wilmette, IL: Bahá'í Publishing Trust, 1985.

Taherzadeh, Adib. *The Covenant of Bahá'u'lláh*. Oxford: George Ronald, 1992.

Taylor, Bonnie, editor. *The Power of Unity: Beyond Prejudice and Racism*. Wilmette, IL: Bahá'í Publishing Trust, 1986.

Thomas, June M. *Planning Progress: Lessons from Shoghi Effendi*. Ottawa, Canada: Bahá'í Studies Publications, 1999.

Thomas, Richard W. *Racial Unity: An Imperative for Social Progress*. Ottawa: Association of Bahá'í Studies, 1993.

Tygiel, Jules. *Baseball's Great Experiment: Jackie Robinson and His Legacy*. New York: Vintage Books, 1984.

van den Hoonard, Will C. *The Origins of the Bahá'í Community of Canada, 1898–1948*. Ontario: Wilfrid Laurier University Press, 1996.

Ward, Allen L. *239 Days: 'Abdu'l-Bahá's Journey in America*. Wilmette, IL: Bahá'í Publishing Trust, 1977.

Williams, James A. and Ted Jefferson. *The Black Men's Bahá'í Gatherings: A Spiritual Transformation*. Wayfarer Publications, 1995.

Wood, Forrest G. *The Arrogance of Faith: Christianity and Race in America from the Colonial Era to the Twentieth Century*. New York: Alfred A. Knopf, 1990.

Index

For more information about the Bahá'í Faith,
or to contact the Bahá'ís near you, visit
http://www.us.bahai.org/
or call
1-800-22-UNITE

Bahá'í Publishing
and the Bahá'í Faith

Bahá'í Publishing produces books based on the teachings of the Bahá'í Faith. Founded nearly 160 years ago, the Bahá'í Faith has spread to some 235 nations and territories and is now accepted by more than five million people. The word "Bahá'í" means "follower of Bahá'u'lláh." Bahá'u'lláh, the founder of the Bahá'í Faith, asserted that he is the Messenger of God for all of humanity in this day. The cornerstone of his teachings is the establishment of the spiritual unity of humankind, which will be achieved by personal transformation and the application of clearly identified spiritual principles. Bahá'ís also believe that there is but one religion and that all the Messengers of God—among them Abraham, Zoroaster, Moses, Krishna, Buddha, Jesus, and Muḥammad—have progressively revealed its nature. Together, the world's great religions are expressions of a single, unfolding divine plan. Human beings, not God's Messengers, are the source of religious divisions, prejudices, and hatreds.

The Bahá'í Faith is not a sect or denomination of another religion, nor is it a cult or a social movement. Rather, it is a globally recognized independent world religion founded on new books of scripture revealed by Bahá'u'lláh.

Bahá'í Publishing is an imprint of the National Spiritual Assembly of the Bahá'ís of the United States.

Other Books
Available from Bahá'í Publishing

Gleanings from the Writings of Bahá'u'lláh
BY BAHÁ'U'LLÁH
A selection of the most characteristic passages from the outstanding works of the Author of the Bahá'í Revelation

As the youngest of the world's independent religions, the Bahá'í Faith comprises several million adherents who can be found in virtually every part of the planet. Its members represent what may well be the most ethnically and culturally diverse association of people in the world. Its phenomenal expansion since its inception in Persia during the nineteenth century has been fueled by a body of teachings that its followers regard as the Revelation of God's guidance for the collective coming of age of humankind. The source of those teachings is Bahá'u'lláh, the Prophet and Founder of the religion, who left a voluminous body of writings.

Gleanings from the Writings of Bahá'u'lláh is an extremely important compilation that sets out the Bahá'í teachings on a myriad of subjects. Among the themes that fall within its compass are the greatness of the day in which we live, the spiritual requisites of peace and world order, the nature of God and His Prophets, the fulfillment of prophecy, the soul and its immortality, the renewal of civilization, the oneness of the Manifestations of God as agents of one civilizing process, the oneness of humanity, and the purpose of life, to name only a few.

To those who wish to acquire a deeper knowledge and understanding of the Bahá'í Faith, *Gleanings* is a priceless treasury. To the members of the Bahá'í Faith, it has been a familiar companion for many decades, bringing spiritual fulfillment to countless people throughout the world. This new edition includes paragraph numbering for easy reference and a revised and expanded glossary.

$12.00 / $15.00 CAN
ISBN 10: 1-931847-22-3
ISBN 13: 978-1-931847-22-3

Selected Writings of Bahá'u'lláh

Though most people see the world's religions as separate, unrelated entities, the Bahá'í Faith sees them as stages in a single process. Each represents a new stage in God's progressive revelation of His will for humanity. These successive revelations have always been the true source of moral values, ideals, and standards.

The revelation of Bahá'u'lláh (1817–1892) is the most recent stage in the process. It marks the collective "coming of age" of humanity and lays the moral foundation for a global society.

Bahá'u'lláh is the founder of the Bahá'í Faith, the youngest of the independent world religions. The cornerstone of his teachings is the establishment of the unity of humankind. Bahá'u'lláh taught that there is but one religion and that all the Messengers of God—among them Krishna, Abraham, Moses, Buddha, Jesus, Muḥammad—have progressively revealed its nature. Together, the world's great religions are expressions of a single, unfolding divine plan.

Selected Writings of Bahá'u'lláh provides an overview of the Prophet's teachings, including sections on God and His Messengers, the path to God, spiritual aspects of the world civilization described by Bahá'u'lláh, the nature of the human soul and its journey after death, and the renewal of God's covenant with humanity. This volume complements new Bahá'í Publishing editions of Bahá'u'lláh's major works that have appeared in recent years: *Gleanings from the Writings of Bahá'u'lláh* (2005), *The Book of Certitude* (2003), and *The Hidden Words* (2002).

$10.00 / $13.00 CAN
ISBN 10: 1-931847-24-X
ISBN 13: 978-1-931847-24-7

Healing the Wounded Soul

BY PHYLLIS K. PETERSON

A powerful story of courage, hope, and faith that offers encouragement to survivors of childhood sexual abuse and gives important information on prevention for everyone else.

A survivor of six years of childhood sexual abuse, Phyllis Peterson tells her intensely personal story of abuse and the lifelong quest to find healing and wholeness. Her incredible journey is marked by a series of traumas, ongoing therapy, misdiagnoses, reverses, and seemingly overwhelming obstacles to personal development.

Propelled by an unquenchable desire to investigate spiritual truths and bolstered by the discovery of the healing power of her faith, Peterson triumphs by achieving a lasting positive self-image and turning outward to help others. Today her spiritual journey continues to evolve through the teachings of the Bahá'í Faith, her service as a performing artist, and further study of issues of anger and codependency.

Includes comforting extracts from Bahá'í scripture for those who are suffering, dispels myths about child sexual abuse, and provides helpful information on prevention and treatment of childhood sexual abuse.

$14.00 / $17.00 CAN

ISBN 10: 1-931847-25-8

ISBN 13: 978-1-931847-25-4

Hope for a Global Ethic

BY BRIAN D. LEPARD

How can we look with confidence to the future in a world traumatized by terror, war, and human rights violations?

Terrorism. Wars and conflicts. Genocide. Ethnic cleansing. Torture. Oppression of women. Abuse of children. Debilitating poverty. Against this backdrop of the current world scene, Brian D. Lepard suggests that only a global ethic—a shared set of ethical principles—can meet the urgent needs of our troubled global community. But where is the evidence that such an ethic even exists? And where is it to be found?

In this provocative and engaging book, Lepard asserts that there is indeed hope for a global ethic. Surprisingly, the source of that hope is embedded in the scriptures of the various world religions. Reviewing selections from the sacred texts of seven world religions—Hinduism, Judaism, Buddhism, Confucianism, Christianity, Islam, and the Bahá'í Faith—Lepard identifies numerous common ethical principles found in the sacred writings of these faiths. He clearly demonstrates how these shared principles, when put into practice, will help us peacefully solve many problems facing the world that today seem so intractable.

This inspiring and uplifting book will be of interest to anyone who cares about global issues and seeks spiritual guidance from the world's religious traditions.

$14.00 / $17.00 CAN
ISBN 10: 1-931847-20-7
ISBN 13: 978-1-931847-20-9

The Purpose of Physical Reality

BY JOHN S. HATCHER

If human beings are essentially spiritual beings, then what is the purpose of our existence in this physical world?

John Hatcher examines this and other fundamental questions. According to Hatcher, the physical world is like a classroom designed by God to stimulate and nurture our spiritual growth. *The Purpose of Physical Reality* explores the classroom of physical existence and demonstrates how everyday life experiences can lead us to spiritual insights. By viewing this physical existence as a place to learn about spiritual realities, we come to appreciate the overall justice of God's plan and the divine assistance available to unleash human potential. Not only does this concept of physical reality enable us to gain spiritual and intellectual understanding while living on earth, it prepares us for further progress in the life hereafter.

$12.00 / $15.00 CAN
ISBN 10: 1-931847-23-1
ISBN 13: 978-1-931847-23-0

To view our complete catalog, please visit
BahaiBooksUSA.com.